BRUCE NAUMAN

OCTOBER Files

Richard Serra, edited by Hal Foster with Gordon Hughes
Andy Warhol, edited by Annette Michelson
Eva Hesse, edited by Mignon Nixon
Robert Rauschenberg, edited by Branden W. Joseph
James Coleman, edited by George Baker
Cindy Sherman, edited by Johanna Burton
Roy Lichtenstein, edited by Graham Bader
Gabriel Orozco, edited by Yve-Alain Bois
Gerhard Richter, edited by Benjamin H. D. Buchloh
Richard Hamilton, edited by Hal Foster
Dan Graham, edited by Alex Kitnick
John Cage, edited by Julia Robinson
Claes Oldenburg, edited by Nadja Rottner
Louise Lawler, edited by Helen Molesworth with Taylor Walsh
Robert Morris, edited by Julia Byran-Wilson
John Knight, edited by André Rottmann
Isa Genzken, edited by Lisa Lee
Hans Haacke, edited by Rachel Churner
Michael Asher, edited by Jennifer King
Mary Kelly, edited by Mignon Nixon
William Kentridge, edited by Rosalind Krauss
Bruce Nauman, edited by Taylor Walsh

BRUCE NAUMAN

edited by Taylor Walsh

essays and interviews by Fidel A. Danieli, Marcia Tucker, Robert Pincus-Witten, Joan Simon, John Miller, Pamela M. Lee, Isabelle Graw, Kathryn Chiong, Janet Kraynak, Anne M. Wagner, Rosalind Krauss, Robert Slifkin, Jeffrey Weiss, and Taylor Walsh

OCTOBER FILES 22

The MIT Press
Cambridge, Massachusetts
London, England

The MIT Press
Massachusetts Institute of Technology
77 Massachusetts Avenue, Cambridge, MA 02139
mitpress.mit.edu

This book was set in Bembo by Toppan Best-set Premedia Limited.

Library of Congress Cataloging-in-Publication Data

Names: Walsh, Taylor, editor.
Title: Bruce Nauman / edited by Taylor Walsh.
Other titles: Bruce Nauman (M.I.T. Press)
Description: Cambridge, MA : The MIT Press, 2017. | Series: October files |
Includes bibliographical references and index.
Identifiers: LCCN 2017059863| ISBN 9780262038362 (hardcover : alk. paper) |
ISBN 9780262535670 (pb : alk. paper)
Subjects: LCSH: Nauman, Bruce, 1941---Criticism and interpretation.
Classification: LCC N6537.N38 B777 2017 | DDC 709--dc23 LC record available at https://lccn.loc.gov/2017059863

151257765

Contents

Series Preface

OCTOBER Files addresses individual bodies of work of the postwar period that meet two criteria: they have altered our understanding of art in significant ways, and they have prompted a critical literature that is serious, sophisticated, and sustained. Each book thus traces not only the development of an important oeuvre but also the construction of the critical discourse inspired by it. This discourse is theoretical by its very nature, which is not to say that it imposes theory abstractly or arbitrarily. Rather, it draws out the specific ways in which significant art is theoretical in its own right, on its own terms, and with its own implications. To this end we feature essays, many first published in *OCTOBER* magazine, that elaborate different methods of criticism in order to elucidate different aspects of the art in question. The essays are often in dialogue with one another as they do so, but they are also as sensitive as the art to political context and historical change. These "files," then, are intended as primers in signal practices of art and criticism alike, and they are offered in resistance to the amnesiac and antitheoretical tendencies of our time.

The Editors of *OCTOBER*

Acknowledgments

Fidel A. Danieli, "The Art of Bruce Nauman"; Marcia Tucker, "PheNAUMANology"; and Robert Pincus-Witten, "Bruce Nauman: Another Kind of Reasoning" were originally published in *Artforum* 6, no. 4 (December 1967); 9, no. 4 (December 1970); and 10, no. 6 (February 1972), respectively. Nauman's wide-ranging discussion with Joan Simon was conducted in January 1987 and published in *Art in America* 76 (September 1988) with the title "Breaking the Silence: An Interview with Bruce Nauman." "Three Statements on the Recent Reception of Bruce Nauman" (*October* 74 [Fall 1995]) was perhaps the first treatment of Nauman's work to appear in an academic journal. The editors of *October* solicited reactions from John Miller, Pamela M. Lee, and Isabelle Graw on the occasion of Nauman's traveling retrospective, co-organized by the Walker Art Center and the Hirshhorn Museum and Sculpture Garden and on view at the Museum of Modern Art, New York, in the spring of 1995. Graw's contribution was a condensed version of an article previously published in German before the exhibition began its tour (*Texte Zur Kunst* 2, no. 7 [October 1992]). Kathryn Chiong's essay "Nauman's Beckett Walk" first appeared in *October* 85 (Fall 1998). Janet Kraynak's essay "Dependent Participation: Bruce Nauman's Environments" was originally published in *Grey Room* 39 (Winter 2003); a revised version of the text forms the fifth chapter of her monograph on the artist, *Nauman Reiterated* (Minneapolis: University of Minnesota Press, 2014). Anne M. Wagner's essay "Nauman's Body of Sculpture" first appeared in *A Rose Has No Teeth: Bruce Nauman in the 1960s*, the catalog of an exhibition organized by Constance M. Lewallen at the Berkeley Art Museum and Pacific Film Archive in 2007. It appeared in revised and expanded form in *October* 120 (Spring 2007). "Video Promenades: Nauman Taking Architecture for a Walk" by Rosalind Krauss was published previously in *Under Blue Cup* (Cambridge, MA: MIT Press, 2011). Robert Slifkin's essay "Bruce Nauman Going Solo" was published on the occasion of the 2012 exhibition *Bruce Nauman, Basements/Early Studio Films, 1967–69*, organized by Stephanie Snyder for the Douglas F. Cooley Memorial Art Gallery at Reed College in Portland, Oregon. The accompanying catalog was published by Companion Editions, Portland, and edited by Snyder. Jeffrey Weiss's text "Deceptive Practice" was included in the catalog that accompanied the 2018 retrospective *Bruce Nauman: Disappearing Acts*, co-organized by Schaulager Basel and The Museum of Modern Art, New York, curated by Kathy Halbreich with Heidi Naef, Isabel Friedli, Magnus Schaefer, and Taylor Walsh. Walsh's essay "*Small Fires* Burning: Bruce Nauman and the Activation of Conceptual Art" appeared previously in *October* 163 (Winter 2018).

The editor wishes to thank sincerely all of the authors for permitting their texts to be republished, with particular appreciation to Joan Simon for her sharp insights and collegiality.

This project could not have been realized without the support of the artist, and I am and will remain deeply grateful. It has been a privilege to work with—and to know—Juliet Myers of the Nauman studio, whose patience is matched only by her enthusiasm. Nauman's New York gallery, Sperone Westwater, has facilitated my work in every way; special thanks are due to Angela Westwater, and to Katherine Borkowski for responding to my many queries with meticulous care. Adam Lehner and Rachel Churner of *October* and Deborah Cantor-Adams, Victoria Hindley, and Gabriela Bueno Gibbs of the MIT Press have ably guided this manuscript to publication; the work benefitted at every turn from Rachel's keen advice.

The encouragement needed to pursue this publication came from Benjamin H. D. Buchloh and Carrie Lambert-Beatty, who have championed my work on Nauman from the start; along with Jennifer Roberts, they have been the most engaging and rigorous of interlocutors as well as my most valued sources of dialogue and editorial critique. Past projects undertaken with Rosalyn Deutsche, Helen Molesworth, Susan

Dackerman, and Julia Robinson have shaped my thinking and modeled a principled approach to the discipline that has stayed with me. For the past several years, daily discussions of Nauman with Kathy Halbreich and Magnus Schaefer have been sustaining—our shared endeavor has shown me that Nauman's work (all fifty years of it and counting) is even richer and more compelling than I had known. The last and deepest word of thanks goes to my parents, whose generosity has been a constant, and to Michael Rudd for his skill in obtaining images—though that's the least of it.

The Art of Bruce Nauman

Fidel A. Danieli

A first encounter with the work of Bruce Nauman is extremely disconcerting. Very little prepares one for the realm of remarkable concepts and surprising forms with which this young sculptor deals. Each work, like the tip of an iceberg, is the barely exposed result of a complicated and fully developed line of interpolation and interpretation. Nauman is working in an extreme corner of the area of bare visibility, for the forms are of unusual proportions and homely materials and, whether titled or not, would appear at first exposure to be a vaguely repulsive caprice.

The response to a Nauman may vary curiously according to the amount of information one possesses about the piece. Untitled, as were his first fiberglass and rubber works, they have a direct impact by being distasteful in surface and substance and kinesthetically architectonic in working with or across the wall and floor. The plaster works shown at the Nicholas Wilder Gallery last year obviously were casts of other shapes, but the lately acquired knowledge that they were formed against and around shelves and brackets and were concerned with shape generation related to practical or normal wall orientation is enormously valuable and helpful.[1] Experiencing a work then learning the title while still baffled is an odd situation; rather than the shock of recognition one receives from an Oldenburg, one is surprised, amused, and even relieved. Yet it is a cheated sort of satisfaction; the puzzling gestalt falls into place with this last link of identification, but there is little to do except disengage the words and the work and try afresh. In such a situation, the particularly illustrative works, like the punning photographs and the

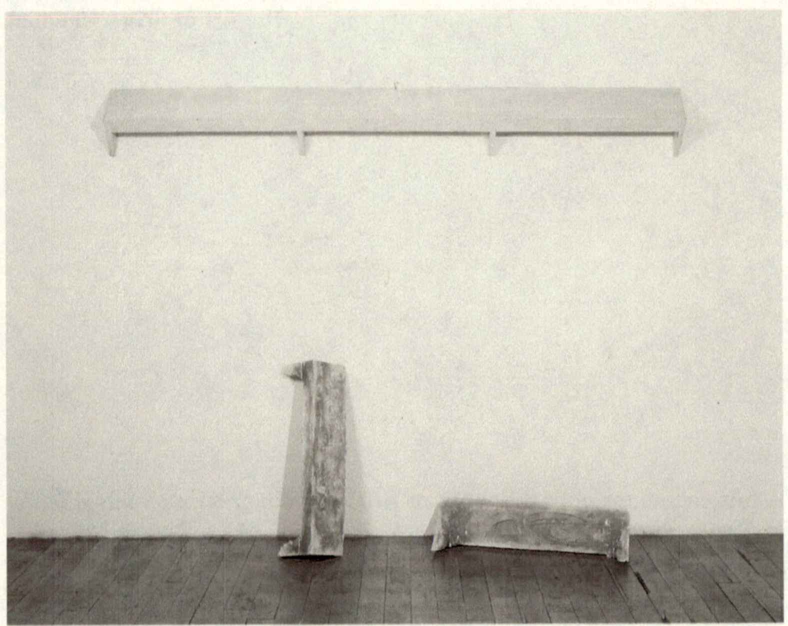

Shelf Sinking into the Wall with Copper-Painted Plaster Casts of the Spaces Underneath, 1966. Wood, plaster, and paint, three parts. Overall: 70 × 84 × 6 in. (177.8 × 213.4 × 15.2 cm). Private collection. Image courtesy Sperone Westwater, New York.

recent figurative wax casts, become obvious, yet a marvelous reverberation takes place. Operating at a lower level, if one accepts the words, the title, as the answer to the search for meaning, the works lapse into another state of invisibility. If one accepts the titles on the level of poetic commentary, a debate arises as to whether the artist is pure and naive or a witty and sophisticated literate. My experience favors an amalgam: an intellect in the service of earnest visualization and scrupulous realization.

As Nauman has put it, he invents long-term projects for himself. This is obviously what any creative worker does, but in the blunt and bald way he states it, it seems even more elementary. One immediately conjures up the image of the slyly lucid Duchamp filling the *Green Box* with his cryptic plans of action. Nauman's ideas come from various sources of inspiration. Some are resolutions of the basic problem of how to originate volumes and where to locate them in a room. Some are a revision or extension of previous plans, leading to completely altered following ones, and a large number are based on word puns and the literal description of common expressions. Alterations occur as ideas hybridize and technical demands press forward. He thinks out a project in terms of visualizations, sets up conditions in which the work will be formed, then accepts what happens.

He is impatient with involved sculptural techniques. His background as a painter directs his preference for manipulative materials or those that fabricate easily. Rubber, wax, and plaster fulfill the requirements of easy handling and are equally appropriate as sketching materials or in casting. That Nauman utilizes all three for finished works indicates a total lack of interest (at least for the present) in traditionally accepted "fine art" sculptural materials and the elevation of the sketch and the mold to the status of art. In fact, he seems to flirt with temporariness and fragility as desirable qualities. He shrugs off knowledge that the rubber used in one series of works will eventually decay and collapse. His use of cardboard, wood, fiberglass, and plastic continues the list out to planar materials easily managed in a studio, while projects in galvanized iron and neon tubing are executed by professionals familiar with working out drawn instructions. The materials, selected, he says, for their color, are handled in a simple, direct manner. He says he makes his sculpture as "hard" as he can. Their poverty of visual appeal suggests a melancholy homeliness and even sadness or, at their most repulsive, a disquieting honesty. Most often the finished product appears rather an end or waste product—the molds a static, frozen chrysalis, the constructions totally useless, the life casts puzzlingly segmented.

The difficulty and the high quality of Nauman's work stem directly from the fact that they are highly conceptual, defined and manipulated in elaborate drawings and executed in the most summary manner. Without discounting the part played by feeling, logic generates the basic considerations of each piece—the size, direction, position, and material. He determines by clear and arbitrary reason each choice or move, though he is somewhat at a loss at times later to recollect why certain features turned out the way they did. He fully realizes that this method courts obscurity but feels this cannot be helped. In notes and drawings, an idea is researched, amplified, and condensed. The drawings are surprisingly rich and explanatory, boldly cartoonish, or generously and incisively expressionistic in style and executed in a variety of materials filled out with color. Often the drawings are executed after a concept has been executed as a sculpture, with the desire to fully terminate it as well as to develop other variants and to pass on to new ideas.

For the past year, he has utilized photographs he has taken to preserve and study altered material that can be made captive in no other way. Some are solely studio references, as are his examinations of various parts of the body pressed against and recorded through a pane of glass. This series ends with the oily impressions collected upon the glass, and the entire sequence extends Jasper Johns's skin-print "drawing," with which Nauman is probably unfamiliar.[2] Another sequence preserves various expressions of the face and mouth that are particularly startling or appropriate for a medical monthly because of the raw vividness of the commercial drug store film processing. In another project (unfinished) for a monument, *Light Trap for Henry Moore*, he imitates that sculptor's cross-contour drawing style with a zigzagging spiral of light captured in a time exposure. This activity recalls and parodies the famed performances of Picasso painting on glass, but Nauman's more resembles the track of a landing helicopter. He anticipates the possibility of publishing at least one group of photos in book form, a set based primarily on illustrating puns and titles. Some, such as *Drill Team* and *Waxing Hot*, are embarrassingly clever and have all the charm of dowdy product demonstrations, complete to tacky, textured material background and heightened, colored side lighting. Others, such as *The Artist Rejecting a Cold Cup of Coffee* and *Self-Portrait as a Garden Fountain*, are highly graphic images recording the flow of liquids.[3]

Recording changes is the motif behind the series *Flour Arrangements*, where a pile of that material was scraped and patted and then photographed from varying angles. Except for the module of the gridded studio floor, one has little accurate indication of scale, and the originally shaped mounds easily become isolated atolls and islands awash in a dark, squared sea.

In a similar manner, recent activities utilize the camera for its potential of distorting and terrain mapping. Suggesting the influence of the recent flood of lunar close-ups, he proposes a neon script of his name projected as a curvature on the horizon. A tentatively titled *Seven Piles of Junk in Bruce Nauman's Studio* will consist of pieced-together views of debris left from previous projects, taken from a height of three feet above the floor.[4]

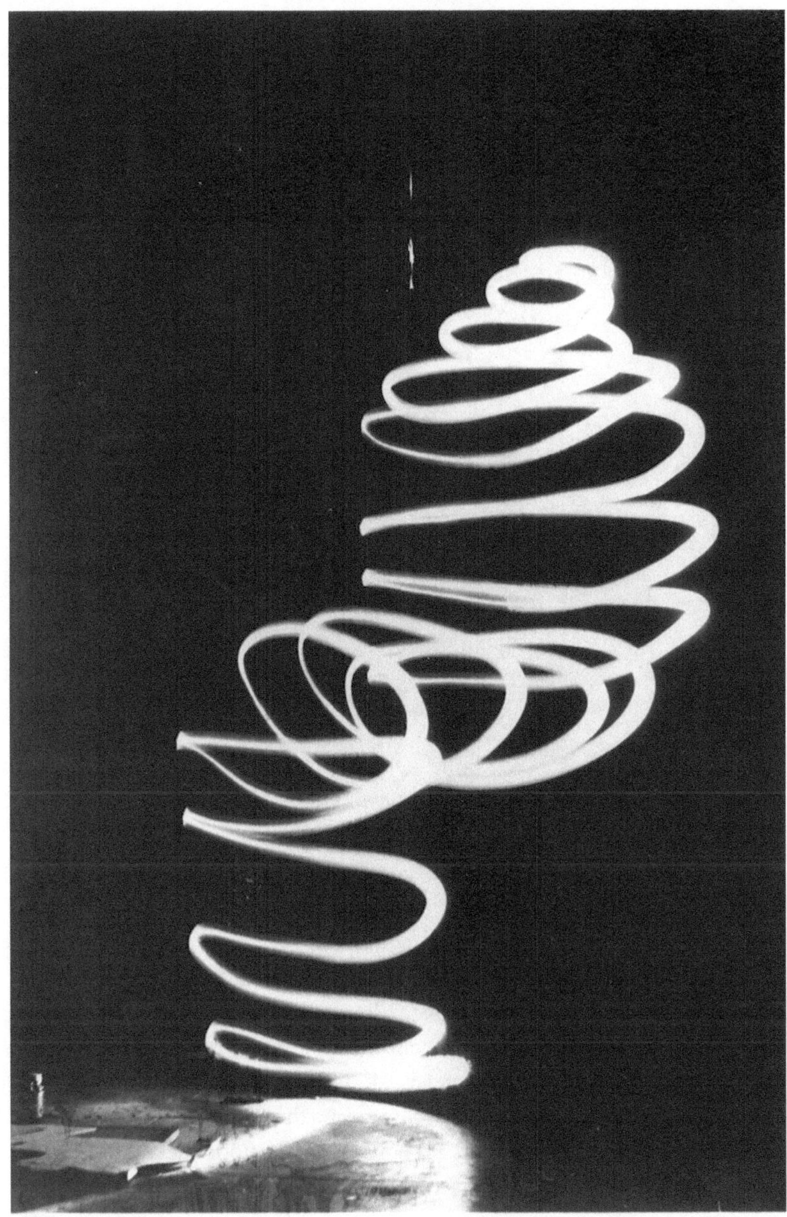

Light Trap for Henry Moore, No. 1, 1967. Black-and-white photograph. 64 × 40 in. (162.6 × 101.6 cm). Glenstone Museum, Potomac, Maryland. Image courtesy Sperone Westwater, New York.

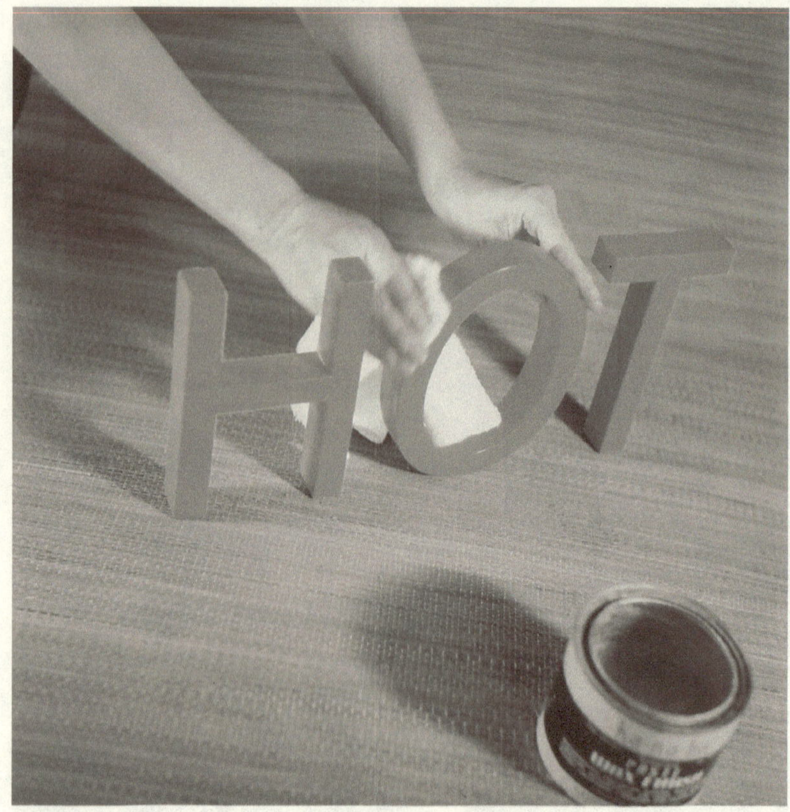

Waxing Hot, 1967, from *Eleven Color Photographs*, 1966–1967/1970. Portfolio of 11 color photographs. Various sizes, approx. 19¾ × 23 in. (50.2 × 58.4 cm) each. Published by the Leo Castelli Gallery, New York. Edition of eight. Image courtesy Sperone Westwater, New York.

To what is "nonart" at first exposure, like the works of the minimalists, he adds a measure of exceedingly bad taste. The early works were constructions, boxes with ventlike openings, with a strong reference to industrial mock-ups, and possessed the character of functionalism, several of which are described by the artist as involving air circulation or viewer position. A slanting metal floor piece is meant to be stood in and is related to a recent green-and-red rubber pad to be stood upon.[5] He conspires to force the incredulous viewer to participate. Several larger, more complex series followed, dividing and occupying space, tying together the elements of a room, or existing in a slender portion of space. One, a cardboard box painted with black tempera, to be hung high in the corner of a room, has as its purpose being hidden or receding from the viewer no matter how hard it is examined. (A hidden partition is kept from view, and black was used to confuse the play of shadows.) *Felt Formed over Sketch for a Metal Floor Piece* operates in a similar area. Several large, stepped sheets, fiberglass molded over plywood, recall 1930s "moderne" curves but were involved in the generation of volumes through repetition and stood in the corner or hung on a nail. A next group revealed the negative spaces molded around the slabs of wall furniture and as awkward and forceful masses revealed the inside outside. Molding, measuring, and recording common but previously undiscovered voids were major intents. Other negatives given form include *Platform Made Up of the Space between Two Rectilinear Boxes on the Floor*, *Neon Templates of the Left Half of My Body Taken at Ten-Inch Intervals*, and *Wax Block with the Impressions of the Knees of Five Famous Artists*. *Platform* qualifies as one of the shabbiest pieces of construction to pass as a finished work and among its flossy neighbors in the *Sculpture of the Sixties* show was nothing if not humble.[6] One must appreciate it as the immediate solidification of a leftover gap, as one considers a Tony Smith plywood and paint mock-up of the economical visualizations of a sculptural projection. Nauman's work bears comparison to the ghost studies of objects of Claes Oldenburg in the similarity of their various orientations in space and their defenseless vulnerability. Nauman's piece is, however, the final version, while the Smiths and the Oldenburgs are to be translated to sterner and finer stuff.

These pieces that demonstrate data are not merely factual, though this is often enough to remove them from everyday experience. He often cheats—that is, imposes other conditions that alter the imagery and meaning. The knees mentioned earlier, for instance, are impressions of the artist's own; a neon version of his handwritten name stretched out of proportion fourteen times higher than wide was also modified to preserve the abstractness, the illegibility, of the letters. The treatment of the name is typical—choosing a familiar known and transferring it systematically to alter the "object" so completely that it is "unreadable." The piece looks like a lavender fall of flowing icicles energetically opposing the organic winding of the black electrical cords.

In form the works are assertive (if fragmentary) and consistently escape definition or clarification. No doubt the artist can explain *Six Inches of My Knee Stretched Out to Six Feet*, but this dark fiberglass hollow length still remains an inert and hermetic item. One work that began as an investigation into the cartoon labyrinths of a Westermann ear drawing ended as a pair of crossed arms echoing the intertwining of heavy rope attached above them. Even if the source is an accurate, life-cast figuration, the mystery remains. *From Hand to Mouth* is exactly the topography of that distance rendered in green wax. It is a moving and

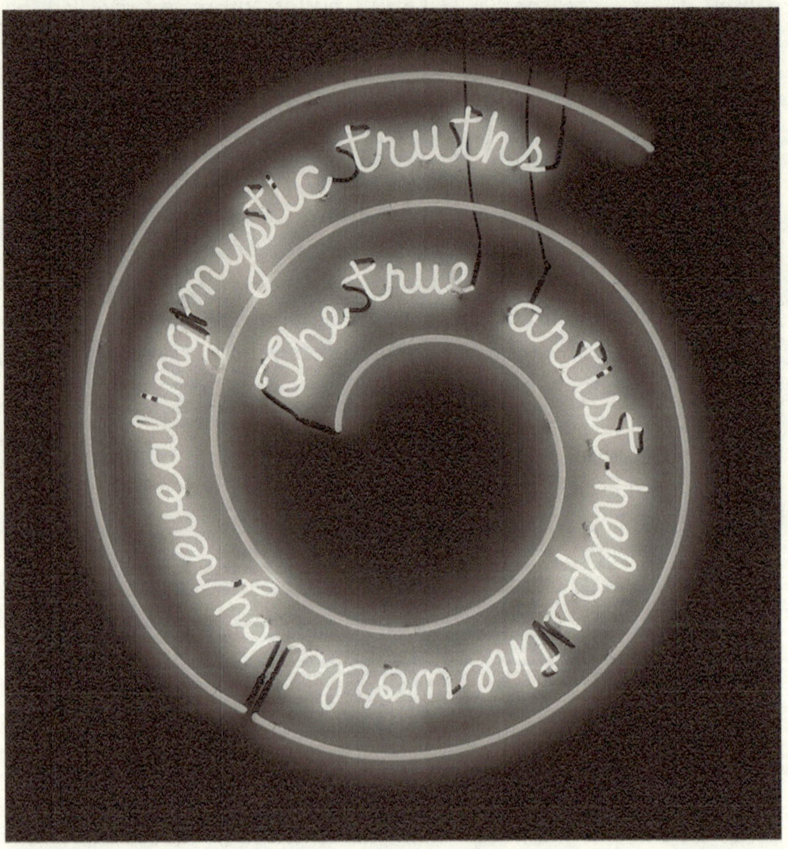

The True Artist Helps the World by Revealing Mystic Truths (Window or Wall Sign), 1967. Neon tubing with clear glass tubing suspension frame. 59 × 55 × 2 in. (149.9 × 139.7 × 5.1 cm). Edition of three, plus artist's proof. Image courtesy Sperone Westwater, New York.

impassively laconic lament, to which the color adds a morbid fascination and the detail found in the soft impression the immediacy of a clinical examination.

When the artist presents as a neon sign "The true artist helps the world by revealing mystic truths" or writes on a window shade, "The true artist is an amazing luminous fountain," he is being poetic in a beautiful, self-flattering way. They also indicate the aspirations of the energetic and fertile mind of a most independent and tough artist.

Notes

1. *Editor's note*: The exhibition the author refers to was Nauman's first solo gallery show, held at the Nicholas Wilder Gallery in Los Angeles, May 10–June 2, 1966.

2. *Editor's note*: The series of skin prints that Danieli observed in Nauman's studio in 1967 do not survive.

3. *Editor's note*: These photographs were ultimately presented as a portfolio entitled *Eleven Color Photographs*, published as an edition of eight in 1970.

4. *Editor's note*: This work is now known as *Composite Photo of Two Messes on the Studio Floor* (1967).

5. *Editor's note*: The slanted metal piece is known as *Device to Stand In* (1966); the red-and-green rubber floor mat with foot-shaped cutouts does not survive.

6. *Editor's note*: Danieli refers here to the group exhibition *American Sculpture of the Sixties* curated by Maurice Tuchman, Los Angeles County Museum of Art, April 28–June 25, 1967.

PheNAUMANology[1]

Marcia Tucker

> Experience shows that human beings are not passive components in adaptive systems. Their responses commonly manifest themselves as acts of personal creation.
>
> —René Dubos, *Man Adapting*

Since his first provocative New York exhibition at the Leo Castelli Gallery in 1968, Bruce Nauman's work has become increasingly complex. We are no longer able to take refuge in art-historical analogies to Duchampian aesthetics or in reference to visual affinities with the work of Johns, Oldenburg, or "process" art. Nauman's roughly built acoustical and performance corridors; his elusive camera/monitor pieces; his unenterable channels of air current; his "dance" pieces and slow-motion, single-image films—all seem to defy our habitual aesthetic expectations. To encounter one of these pieces is to experience basic phenomena that have been isolated, inverted, taken out of context, or progressively destroyed.

Nauman does not represent or interpret phenomena, such as sound, light, movement, or temperature, but uses them as the basic material of his new work. Our responses to the situations he sets up are not purely physical, however. Man alone among animals is able to symbolize, to respond not only to the direct effect of a stimulus on his body but also to a symbolic interpretation of it. This interpretation (and its emotional or psychological corollaries) is conditioned by all other experiences a person has had and involuntarily brings to bear on every new situation. Each person will, therefore, respond to the physical experience of Nauman's work in a different way.

Nauman carefully constructs his pieces to create a specific physical situation. Although he is no longer interested in ways of making art or in the "interpretation" of a made object, he feels it is still important that a piece be neither over- nor underrefined. In this way focus can be directed to the experience and our response to it rather than to the object itself.

The structures of sound and movement as a basic function of human behavior and communication are the phenomena that provide not only the artist but also the linguist, the anthropologist, the philosopher, and the social scientist with the sources of our knowledge of man. These are Nauman's concerns, and he sees his art as more closely related to man's nature than to the nature of art. This attitude is evidenced by his evolution from the making of objects and the recording of activities to his present concern with manipulations of phenomena.

He has utilized progressively intricate "extensions" of the human body, the same extensions that man has evolved in order to live, to communicate, and to adapt to his environment. They range from writing, which extends language, and the telephone, which extends the voice, to complicated mechanisms such as the computer, allowing memory and calculation far beyond the capacity of any human source.

Because Nauman's earlier work consists of visual puns, verbal plays, and manipulations of nonart materials, the intent of this work resides largely in the objects themselves. Recently, by dealing with the ways things are experienced instead of how they are made or perceived, the intent of the work is realized only through the physical involvement of the spectator. To this end, Nauman has investigated a wide variety of modes of communication, each of which is increasingly complex in the responses it is capable of effecting. They include language (both spoken and written); nonverbal sounds, both natural (breathing, walking) and artificial (clapping, making music); physical gesture (facial expressions, body manipulations, dance); and the extension of any or all of these by artificial or technological means.

Our bodies are necessary to the experience of any phenomenon. It is characteristic of Nauman's work that he has always used his own body and its activities as both the subject and the object of his pieces. He has made casts from it (*From Hand to Mouth*, *Neon Templates of the Left Half of My Body Taken at Ten-Inch Intervals*, etc.) and manipulated it (in earlier performances using his body in relation to a T-bar or neon tube as well as in the holograms). He has made videotapes of his own activities (*Bouncing Balls*) and films of parts of his body being acted upon; *Bouncing Balls* and *Black Balls* are slow-motion films of Nauman's testicles moving and being painted black. He has questioned, in various pieces, his behavior as an artist and his attitudes toward himself as such. He has contorted his body and face to the limits of physical action as well as representation. By making audiotapes of himself clapping, breathing, whispering, and playing the violin, he has also explored a range of noises made and perceived by his own body.

This concern with physical self is not simple artistic egocentrism but use of the body to transform intimate subjectivity into objective demonstration. Man is the perceiver and the perceived; he acts and is acted upon; he is the sensor and the sensed. His behavior constitutes a

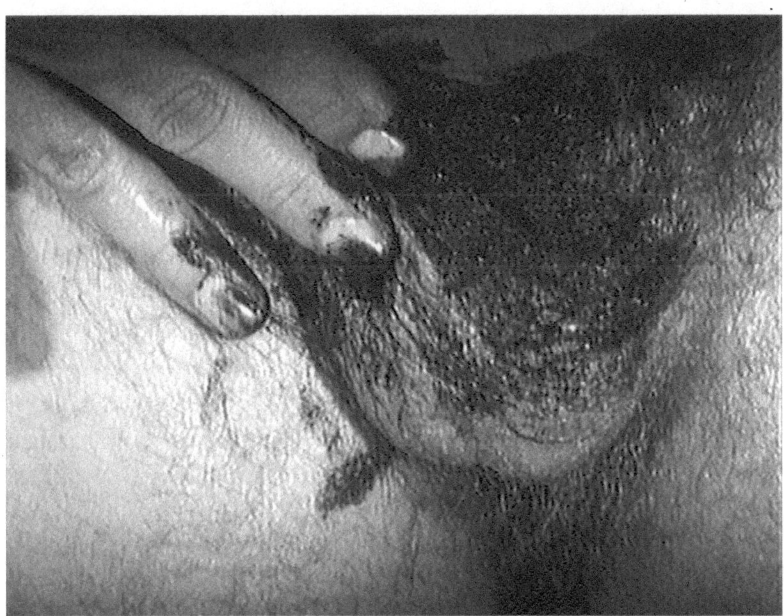

Black Balls, 1969. 16-mm film (black-and-white, silent). 8 min. Distributed by Electronic Arts Intermix. Image courtesy Sperone Westwater, New York.

dialectical interchange with the world he occupies. Maurice Merleau-Ponty, in *The Structure of Behavior*, stresses that man *is*, in fact, his body, despite the essential ambiguity of its being at once lived from the inside and observed from the outside.[2] Nauman has used himself in this way as a prototypical subject for the pieces. These works are meant, essentially, to be encountered privately by one person at a time. Where earlier the artist was the subject and object of recorded situations, now it is the spectator who becomes the actor and observer of his own activity.

Ordinarily we are unable to experience both things simultaneously, at least not without a mirror and an extraordinary degree of self-consciousness. At the Nicholas Wilder Gallery in Los Angeles, Nauman set up a series of wallboard panels running parallel along the length of the gallery. Cameras and videotape monitors were set up in such a way that a person walking the length of one corridor and turning into the next would see himself on a monitor only as he turned the corner. The space set up is longer and narrower than most spaces we find or make for ourselves. The corridors therefore occupy an ambiguous and uncomfortable realm between too much space, which creates feelings of isolation and disorientation, and too little space, which causes cramping and tension. In this case, both are experienced simultaneously. At the same time, the image on the screen further disorients the viewer because he sees himself at a distance, from below and behind. He is prevented from being intimate with himself because he is not even allowed to meet his image head-on. Ordinary experience of the space between man and his image is the frontal, 12-to-16-inch space we normally allow when looking into a mirror.

As in most of his work, this situation does not deal with a concept of space but with the sensation of it. Its effect goes beyond that of a purely physiological reaction to become a highly charged emotional experience. It is similar in feeling to the impact of seeing but not immediately recognizing yourself in the reflective surface of a store window as you pass it.

Other pieces deal more specifically with the physiological and emotional effects of time. Even according to the most stringent scientific analyses of time, pure (or absolute) time cannot be measured because every lapse of time must be connected with some process in order to be perceived. We define time, therefore, according to our experience of it. When looking at a static object, the phenomenon of time, of *how* we

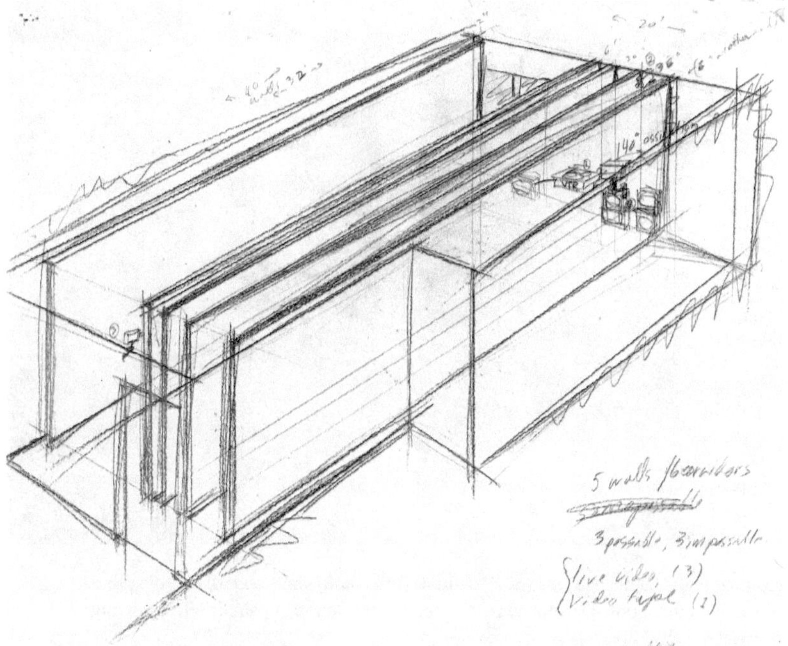

(Wilder Installation) 5 walls/6 corridors/3 passable, 3 impassable/live video (3)/videotape, 1969. Graphite and ink on paper. 23 × 25 in. (58.4 × 73.6 cm). Raussmüller Collection, Basel. Image courtesy Sperone Westwater, New York.

perceive something, can be separated from *what* we are looking at, which does not change. In Nauman's slow-motion films, he uses uncut footage, taken from an unchanging vantage point. In them, a repeated simple change occurs in the object itself, while the way we perceive it does not change. *Bouncing in the Corner, No. 1, Bouncing Balls,* and similar films confound our experience of time by a transference of the functions usually assigned to objects and phenomena.

The performance pieces, which Nauman says have duration but no specific time, operate in a similar fashion. For example, two dance proposals require a performer to work on one exercise for 10 to 14 days before giving an hour-long performance of it. One process involves the use of the body as a cylinder, in which the dancer lies along the junction of wall and floor, facing into the angle formed by them. He straightens and lengthens the body through its center into the angle. A second piece

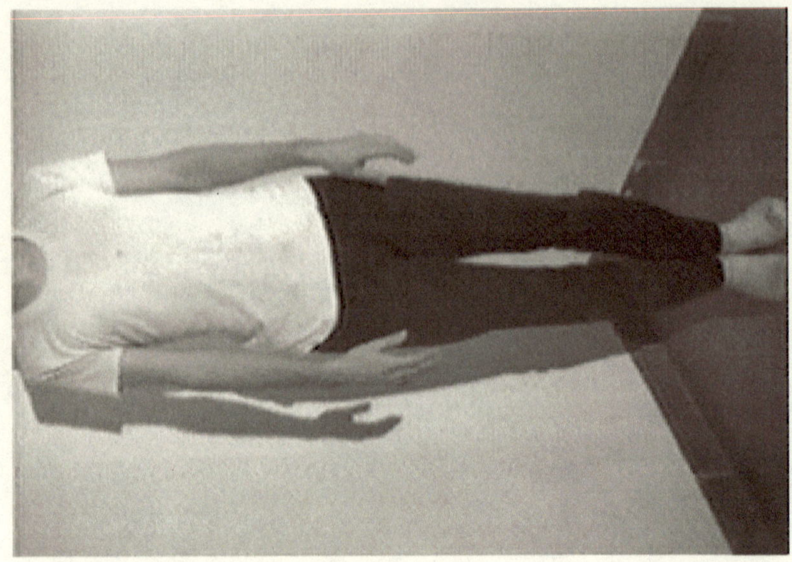

Bouncing in the Corner, No. 1, 1968. Videotape (black-and-white, sound). 60 min., to be repeated continuously. Distributed by Electronic Arts Intermix. Image courtesy Sperone Westwater, New York.

uses the body as a sphere, curled into a corner. The dancer attempts to compress his body toward the central point of the sphere and then toward the corner. Changes in movement during the performance would be barely perceptible to the audience, but the discrepancy between our normal expectation of how long it takes to perform or perceive a given activity and Nauman's distension of that time creates extreme tension.

Other kinds of tension resulting from the physiological effect of changes in pressure on the auditory system are used by Nauman. One such piece is an acoustically paneled corridor whose two walls converge. Another is a parallel, staggered group of 8-foot acoustical panels to be walked between. Nauman has pointed out an analogous situation existing in nature, when certain winds or approaching storms can create even minute pressure changes in the atmosphere, which are said to account for widespread emotional instability and increased suicide rates in a given area.

The "emotional overload" that he is interested in can be partly accounted for in these kinds of terms but is also due, in a less definable way, to how much of his own ideas and feelings he has been able to incorporate into the work—to how personal it is. For him, this quality is essential, even if it is impossible to measure or evaluate.

> I think when you attempt to engage people that way—emotionally—in what you're doing, then it's difficult because you never know if you succeed or not, or to what extent. In other words, it's easier to be professional, because then you can step outside the situation. When you bring things to a personal level then you're just much less sure whether people can accept what's presented.[3]

Since the emotional responses to each piece differ according to the receptor, it is almost impossible to name them; loneliness, delight, anxiety, surprise, frustration, serenity, and other private feelings provide the sensory poetry of this work.

> Even a long time ago, when I was painting, I could get to the point where everything worked except for one part of the painting which was a mess, and I couldn't figure out what to do with it. One way was to remove that part of the painting. The other way was to make that the important part of the painting; that always ended up the most interesting.

The artist's concern with making the "difficult" aspect of a work its focus need not be seen as perversity or artistic sadism but as a viable working method. For example, Nauman has stated that art generally adds information to a situation and that it seems reasonable also to make art by removing information from a situation. In fact, sensory-deprivation experiments have shown that only the essential information needed to identify a thing tends to be picked up from a surrounding group of stimuli.

One of a group of pieces operating on this principle consists of an empty sealed room and an accessible room. An oscillating picture of the open room and its occupants (if any) is projected onto a monitor in the sealed room. Spectators witness only the videotape of the closed space rather than the expected image of themselves. The elimination of extraneous material here clarifies the work's intent by making its focus immediately apprehensible.

Mixing up two kinds of information that are similar but not quite the same is still another means of effecting sensory dislocation. For instance, at Galleria Sperone in Turin last year Nauman made a piece in which touching one wall of the gallery produced the sound of that touch on another wall. He relates this phenomenon to the use of skew lines in mathematics, where two nonparallel lines are situated in relation to each other in space but never meet.

> If you make the lines very close … it's the point at which you get to an optical illusion. Even though you understand how it works, it works every time. It's sort of the way I felt about how these pieces worked. Touching and hearing later, there were two kinds of information that occurred that were very close. You couldn't quite separate them, and you couldn't quite put them together. And so the experience has to do with that confusion that occurs. It's very hard to understand why that turns out to be a complete experience, but it does.

Another method used by Nauman in *Second Poem Piece* is to radically alter the sentence "YOU MAY NOT WANT TO SCREW HERE" by progressive removal of words. Differences in the degree of information and changes in our emotional response to each line occur immediately upon reading (i.e., participating in) the work. By removing semantic information until only the words "YOU WANT" are left, the degree of emotive content is increased.

In the audiotapes of breathing, pacing, clapping, and playing violin scales, sounds are differentiated from "noises" by periodicity, which arouses the expectation of pattern in the listener. Intent is thereby revealed through rhythmic structuring. In another tape, Nauman whispers over and over, "GET OUT OF THE ROOM. GET OUT OF MY MIND." This highly charged message, delivered regularly and repeatedly, confuses us because we generally associate repetitive messages with a low expressive content.

In a performance at the Whitney Museum last year [1969], a similar situation was structured by using an abrupt, emotionally charged

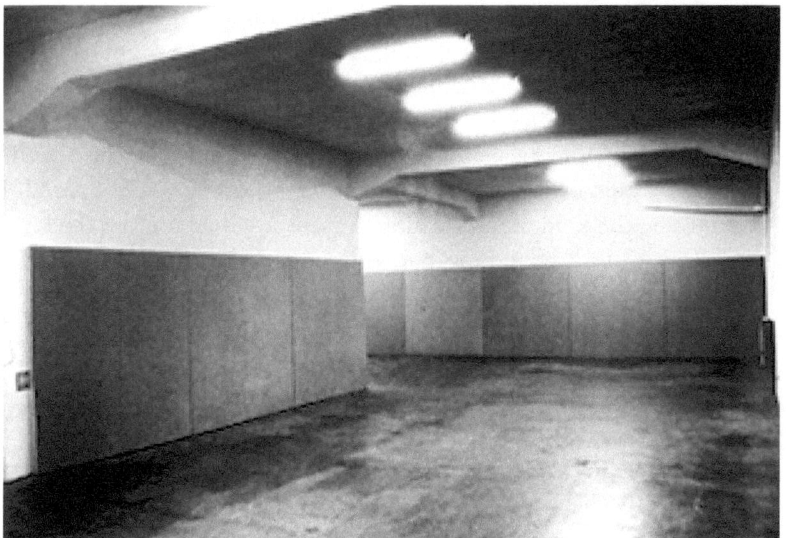

Touch and Sound Walls, 1969. Wallboard, acoustic material. Dimensions variable. Solomon R. Guggenheim Museum, New York. Panza Collection, gift, 1992. Image courtesy Sperone Westwater, New York.

movement. Nauman, his wife, Judy, and Meredith Monk stood about a foot away from respective corners and bounced the upper part of their bodies into them repeatedly for an hour. In both kinds of work, Nauman is also interested in how a movement or sound becomes an exercise, how an exercise becomes a performance, and how specific responses to the performance can be controlled.

In some informal and unpublished notes entitled "Withdrawal as an Art Form," Nauman describes a diverse group of phenomena and possible methods for manipulating them. He is involved with the amplification and deprivation of sensory data; with an examination of physical and psychological responses to simple situations that yield clearly experienceable phenomena; with our responses to extreme or controlled situations, voluntary and involuntary defense mechanisms, and biological rhythms.

Among his notes, there is a plan for a piece that is at present impossible to execute:

> A person enters and lives in a room for a long time—a period of years or a lifetime. One wall of the room mirrors the room but from the opposite side; that is, the image room has the same left–right orientation as the real room. Standing facing the image, one sees oneself from the back in the image room, standing facing a wall. There should be no progression of images; that can be controlled by adjusting the kind of information the sensor would use and the kind the mirror wall would put out. After a period of time, the time in the mirror room begins to fall behind the real time—until after a number of years, the person would no longer recognize his relationship to his mirrored image. (He would no longer relate to his mirrored image or a delay of his own time.)[4]

This piece, he says, is related to a dream that he had a long time ago and could only be done eventually with the aid of a vast computer network.

The experience of such a room, were it possible to build, would slowly alter the way in which we, as human beings, know ourselves in relation to the world we inhabit. If what we know of the world is the sum of our perceptions and our physical, emotional, and intellectual reactions to our environment, then to effectively manipulate these factors is to effect a virtual change in that world.

Nauman's work continues to explore these possibilities. Like the mirror piece, the computer and the dream exemplify the polarities of man's nature and consequently of his art.

Notes

1. © J. Paul Getty Trust. Getty Research Institute, Los Angeles (2004.M.13).
2. Maurice Merleau-Ponty, *The Structure of Behavior*, trans. Alden L. Fisher (Cambridge, MA: Beacon Press, 1963).
3. All statements by Bruce Nauman are taken from taped interviews by the author made during August 1970.
4. *Editor's note*: These notes were published as a short text piece, "Withdrawal as an Art Form," in *Artforum* 9 no. 4 (December 1970): 44.

Bruce Nauman: Another Kind of Reasoning

Robert Pincus-Witten

I

In 1968, the cutting edge of postminimalist sensibility could have sectioned between Richard Serra, Keith Sonnier, and Bruce Nauman. And yet each of Nauman's successive appearances presents us with a growing insipidness, the one quality that, whatever else may have been wrong, he certainly was not thought to possess.

When Nauman worked with verbal problems in Duchamp's oeuvre, he was answering a central problem of contemporary art: where to stand in relation to Duchamp. Duchamp demonstrates, as no other artist does, that the ultimate basis of meaning in art is linguistic and not formal, whatever the formal properties his work may possess. In establishing his connection, Nauman settled on the baldest examination of the pun and arrogated a messianic mysticism—the banners and slogans—to himself as well. (The relation to Duchamp in Nauman's early work will be examined in part II of this essay.)

Nauman's solution, on the basis of a self-referential interpretation of Duchamp's enigmatic three small, sexual works of 1951 and the linguistic commitment of Duchamp's total body of work, finally has led him to a production that, in fashionable terms, is called "phenomenological" and that I have tried to indicate is merely ontological in nature; that is, it answers the problem of how to make conceptual art that looks like art and that, in looking like art, supplies no information except that of style.[1]

In my view, then, it appears that Nauman went wrong at the moment he read the lesson Duchamp as a public rather than a private one, the moment that he moved from a cryptic and introverted position to a democratic behaviorism. This shift indicates an art free of any basis in Duchamp but that instead borrows premises from behavioral psychology and a nostalgia for a purportedly lost human interchange in modern American culture. In short, Nauman now offers up a set of simplistic tests rooted in behavioral phenomenology; he has become interested in the exposure and experience of specific and isolated sensory phenomena rather than in an integrative theory of function. Nauman has exchanged

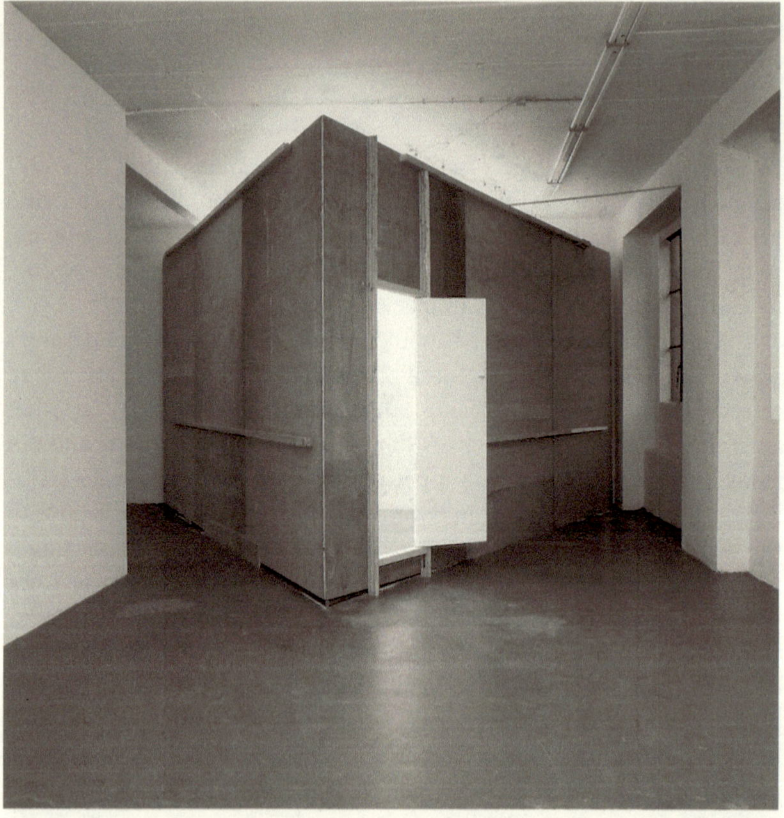

Yellow Room (Triangular), 1973. Wallboard, plywood, yellow fluorescent light. Dimensions variable; 120 × 177 × 157 in. (304.8 × 449.6 × 398.8 cm) as installed at Galerie Konrad Fischer, Düsseldorf, 1974. Solomon R. Guggenheim Museum, New York. Panza Collection, 1991. Image courtesy Sperone Westwater, New York.

elitism for populism and, devoid of the verbal flourish that his work once possessed, gives us only sensitivity boxes that he imagines turn his observer on to the fresh experience of color and sound. In proselytizing for the "WOW" experience—"WOW," sound proofing; "WOW," yellow fluorescent light; "WOW," the room is built on a diagonal axis[2]—he has now abandoned Duchamp and, in leaving Duchamp, has abandoned his claim to being interesting, at least for the moment.

Behavioral phenomenology at best tends to locate discrete phenomena rather than the ongoing product of continuous variables. In other words, instead of dealing with a constant field of activity, this view tends to isolate discrete phenomena. The location of neural processes is not important in Nauman's case except insofar as he sets a prestigious example in this activity.[3] Said another way, what Nauman is doing is not important because it has been done; and Pavlov, Skinner, Bender, and Gibson (the behavioral psychologist), working out of Heidegger and Husserl, are the original major contributors to this field of data.

The recent installation at Castelli Downtown presents a set of disorienting chambers of eccentric proportions. Moving through one room funneled into another, one passes through a yellow Flavin fluorescent atmosphere (the retina supplies the neutralizing lavender spurts) and then into a kind of boardwalk more or less enclosed by soundproof panels, in which the experience of sound is structured to become possibly more physically sensate or tangible on the viewer's body.

What seems to be regrettable in all of this is not that these tired experiments in behavioral phenomenology are presented as art—that, in itself, is an arresting idea if an equally tired one—but that Nauman has been reduced to making "pieces" to answer the pressures of celebrity by doing what he has already done. What Nauman presents is another jerry-built version of last year's Whitney show. And in this he makes "artworks" or replicated "pieces" but gives no new information or new idea.

II

> Generally, they were pieces of rubber shower caps, which I cut up and I glued together and which had no special shape. At the end of each piece there were strings that one attached to the four corners of the room. Then, when one came in the room, one couldn't walk around, because of the strings! The length of the strings could

> be varied; the form was *ad libitum.* That's what interested me. This game lasted three or four years, but the rubber rotted and it disappeared.
>
> —Marcel Duchamp (in conversation with Pierre Cabanne)

Bruce Nauman's career has been based almost exclusively in California. A lack of vigorous firsthand acquaintance with this ambience has made me acutely conscious of—though not necessarily sympathetic to—certain California qualities, which I often sense as outlandish. The central Californian characteristic seems to me to be a pervading narcissism expressed through mirroring and colorism predicated in a technically oriented automotive culture and a geographical metaphor. I think this originates and has been intensified by the comparative smallness of the scene, a feature that has tended to a stylistic inbreeding. This is a quality, not necessarily pejorative, historically noted in all regional art centers. It can be said as easily of London art today as of Dutch art at the height of the de Stijl movement.

The chief distinction separating the arts of the two seaboards, at least through the end of the 1960s, appears to be between an art concerned with the *characterological* functionings of its *creators* (California) and the *morphological* processes of *creation* (New York). Tersely, the distinction is between "being" and "doing." Despite the broadness of this distinction, it permits one to close in on Nauman, who, if nothing else, stresses confession, autobiography, and narcissism—certainly in the work after 1966, when Nauman's art seems or seemed to be primarily about the artist's ability to reconstruct himself before an audience. Such a theatrical intention is congruent in many respects with those episodes that have been variously named process, phenomenological, or conceptual art (Marcia Tucker once punned "pheNAUMANology"[4]) and that I group under the umbrella term *postminimalism.* But in Nauman's case it is essentially a received art, stemming from Marcel Duchamp and given vitally important refurbishment in the work of Jasper Johns, in whose tradition Nauman continued to be nourished, at least through the end of 1969.

Fidel Danieli, a California critic who wrote the first intelligent article on Nauman, observed that Nauman's work "would appear at first exposure to be a vaguely repulsive caprice."[5] Danieli also affiliated Nauman to Marcel Duchamp (the *Green Box*) and to Jasper Johns (the skin print drawings). He recognized that Nauman was not above a certain duplicity, citing as an example of "cheating" the knees referred to in *Wax Block with the Impressions of the Knees of Five Famous Artists*, 1966, which the critic knew to be impressions of the artist's own knees. Nor was Danieli deceived by the arch double-dealing of the title, a problem to which I will return. In a like manner, the romantic and mystical stance of the neons and banners (e.g., "The artist is an amazing luminous fountain") was seen for what it was—namely, "being poetic in a beautiful, self-flattering way."[6]

Subsequent criticism seems to have consistently stressed the theme of Nauman's relation to Duchamp and Johns. In a statement by the artist published in the catalog *American Sculpture of the Sixties*, Nauman also recognized a derivation in Dadaism:

> I suppose some work has to do in part with some of the things that the Dadaists and Surrealists did. I like to give the pieces elaborate titles the way they did, although I've only been titling them recently. That all came from not trying to figure out why I make those things. It got so I just couldn't do anything. So like making the impressions of knees in a wax block … was a way of having a large rectangular solid with marks in it so *I had to make this other kind of reasoning. It also had to do with trying to make a less important thing to look at.*[7]

After 1966, that "other kind of reasoning" accelerated toward the art object invested with extraformal meaning on the basis of the *title as pun*—for example, *Henry Moore Bound to Fail* (1967). As a literary formula, the pun is a loaded area of intellectual experience, for, as Duchamp knew, the circularity of the pun appears to provide information without getting you anywhere. Toby Mussman correctly observed in his study of Duchamp's film *Anemic Cinema* (made in conjunction with Man Ray) that "puns, unlike ordinary sentences, do not attempt to make a definite statement but rather they cast ironic doubt on the ability of any written sentence to make ultimate and absolutely conclusive sense."[8]

Reactions to Nauman's punning ranged from the positive ("we all secretly enjoy the hideous sinking sensation engendered by a really bad pun"[9]) to the negative ("the most vexing portion of Mr. Nauman's work is related to his ingenuous literary punning"[10]). A middle road is possible: "If one accepts the title on the level of poetic commentary, a debate arises as to whether the artist is pure and naïve, or a witty and sophisticated literate. My experience favors an amalgam."[11] The works that led to these reactions were a set of color photographs in which the artist was seen performing such elementary activities as *Eating My Words*. In this instance, the word *words* had been literally shaped out of bread and was being eaten. Similarly, *Waxing Hot* depicted the artist literally waxing the letters of the word *HOT*. The photograph *Feet of Clay* (1967) depicts the artist's feet literally covered over with clay pellets.[12] The images, therefore, have been given "meaning" and "recognizability" by fusing them to a cliché. The model for such an activity is obviously Marcel Duchamp. For example, *With My Tongue in My Cheek*, an assemblage relief of 1959 and a late self-portrait, combines a drawn profile of the artist with a plaster cast of the artist's jaw. Similarly, Nauman's green-wax piece *From Hand to Mouth* (1967, the color and substance deriving from Johns's early encaustic *Green Target*) is a cast of the artist's right hand, arm, shoulder, throat, jaw, and lips.[13] Another work of 1967 presents the artist's crossed arms cast in green wax, from whose severed biceps there emerges a heavy rope tied into a square knot. Although the work is untitled, its verbal/visual interplay turns on the following equation: as the arms are folded, so the rope is knotted, or vice versa. In short, the rope and arms are permutations of the same knotted condition: they are tied up in knots. In addition to the obvious relationship to Johns in terms of the cast elements of these works, they are also distinctly Johns-like in terms of the work's insistent proliferation of the *same* thing projected into a *different* state, diagrammatic or otherwise. Johns's celebrated *Ballantine Ale Cans*, 1962, one a cast and the other modeled by hand, is a well-known example of this kind of pairing. Nauman also stated in the catalog quote in *American Sculpture of the Sixties* that part of his effort was directed toward making "a less important thing to look at."[14] I take this to reflect an active indifference to the issues of reductivist abstraction as they were then being explored and a desire to make works that would *obviously* have no relevance to the solemn earnestness, for example, of minimalist sculpture then at its apogee.

From 1965 on, one sees a hyperbolic attempt on Nauman's part to create forms never before seen, made of substances and colored in ways equally unknown.[15] I do not quarrel with the aspiration; it is the very fiber of art. But the quest, though stated and perhaps even "felt" in these exalted terms, is equally arbitrary, notwithstanding the fact that between

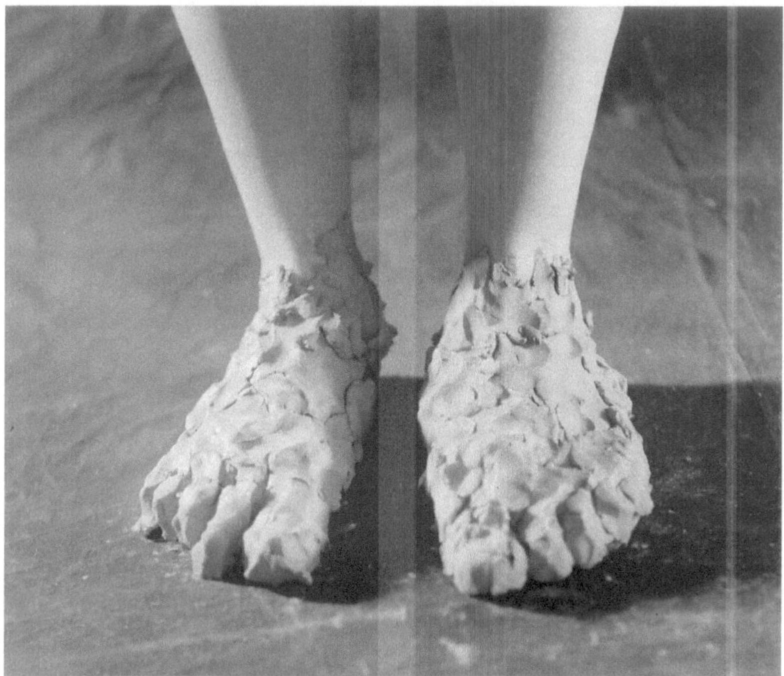

Feet of Clay, 1967, from *Eleven Color Photographs*, 1966–1967/1970. Portfolio of 11 color photographs. Various sizes, approx. 19¾ × 23 in. (50.2 × 58.4 cm) each. Published by the Leo Castelli Gallery, New York. Edition of eight. Image courtesy Sperone Westwater, New York.

1965 and 1967 Nauman came close to realizing such an ambition. The forms that Nauman took to making at the time were spindly affairs, loaf-like and split into arching rails. They were of two kinds, soft and hard; the soft group were made of colored rubber latex and the hard of cast fiberglass. The works give off an aura of undernourishment and eccentricity. In many respects, these "impoverished" works, supported directly by the wall and floor, anticipate many of the experiments associated with the rise of postminimalism—particularly the early rubber and neon work of Richard Serra—a history that I have attempted to write in my essays on Richard Serra, Keith Sonnier, and Eva Hesse.[16] I would be hard put not to acknowledge the seminal role played by Nauman's untitled rubber, fiberglass, and neon works in redirecting the nature of artistic aspiration in the late 1960s.

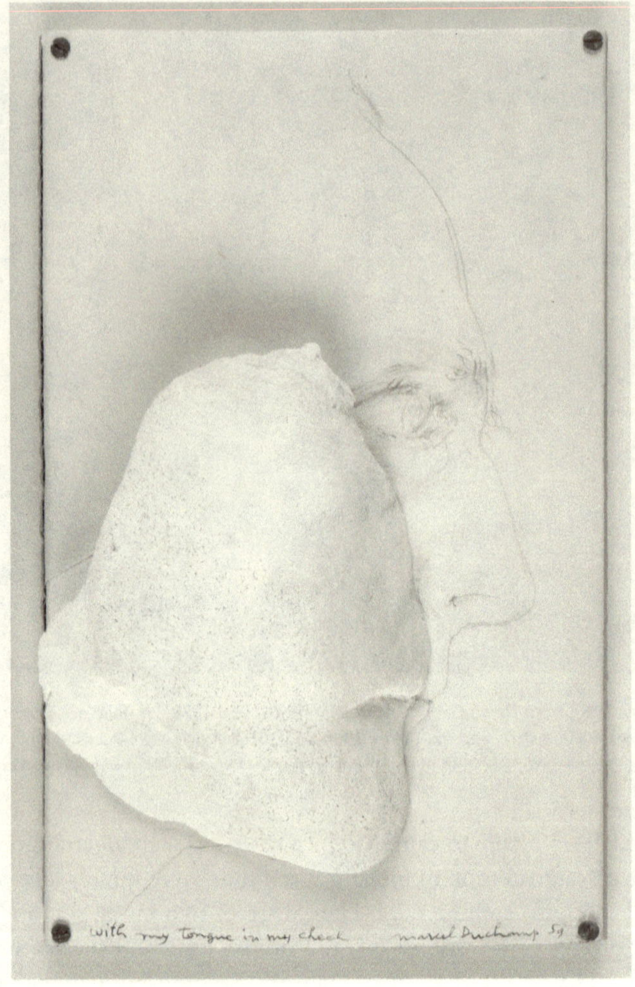

Marcel Duchamp, *With My Tongue in My Cheek*, 1959. Plaster, pencil, and paper, mounted on wood. $9\frac{13}{16} \times 5\frac{7}{8}$ in. (24.92×14.91 cm). Musée national d'art moderne, Centre Georges Pompidou, Paris. Art © Association Marcel Duchamp / ADAGP, Paris / Artists Rights Society (ARS), New York. Photograph: Jacques Faujour, © CNAC/MNAM/Dis. Réunion des musées nationaux/Art Resource, New York.

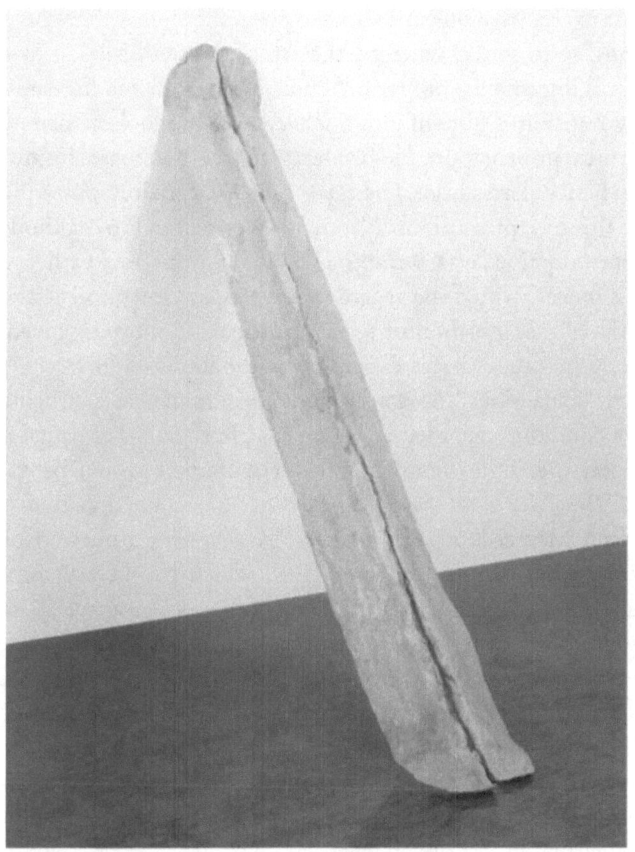

Untitled, 1965. Fiberglass, polyester resin. Approx. 68 × 16 × 3 in. (172.7 × 40.6 × 7.6 cm). Tate. Purchased with funds provided by an anonymous donor, 2009. Image courtesy Sperone Westwater, New York.

In November 1966, Nauman figured prominently in an exhibition held in New York's Fischbach Gallery called *Eccentric Abstraction*, which represented the real surfacing of this counterminimalist taste in the gallery context. Works by Keith Sonnier and Eva Hesse were included, among others. The exhibition was organized and introduced by the critic Lucy Lippard, who undertook to clarify "an aspect of visceral identification that is hard to escape, an identification that psychologists have called 'body ego.'"[17] Lippard was referring to the capacity of the viewer to empathetically respond to unfamiliar forms in visceral terms.

Yet the term *body ego* suggests another possibility—that the work may be the means, so to speak, whereby the artist employs his body or sections thereof, his lineaments, his personal possessions, or even his name and in so doing transforms himself into a self-exploitable tool or the raw material of artistic presentation. He becomes, in a certain sense, his own objet trouvé—hence narcissistic. The term *body ego* certainly poses the possibility of this interpretation in Nauman's work after 1967, although Lippard's introduction was written on the basis of the earlier untitled fiberglass pieces, which she regarded as vehicles "unconcerned with the conventional manipulation of forms in space and more involved with a perverse, sometimes bizarre expansion of the limits of art."[18]

Such "expansions" obviously posit formlessness as a structural possibility, a condition recorded in Nauman's photographs of patted mounds of flour on the studio floor. Another counterpart would be *Composite Photo of Two Messes on the Studio Floor* (1967). The affiliation of these works with Marcel Duchamp's *Élevage de Poussière*, a photograph taken in 1920 by Man Ray of the *Large Glass*, which had been lying flat and gathering dust in Duchamp's New York studio, is inescapable. The works are alike in that they refer to insubstantial and amorphous substances. It is of larger critical interest, however, that they exist at several removes from the original, the "real" works having been replaced by *photographs*, which are or have become by default the central document of experience, hence the central emotional repository of the works. It is obvious that with Nauman the "real" or "original" work had all along been an auxiliary effort. The shift away from an *original* by whatever means—photography, cinematography, tape-recording, private journals, notations, memos, or ultimately merely the unexecuted idea or conception, allied to a valorization of the technological, cognitive, mental, or other processes—is the chief characteristic of Nauman's work. This most clearly identifies him as a founder of the conceptualist movement, a postminimalist episode that is, in Nauman's expression of it, Dada in spirit.

The lateral spread of *Composite Photo of Two Messes on the Studio Floor* is assembled in a manner similar to an aerial reconnaissance map. In this way it resembles a work called *Composite Photo of My Name as Though It Were Written on the Surface of the Moon* (1967), which appears as if a repeatedly beamed electronic signal forming the letters of Nauman's first name had bounced off the moon and returned to earth at constant intervals. The work is predicated on dubbing, on christening, and

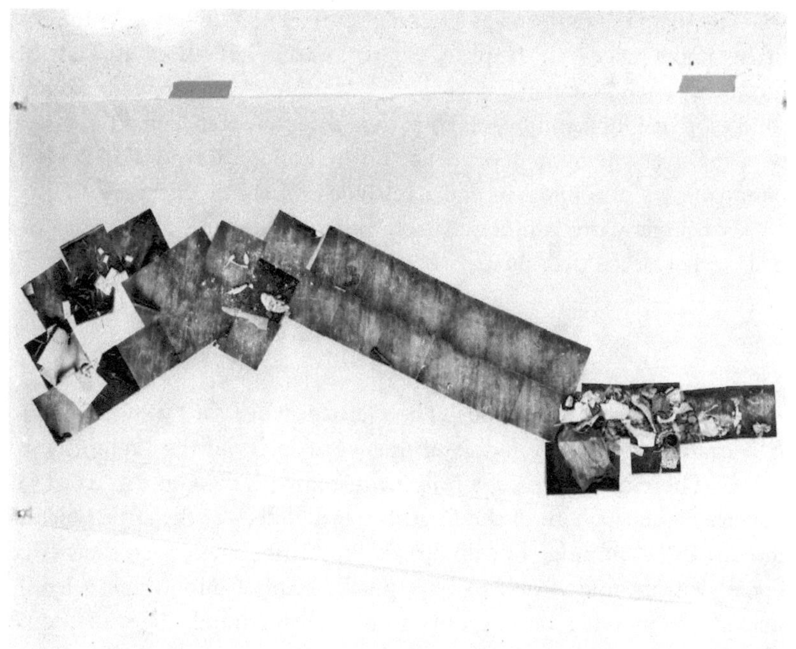

Composite Photo of Two Messes on the Studio Floor, 1967. Gelatin silver print. 40½ × 123 in. (102.9 × 312.4 cm). The Museum of Modern Art, New York. Gift of Philip Johnson. Image courtesy Sperone Westwater, New York.

though the similarity to Duchamp's readymades may appear tenuous, the connection is still discernible. Duchamp's investment of artistic identity in a neutral common object (a snow shovel or a bottle rack) was also in part based on a kind of baptism, on arrant say-so. As the snow shovel and the bottle rack were Duchamp's readymades, so is Nauman's first name his readymade. Nauman's name, of course, is subjected to a complex alteration, whereas Duchamp's readymades were scarcely adjusted, if at all. Each individual letter of the name "Bruce" is arbitrarily repeated, similar to the repetitions in *Six Inches of My Knee Extended to Six Feet* (1967) or any of the duplications of measurements and sections taken from the artist's body. Perhaps the most striking alterations occur in the neon work, which fudges the script of Nauman's *My Last Name Exaggerated Fourteen Times Vertically* (1967).[19] In the latter work, the legibility is all but obliterated by the vertical scaling, and one reads the name "Nauman" as a neon gesture. The title serves, as in most of his neon pieces, to "explain" or to "justify." In short, it is at this moment, when Nauman comes more and more to rely on technological sources, that Duchamp begins to fade as a central preoccupation. Now, with the overwhelming dependence on technological recording devices, Nauman's art announces its entire reliance on behavioral theory.

No single work is more characteristic of Nauman's use of extraformal, verbal tactics than the two steel wedges of 1968; they are inscribed:

$$\frac{\text{LIKE}}{\text{KEIL}} \text{ and } \frac{\text{WEDGE}}{\text{KEIL}}$$

The wordplay is facetious. The German word for "wedge" is *Keil.* A rearrangement of the letters of this word spell out the English word "like." Therefore, the wedge *form* is equated with the German word for "wedge," the anagram of the English word "like," or the same word as the first LIKE: punning or palindromic circularity. Moreover, the wedge shape is easily understood to be a phallic symbol into which a lentil-shaped chamfer has been grooved, a vaginal symbol. This additional

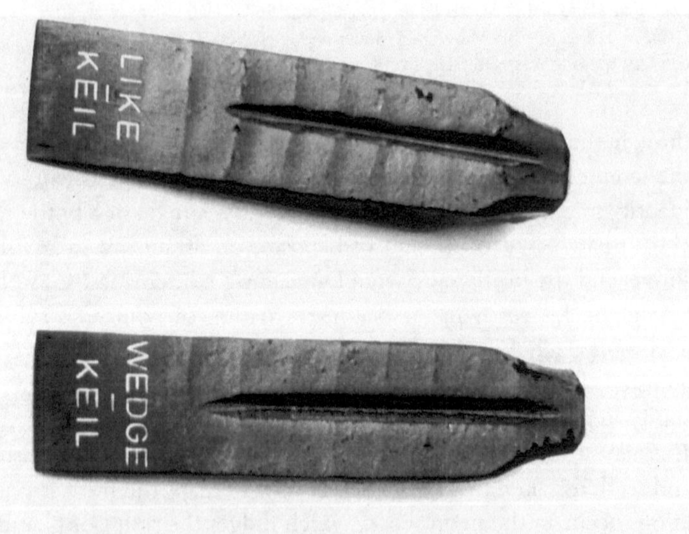

Wedge Piece, 1968. Steel, paint. Two parts: approx. 1½ × 11 in. (3.8 × 27.9 cm) each. Fischer Family Collection, Düsseldorf. Image courtesy Sperone Westwater, New York.

orchestration may derive from the sexual and poetic object of Duchamp's late work, *Coin de chasteté* of 1951,[20] in which a wedge has been pressed into dental plastic. The verbal fixation of such exercises are linked to Duchamp, from the quasi-pornographic caption of *LHOOQ (elle a chaud au cul)*, or "Mona Lisa's Moustache," as it is popularly called, to the punning titles such as the *Anemic Cinema*. This kind of closed and perfect verbal/visual decoction leads to a chain of equally absurd neutral elements. Such verbal/visual puns are curiously self-referential and hidebound. As experiences, they tend toward introversion rather than extroversion. Even after one "gets" them, one is irked by the tightness of their boundaries because of their obviously axiomatic and tautological nature.

From all this, one would imagine that Bruce Nauman was a mere Dadaistic *pasticheur* haunted by the specter of Duchamp. But, added to Nauman's verbal/visual juggling, there remains his equal commitment to sheer materiality and physicality, which alone would mark him as foreign to Dadaism. Because of this latter aspect, Nauman is a bedfellow of Andre, Hesse, Morris, Serra, Sonnier, Smithson, and any of half-a-dozen artists whose names readily come to mind. Nauman's uniquely private employment of neon would serve to rank him as an important figure.

Nauman's work exhibited at the Castelli Gallery in June 1969 consisted of a set of holograms (photographs made with laser beams that manneristically exaggerate stereometry) that showed the artist viewed from below in multiple crouched and fetal positions. These holograms alter one's spatial apperceptions in an odd way; they induce a sensation of looking into a stereopticon of a greenish coloration.

In May 1969, a freestanding passageway that could be walked through was included at the Whitney Museum's *Anti-Illusion: Procedures/ Materials* exhibition. Its oddness was a function of its seeming neutrality, but as passageway it gained meaning when the viewer watched a videotape shown at Nauman's subsequent one-man exhibition held shortly thereafter at the Leo Castelli Gallery. The videotape image revealed Nauman entering and exiting from this narrow corridor. It became evident that the width of the odd corridor was delimited to accommodate the deliberately exaggerated swing of the artist's hips. The passageway itself was virtually without meaning, which it subsequently and suddenly assumed only to the degree that it was revealed to be a visual boundary for the setting of the videotape.

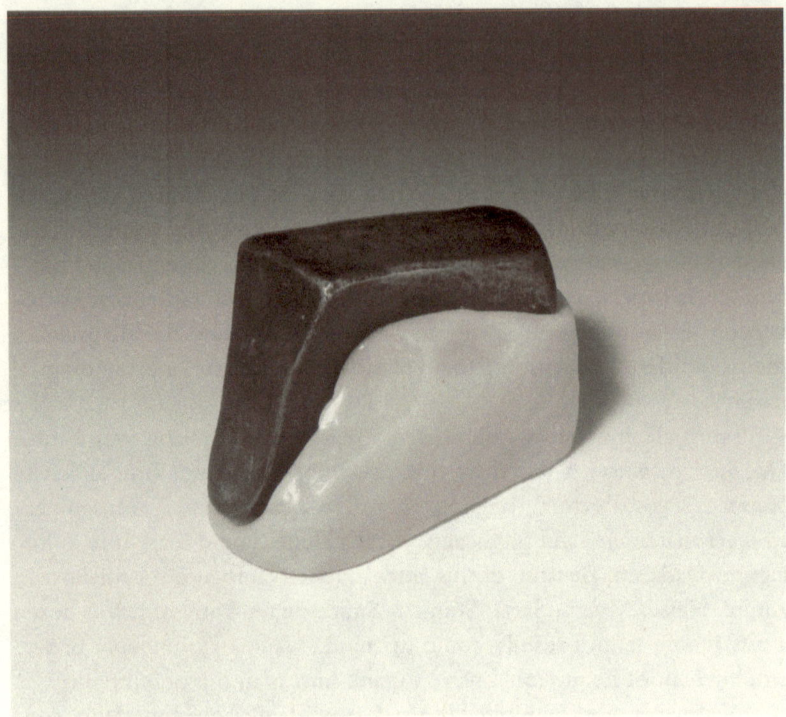

Marcel Duchamp, *Coin de chasteté* (*Wedge of Chastity*), 1954/1963. Bronze and plastic. $2^{3}/_{16} \times 3^{3}/_{8} \times 1^{5}/_{8}$ in. (5.6 × 8.6 × 4.1 cm). The Menil Collection, Houston. Art © Association Marcel Duchamp / ADAGP, Paris / Artists Rights Society (ARS), New York. Photograph: Paul Hester.

Because of his use of cryptic self-reference, linguistic attachment, resistance to received notions of good taste (and therefore good sense and good behavior), and experimentation as an end in itself, Nauman *in the phase of his allegiance to Duchamp* can be regarded as a significant artist whose work is important because—like much of Johns's later work—he continued to vitally extrapolate on the lessons of Duchamp.

The inferences, then, of these views are that Nauman's contribution as a critical artist is supported to the degree that he was able to expressively prevaricate on Duchamp. But with the introduction of laser-beam holograms and the greater reliance on technology and behavioral phenomenology, Nauman cut himself off from the experience that centrally formed his art.

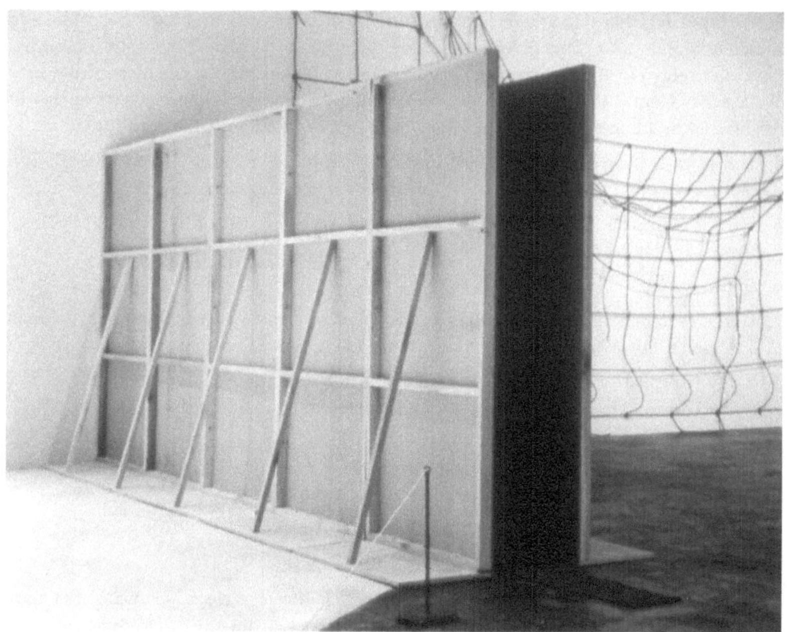

Performance Corridor, 1969. Wallboard, wood. 96 × 240 × 20 in. (243.8 × 609.6 × 50.8 cm). Solomon R. Guggenheim Museum, New York. Panza Collection, gift, 1992. Image courtesy Sperone Westwater, New York.

It is apparent that two options were open to Nauman: he had either to continue to develop his attachments to Duchamp or to exposit purely epistemological information. But the very fact that his postminimal production was linked to Dadaism obviated an epistemological response and promoted an art of continuing self-exposure in the context of conceptualism. However, the latter context is unable to support this kind of externalization since it cannot support objectification. And in being unable to support an art of things or of making objects, Nauman's postminimalism is betrayed by both his beginnings and his conclusions.

Notes

1. See "Bochner at MOMA," *Artforum* 10, no. X (December 1971): 28–30.
2. I have adopted this terminology from the teaching practice of Mel Bochner, who always warns his students to beware of the "WOW" experience.

3. Recognizing that fluorescent light functioning as color may no longer be considered sufficiently ambitious, Dan Flavin has of late forced colored light to function as another kind of energy. In the fluorescent "plaid" corridor set up for the opening of the new Walker Art Center this past summer, the essential experience of the viewer was that of the light as heat contained by the passageway as he passed through the corridor.

4. See Marcia Tucker, "PheNAUMANology," *Artforum* 9, no. 4 (December 1970): 38–44 [reprinted in this volume].

5. Fidel A. Danieli, "The Art of Bruce Nauman," *Artforum* 6, no. 4 (December 1967): 15 [reprinted in this volume].

6. Ibid., 19.

7. Bruce Nauman, statement in *American Sculpture of the Sixties*, ed. Maurice Tuchman (Los Angeles: Los Angeles County Museum of Art, 1967), 49, emphasis added.

8. Toby Mussman, "Marcel Duchamp's Anemic Cinema" (1966), reprinted in *The New American Cinema: A Critical Anthology*, ed. Gregory Battcock (New York: Dutton, 1967), 151.

9. John Perreault, writing on Nauman's first New York one-man show, *Village Voice*, February 8, 1968.

10. Robert Pincus-Witten, "New York Review," *Artforum* 6, no. 8 (April 1968): 64.

11. Danieli, "Bruce Nauman."

12. *Editor's note*: It was a common assumption that the feet were Nauman's, but they were actually those of Nauman's wife at the time, Judy Govan.

13. *Editor's note*: Again, Govan, not the artist himself, served as the model for *From Hand to Mouth*.

14. Nauman, statement in *American Sculpture of the Sixties*, 49.

15. David Whitney's picture folder of 44 works by Bruce Nauman, published by Leo Castelli Gallery, is helpful in dating the early shift in the direction of Nauman's work.

16. Robert Pincus-Witten, "Richard Serra—Slow Information," *Artforum* 8, no. 1 (September 1969): 34–39; "Keith Sonnier: Materials and Pictorialism," *Artforum* 8, no. 2 (October 1969): 39–45; "Eva Hesse: Post-minimalism into Sublime," *Artforum* 10, no. 3 (November 1971): 32–43.

17. Lucy Lippard, broadside to an exhibition called *Eccentric Abstraction*, Fischbach Gallery, New York, September 1966.

18. Ibid.

19. Neon appears in many of Nauman's constructions. Philip Glass, a musician and intimate of both Nauman and Richard Serra, contends that the neon spiral maxim "The true artist helps the world by revealing mystic truths" is directly related to the optical spiral of Duchamp's *Rotary Demisphere* of 1925. This information was supplied by Philip Leider, to whom, although he will probably not subscribe to the changing "politics" inherent in this article, I nevertheless respectfully dedicate it.

20. *Wedge of Chastity*.

Breaking the Silence: An Interview with Bruce Nauman

Joan Simon

Last year two major retrospective exhibitions in Europe of the work of Bruce Nauman made it possible to see, comprehensively and for the first time, the tremendous diversity and at the same time the consistency of vision that characterize his work. Inevitably, these exhibitions recalled the fact that Nauman's only other retrospective (aside from a survey of the neons at the Baltimore Museum in 1982) was more than 15 years ago—when the artist had just turned 31. That 1972 retrospective, organized by the Los Angeles County Museum of Art and the Whitney Museum, included many of Nauman's now classic early works: fiberglass casts, neon pieces, photographs, films, videos, drawings, and environments (including several corridor installations). The heterogeneity of Nauman's early work not only challenged the purity of minimal or late-formalist sculpture but also demonstrated Nauman's characteristic attitude toward art making, which often treats linguistic fragments and material issues as interchangeable.

Nauman was raised in the Midwest. He was born in Fort Wayne, Indiana, in 1941, and while he was still young, his family moved to Milwaukee. There Nauman attended the University of Wisconsin, studying mathematics and art. Following graduation from Wisconsin in 1964, Nauman went to the University of California at Davis to continue his art studies. Though initially a painter, Nauman soon began producing quirky sculptures, performances, and films under the influence of his instructors, William Wiley and Robert Arneson.

During 1965–1966, Nauman produced his first fiberglass pieces and performances based on simple procedures and body movements. In 1966, Nauman finished his MA at Davis and moved to San Francisco, where he had a studio in an old storefront. There his work began to reflect more directly his relationship to his own body and to the space where he worked. These themes were explored in a neon (*Neon Templates of the Left Half of My Body Taken at Ten-Inch Intervals*, 1966), wax casts (*From Hand to Mouth*, 1967), holograms (*Making Faces*, 1968), film (*Art Make-Up*, 1967–1968), and fiberglass sculpture (*Six Inches of My Knee Extended to Six Feet*, 1967). In 1968, Nauman had his first solo show at the Leo Castelli Gallery in New York.

In the 1970s, Nauman's work shifted from the body and elements in the studio to quasi-architectural installations (including many corridor pieces), which often incorporated sound or video. Nauman himself was no longer the ostensible subject; instead, the cameras were often turned on the viewer. A recurrent motif was his exhortation of the viewer to pay attention. In the claustrophobic corridor pieces, Nauman confronted the viewer with seemingly playful or gamelike situations, but they were often quite terrifying to experience. The viewer's self-image was at stake, as video cameras recorded him or her in the corridor from behind or upside down. This use of emotionally charged architectural space sometimes comprised whole rooms—such as *Double Steel Cage Piece*, 1974, a doubled prison cell within a cell—that served as moral statements or political metaphors. During the 1970s, Nauman almost entirely abandoned photography, film, and video, although he continued to use video and audio technology in his installations.

Nauman's work in the 1980s focuses increasing attention on social and political subject matter. His large-scale steel sculptures, such as *Diamond Africa Chair Tuned D.E.A.D.*, 1981, and *South America Triangle*, 1981, use abstract elements (such as a steel chair or a huge hanging steel triangle) to suggest the threat of political torture or the cold surface of alienation. The abstracted chairs in these works also reintroduce a surrogate figurative presence. This figuration is reiterated in Nauman's recent neons and videos. In both forms, Nauman's work frequently starts with a banal situation or an innocent joke—as in pulling a chair out from under someone in *Violent Incident*, 1986. In a series of videos made since 1987, featuring actors dressed as clowns, Nauman has continued to investigate the darker side of humor.

BRUCE NAUMAN: There is a tendency to clutter things up, to try to make sure people know something is art, when all that's necessary is to present it, to leave it alone. I think the hardest thing to do is to present an idea in the most straightforward way.

What I tend to do is see something, then remake it and remake it and remake it and try every possible way of remaking it. If I'm persistent enough, I get back to where I started. I think it was Jasper Johns who said, "Sometimes it's necessary to state the obvious."

Still, how to proceed is always a mystery. I remember at one point thinking that someday I would figure out how you do this, how you do art—like, "What's the procedure here, folks?"—and then it wouldn't be such a struggle anymore. Later, I realized it was never going to be like that; it was always going to be a struggle. I realized I would never have a specific process; I would have to reinvent it, over and over again. That was really depressing.

After all, it was hard work; it was a painful struggle and tough. I didn't want to have to go through all that every time. But of course you do have to continually rediscover and redecide, and it's awful. It's just an awful thing to have to do.

On the other hand, that's what's interesting about making art and why it's worth doing: it's never going to be the same; there is no method. If I stop and try to look at how I got the last piece done, it doesn't help me do the next one.

JOAN SIMON: What do you think about when you're working on a piece?

BN: I think about Lenny Tristano a lot. Do you know who he was? Lenny Tristano was a blind pianist, one of the original—or maybe second-generation—bebop guys. He's on a lot of the best early bebop records. When Lenny played well, he hit you hard, and he kept going until he finished. Then he just quit. You didn't get any introduction, you didn't get any tail—you just got full intensity for 2 minutes or 20 minutes or whatever. It would be like taking the middle out of [John] Coltrane—just the hardest, toughest part of it. That was all you got.

From the beginning I was trying to see if I could make art that did that. Art that was just there all at once. Like getting hit in the face with a baseball bat. Or better, like getting hit in the back of the neck. You never see it coming; it just knocks you down. I like that idea very much:

the kind of intensity that doesn't give you any trace of whether you're going to like it or not.

JS: In trying to capture that sort of intensity over the past 20 or so years, you've worked in just about every medium: film, video, sound, neon, installation, performance, photography, holography, sculpture, drawing—but not painting. You gave that up very early on. Why?

BN: When I was in school, I was a painter. And I went back and forth a couple of times. But basically I couldn't function as a painter. Painting is one of those things I never quite made sense of. I just couldn't see how to proceed as a painter. It seemed that if I didn't think of myself as a painter, then it would be possible to continue.

It still puzzles me how I made decisions in those days about what was possible and what wasn't. I ended up drawing on music and dance and literature, using thoughts and ideas from other fields to help me continue to work. In that sense, the early work, which seems to have all kinds of materials and ideas in it, seemed very simple to make because it wasn't coming from looking at sculpture or painting.

JS: That doesn't sound simple.

BN: No, I don't mean that it was simple to do the work. But it was simple in that in the '60s you didn't have to pick just one medium. There didn't seem to be any problem with using different kinds of materials—shifting from photographs to dance to performance to videotapes. It seemed very straightforward to use all of those different ways of expressing ideas or presenting material. You could make neon signs, you could make written pieces, you could make jokes about parts of the body or casting things or whatever.

JS: Do you see your work as part of a continuum with other art or other artists?

BN: Sure there are connections, though not in any direct way. It's not that there is someone in particular you emulate. But you do see other artists asking the same kinds of questions and responding with some kind of integrity.

There's a kind of restraint and morality in Johns. It isn't specific. I don't know how to describe it, but it's there; I feel it's there. It's less there but still important in Duchamp. Or in Man Ray, who also interests me. Maybe the morality I sense in Man Ray has to do with the fact that while he made his living as a fashion photographer, his artworks tended to be jokes—stupid jokes. The whole idea of Dada was that you didn't have to make your living with your art, so that generation could be more provocative with less risk. Then there is the particularly American idea about morality that has to do with the artist as workman. Many artists used to feel all right about making a living with their art because they identified with the working class. Some still do. I mean, I do, and I think Richard Serra does.

JS: No matter how jokey or stylistically diverse or visually dazzling your works are, they always have an ethical side, a moral force.

BN: I do see art that way. Art ought to have a moral value, a moral stance, a position. I'm not sure where that belief comes from. In part it just comes from growing up where I grew up and from my parents and family. And from the time I spend in San Francisco going to the Art Institute and before that in Wisconsin. From my days at the University of Wisconsin, the teachers I remember were older guys—they wouldn't let women into teaching easily—and they were all WPA [Works Progress Administration] guys. They were socialists, and they had points to make that were not only moral and political but also ethical. Wisconsin was one of the last socialist states, and in the '50s, when I lived there and went to high school there, Milwaukee still had a socialist mayor. So there were a lot of people who thought art had a function beyond being beautiful—that it had a social reason to exist.

Early Work

JS: What David Whitney wrote about your *Composite Photo of Two Messes on the Studio Floor* (1967)—that "it is a direct statement on how the artist lives, works, and thinks"—could apply in general to the variety of works you made in your San Francisco studio from 1966 to 1968.

BN: I did some pieces that started out just being visual puns. Since these needed body parts in them, I cast parts of a body and assembled them or presented them with a title. There was also the idea that if I was in the studio, whatever I was doing was art. Pacing around, for example. How do you organize that to present it as art? Well, first I filmed it. Then I videotaped it. Then I complicated it by turning the camera upside down or sideways or organizing my pacing to various sounds.

In a lot of the early work, I was concerned with ideas about inside and outside and front and back—how to turn them around and confuse them. Take the *Window or Wall Sign*—you know, the neon piece that says, "The true artist helps the world by revealing mystic truths." That idea occurred to me because of the studio I had in San Francisco at the time. It had been a grocery store, and in the window there was still a beer sign which you read from the outside. From the inside, of course, it was backwards. So when I did the earliest neon pieces, they were intended to be seen through the window one way and from the inside another way, confusing the message by reversing the image.

JS: Isn't your interest in inverting ideas, in showing what's "not there," and in solving—or at least revealing—"impossible" problems related in part to your training as a mathematician?

BN: I was interested in the logic and structure of math and especially how you could turn that logic inside out. I was fascinated by mathematical problems, particularly the one called "squaring the circle." You know, for hundreds of years mathematicians tried to find a geometrical way of finding a square equal in area to a circle—a formula where you could construct one from the other. At some point in the nineteenth century, a mathematician—I can't remember his name—proved it can't be done. His approach was to step outside the problem rather than struggling inside the problem; by stepping outside of it, he showed that it was not possible to do it at all.

Standing outside and looking at how something gets done or doesn't get done is really fascinating and curious. If I can manage to get outside of a problem a little bit and watch myself having a hard time, then I can see what I'm going to do—it makes it possible. It works.

JS: A number of early pieces specifically capture what's "not there." I'm thinking about the casts of "invisible spaces": the space between two crates on the floor, for example, or the "negative" space under a chair.

BN: Casting the space under a chair was the sculptural version of de Kooning's statement: "When you paint a chair, you should paint the space between the rungs, not the chair itself." I was thinking like that: about leftovers and negative space.

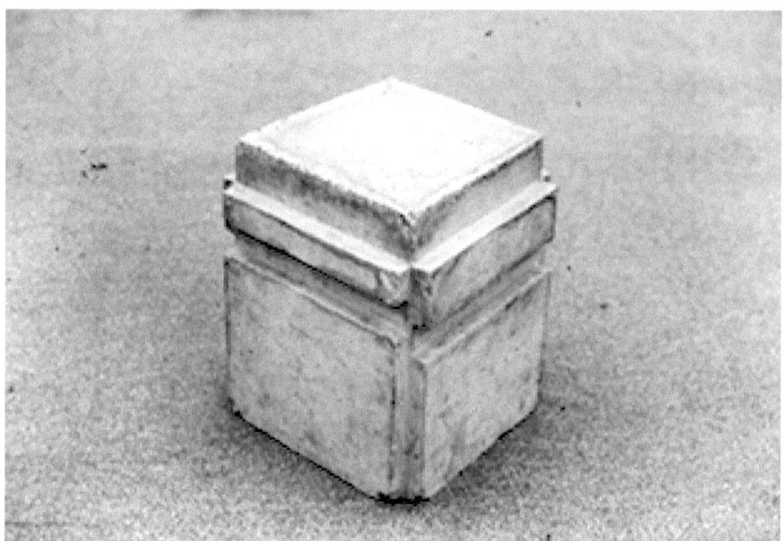

A Cast of the Space under My Chair, 1965–1968. Concrete. 17½ × 15⅜ × 14⅝ in. (44.5 × 39.1 × 37.1 cm). Kröeller-Müller Museum, Otterlo, Netherlands. Image courtesy Sperone Westwater, New York.

JS: But your idea of negative space is very different from the sculptor's traditional problem of locating an object in space or introducing space into a solid form.

BN: Negative space for me is thinking about the underside and the backside of things. In casting, I always like the parting lines and the seams—things that help to locate the structure of an object but in the finished sculpture usually get removed. These things help to determine the scale of the work and the weight of the material. Both what's inside and what's outside determine our physical, physiological, and psychological responses—how we look at an object.

JS: The whole idea of the visual puns, works like *Henry Moore Bound to Fail* and *From Hand to Mouth*, complicates this notion of how we look at an object. They are similar to readymades. On the one hand, they translate words or phrases into concrete form—in a sense literalizing them. On the other hand, they are essentially linguistic plays, which means abstracting them. I'm curious about the thought process that went into

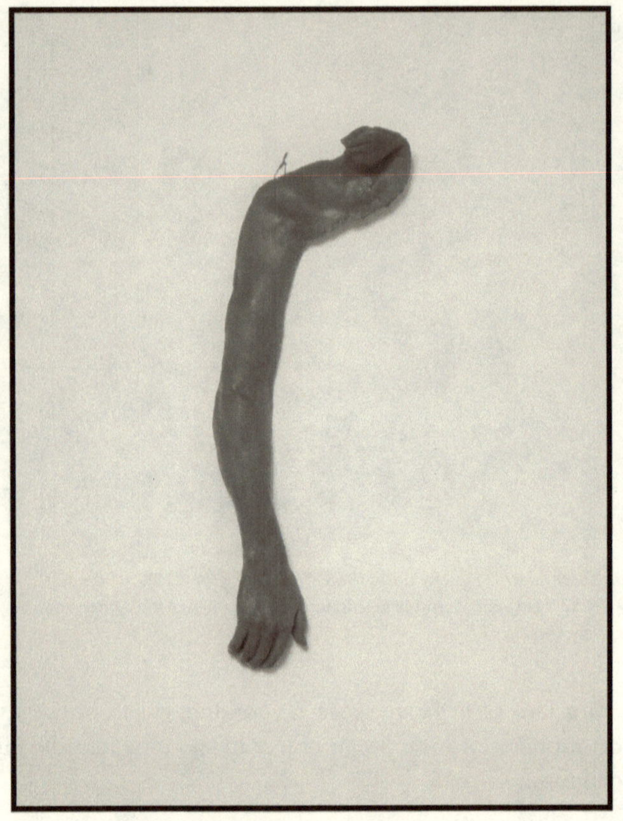

From Hand to Mouth, 1967. Wax over cloth. 28 × 10⅜ × 4⅜ in. (71.1 × 26.4 × 11.1 cm). Hirshhorn Museum and Sculpture Garden, Smithsonian Institution, Washington, DC, Joseph H. Hirshhorn Purchase Fund and Holenia Purchase Fund, in memory of Joseph H. Hirshhorn, and Museum Purchase, 1993. Image courtesy Sperone Westwater, New York.

conceiving those works. For instance, how did *From Hand to Mouth* come about?

BN: In that case, the cast was of someone else, not of myself, as has generally been assumed—but that doesn't really matter. It was just supposed to be a visual pun or a picture of a visual pun.

I first made *From Hand to Mouth* as a drawing—actually there were two or three different drawings—just the idea of drawing "from hand to mouth." But I couldn't figure out exactly how to make the drawing.

My first idea was to have a hand in the mouth with some kind of connection—a bar or some kind of mechanical connection. I finally realized that the most straightforward way to present the idea would be to cast that entire section of the body. Since I couldn't cast myself, I used my wife as the model.

I worked with the most accurate casting material I could find, something called "moulage." I found the stuff at some police shop. You know, they used it to cast tire prints and things like that. It's actually a very delicate casting process; you could pick up fingerprints in the dust with it. The moulage is a kind of gel you heat up. Because it's warm when you apply it to a body, it opens up all the pores—it picks up all that, even the hairs. But it sets like five-day-old Jell-O. You have to put plaster or something over the back of it to make it hold its shape. Then I made the wax cast, which became very superrealistic—hyperrealistic. You could see things you don't normally see—or think about—on people's skin.

JS: All your work seems to depend not only on this kind of tactile precision but also on a kind of incompleteness—a fragmentariness, a sense of becoming. As a result, your pieces accrue all sorts of meaning over time. With *From Hand to Mouth*—completed over 20 years ago—what other meanings have occurred to you?

BN: Well it's funny you should ask that because not long ago I read this book in which a character goes to funeral homes or morgues and puts this moulage stuff on people and makes plaster casts—death masks—for their families. I had no idea that this was a profession. But it turns out that this moulage is a very old, traditional kind of material and was often used this way. But it just connects up in a strange sort of way with my more recent work since over the past several years I have been involved with both the idea of death and dying and the idea of masking the figure.

Masks and Games

JS: An early example of masking the figure—your figure, to be precise—was your 1967–1968 film *Art Make-Up*.

BN: That film—which was also later a videotape—has a rather simple story behind it. About 20 years ago—this was in '66 or '67—I was living in San Francisco, and I had access to a lot of film equipment. There were a lot of underground filmmakers there at that time, and I knew a bunch of those guys. And since everybody was broke, I could rent pretty good 16-mm equipment for $5 or $6 a day—essentially the cost of gas to bring it over. So I set up this *Art Make-Up* film.

Of course, you put on makeup before you film in the movies. In my case, putting on the makeup became the activity. I started with four colors. I just put one on over the other, so that by the time the last one went on, it was almost black. I started with white. Then red on the white, which came out pink; then green on top of that, which came out gray; then something very black on top of that.

One thing which hadn't occurred to me when I was making the film was that when you take a solid color of makeup—no matter what color—it flattens the image of the face on film. The flatness itself was another kind of mask.

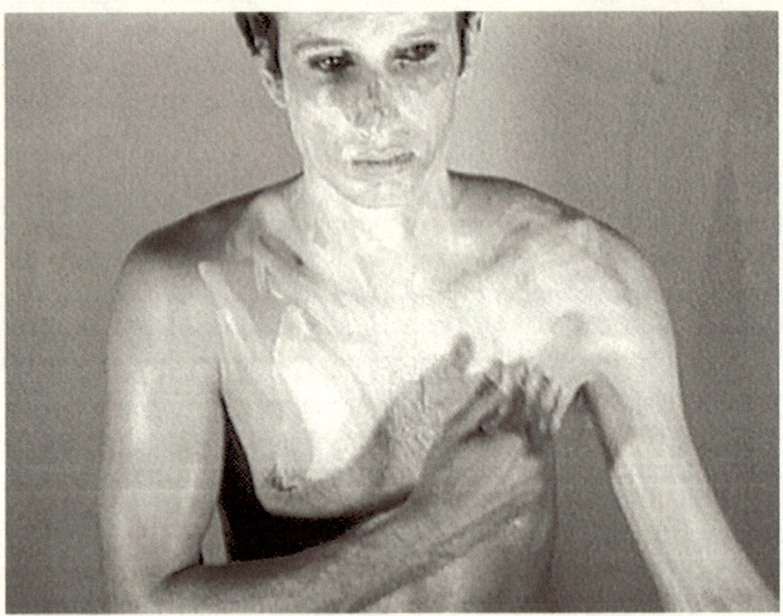

Art Make-Up, No. 1: White, No. 2: Pink, No. 3: Green, No. 4: Black, 1967–1968. Four 16-mm films (color, silent). 400 feet, approx. 10 min. each. Distributed by Electronic Arts Intermix. Image courtesy Sperone Westwater, New York.

JS: The whole idea of the mask, of abstracting a personality, of simultaneously presenting and denying a self, is a recurring concern in your work.

BN: I think there is a need to present yourself. To present yourself through your work is obviously part of being an artist. If you don't want people to see that self, you put on makeup. But artists are always interested in some level of communication. Some artists need lots, some don't. You spend all of this time in the studio, and then when you do present the work, there is a kind of self-exposure that is threatening. It's a dangerous situation, and I think that what I was doing and what I am going to do and what most of us probably do is to use the tension between what you tell and what you don't tell as part of the work. What is given *and* what is withheld become the work. You could say that if you make a statement, it eliminates the options; on the other hand, if you're a logician, the opposite immediately becomes a possibility. I try to make work that leaves options or is open-ended in some way.

JS: The tenor of that withholding—actually controlling the content or subject—is changed significantly when you stopped performing and began to allow the viewer to participate in some of your works. I'm thinking of the architectural installations, in particular the very narrow corridor pieces. In one of them, the viewer who could deal with walking down such a long claustrophobic passage would approach a video monitor on which were seen disconcerting and usually "invisible" glimpses of his or her own back.

BN: The first corridor pieces were about having someone else do the performance. But the problem for me was to find a way to restrict the situation so that the performance turned out to be the one I had in mind. In a way, it was about control. I didn't want somebody else's idea of what could be done.

There was a point in American art, in the '60s, when artists presented parts of works, so that people could arrange them. Bob Morris did some pieces like that, and Öyvind Fahlström did those political coloring-book-like things with magnets that could be rearranged. But it was very hard for me to give up that much control. The problem with that approach is that it turns art into game playing. In fact, at that time a number of artists were talking about art as though it were some kind of game you could play. I think I mistrusted that idea.

Of course, there is a kind of logic and structure in art making that you can see as game playing. But game playing doesn't involve any responsibility—any moral responsibility—and I think that being an artist does involve moral responsibility. With a game you just follow the rules. But art is like cheating—it involves inverting the rules or taking the game apart and changing it. In games like football or baseball, cheating is allowed to a certain extent. In hockey, breaking the rules turns into fighting—you can't do that in a bar and get away with it. But the rules change. It can only go so far, and then real life steps in. This year warrants were issued to arrest hockey players; two minutes in the penalty box wasn't enough. It's been taken out of the game situation.

JS: Nevertheless, many of your works take as their starting point very specific children's games.

BN: When I take the game, I take it out of context and apply it to moral or political situations. Or I load it emotionally in a way that it is not supposed to be loaded. For instance, the *Hanged Man* neon piece (1985) derives from the children's spelling game. If you spell the word, you win; if you can't spell the word in a certain number of tries, then the stick figure of the hanged man is drawn line by line with each wrong guess. You finally lose the game if you complete the figure—if you hang the man.

With my version of the hanged man, first of all I took away the part about being allowed to participate. In my piece, you're not allowed to participate—the parts of the figure are put into place without you. The neon "lines" flash on and off in a programmed sequence. And then the game doesn't end. Once the figure is complete, the whole picture starts to be re-created again. Then I added the bit about having an erection or ejaculation when you're hanged. I really don't know if it's a myth or not.

I've also used the children's game "musical chairs" a number of times. The simplest version was *Musical Chairs (Studio Piece)* in 1983, which has a chair hanging at the outside edge of a circumference of suspended steel Xs. So when the Xs swing or the chair swings, they bang into each other and actually make noise—make music. But of course it was more than that because musical chairs is also a cruel game. Somebody is always left out. The first one to be excluded always feels terrible.

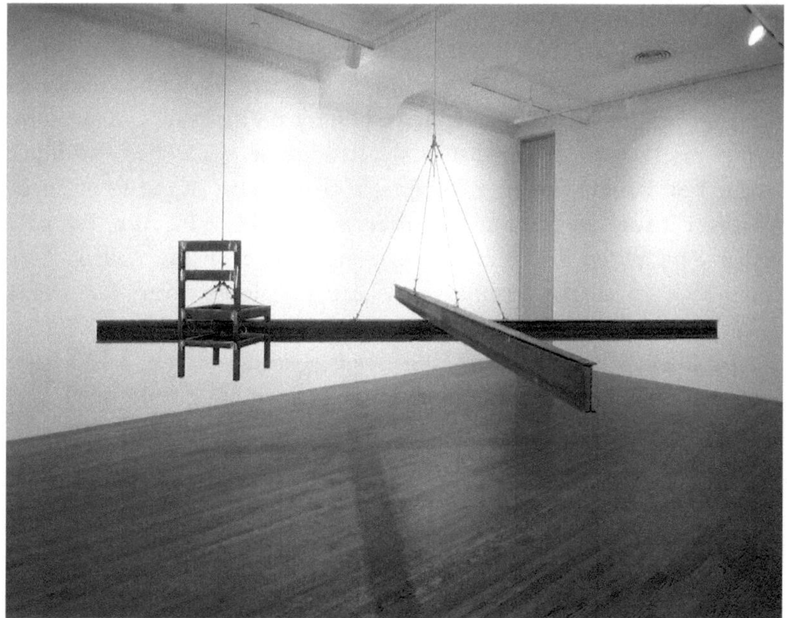

Musical Chair, 1983. Steel, wire. 34 × 192⅛ × 200¾ in. (86.4 × 488 × 510 cm). Friedrich Christian Flick Collection. Image courtesy Sperone Westwater, New York.

That kid doesn't get to play anymore, has nothing to do, has to stand in the corner, or whatever.

Large-Scale Sculpture

JS: There seems to be something particularly ominous about your use of chairs—both in this and other works. Why a chair? What does it mean to you?

BN: The chair becomes a symbol for a figure—a stand-in for the figure. A chair is used, it is functional, but it is also symbolic. Think of the electric chair or that chair they put you in when the police shine the lights on you. Because your imagination is left to deal with that isolation, the image becomes more powerful, in the same way that the murder offstage can be more powerful than if it took place right in front of you. The symbol is more powerful.

I first began to work with the idea of a chair with that cast of the space underneath a chair—that was in the '60s. And I remember, when I think back to that time, a chair [Joseph] Beuys did with a wedge of suet on the seat. I think he may have hung it on the wall. I'm not sure. In any case, it was a chair that was pretending it was a chair—it didn't work. You couldn't sit in it because of that wedge of grease or fat or whatever it was—it filled up the space you would sit in. Also, I'm particularly interested in the idea of hanging a chair on the wall, so they could pick up all the furniture and keep the floors clean. The chairs didn't have to be on the floor to function.

In 1981, when I was making *South America Triangle*, I had been thinking about having something hanging for quite a long time. The *Last Studio Piece*, which was made in the late '70s when I was still living in Pasadena, was made from parts of two other pieces—plaster semicircles that look like a cloverleaf and a large square—and I finally just stuck them together. I just put one on top of the other and a metal plate in between and hung it all from the ceiling. That was the first time I used a hanging element. I was working at the same time on the "underground tunnel pieces." These models for tunnels I imagined floating underground in the dirt. The same ideas and procedures, the same kind of image, whether something was suspended in water, in earth, in air.

JS: *South America Triangle* in a certain sense continues the ideas of game playing, suspension, inside and outside, and the chair as a stand-in for the figure. In this case, though, we're talking about a big steel sculpture hanging from the ceiling, with the chair isolated and suspended upside down in the middle of the steel barrier. This seems considerably more aggressive than the earlier work, though the content is till covert, an extremely private mediation. But the title hints at its subject matter and begins to explicate its intense emotional and political presence. I'm wondering what your thoughts were when you were making this piece.

BN: When I moved to New Mexico and was in Pecos in '70, I was thinking about a piece that had to do with political torture. I was reading V. S. Naipaul's stories about South America and Central America, including "The Return of Eva Perón" and especially "The Killings in Trinidad"—that's the one that made the biggest impression on me. Reading the Naipaul clarified things for me and helped me continue. It helped me to name names, to name things. But it didn't help me to

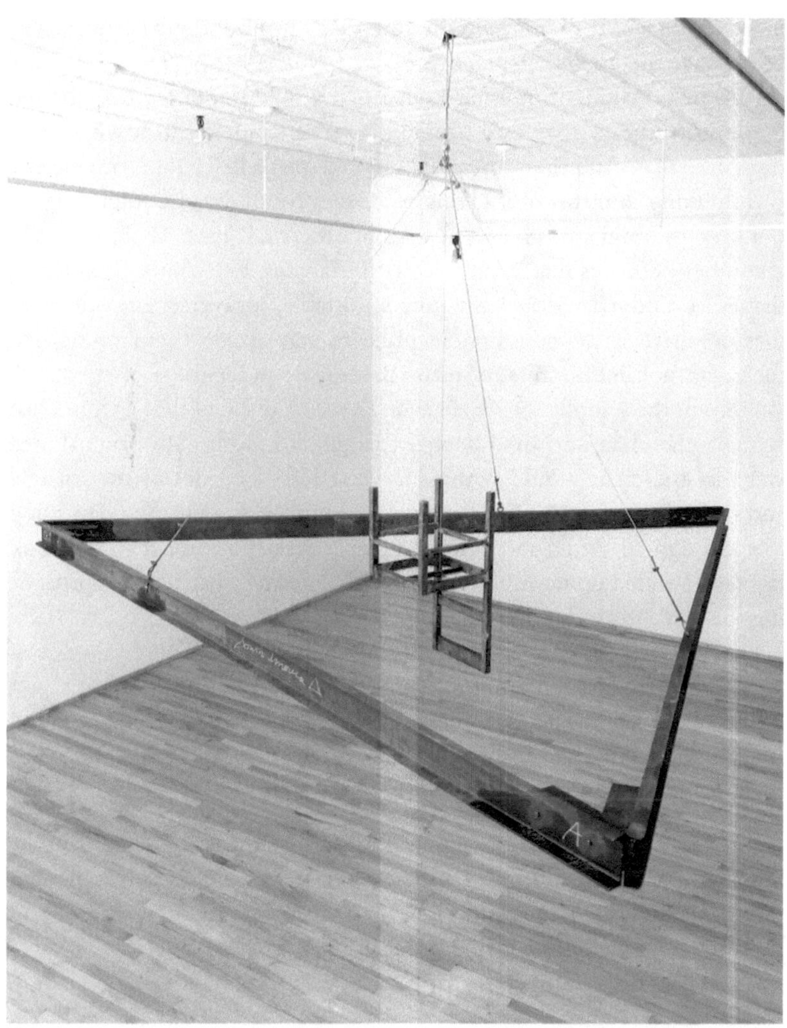

South America Triangle, 1981. Steel beams, steel cable, cast-iron chair. 39 × 169 × 169 in. (99.1 × 429.3 × 429.3 cm); suspended 60 in. (152.4 cm) above floor. Hirshhorn Museum and Sculpture Garden, Smithsonian Institution, Washington, DC. Holenia Purchase Fund, in memory of Joseph H. Hirshhorn, 1991. Image courtesy Sperone Westwater, New York.

make the piece. It didn't help me to figure out how the bolts went on. It just gave me encouragement.

At first, I thought of using a chair that would somehow become the figure: torturing a chair and hanging it up or strapping it down, something like that. And then torture has to take place in a room, or at least I was thinking in terms of it taking place in a room, but I couldn't figure out how to build a room and how to put the chair in it. Well, I'd made a number of works that had to do with triangles, like rooms in different shapes. I find triangles really uncomfortable, disconcerting kinds of spaces—there is no comfortable place to stay inside them or outside them. It's not like a circle or square that give you security.

So, in the end, for *South America Triangle* I decided that I would just suspend the chair and then hang a triangle around it. My original idea was that the chair would swing and bang into the sides of the triangle and make lots of noise. But then when I built it so that the chair hung low enough to swing into the triangle, it was too low. It didn't look right, so I ended up raising it. The triangle became a barrier to approaching the chair from the outside.

Again, it becomes something you can't get to. There is a lot of anger generated when there are things you can't get to. That's part of the content of the work—and also the genesis of the piece. Anger and frustration are two very strong feelings of motivation for me. They get me into the studio, get me to do the work.

JS: That sense of frustration and anger also becomes the viewer's problem in approaching and making sense of your work, especially a piece as disturbing as *South America Triangle*. One critic, Robert Storr, said recently, "Unlike setting into the reassuring 'armchair' of Matisse's painting, to take one's seat in Nauman's art is to risk falling on one's head."

BN: I know there are artists who function in relation to beauty—who try to make beautiful things. They are moved by beautiful things, and they see that as their role: to provide or make beautiful things for other people. I don't work that way. Part of it has to do with an idea of beauty. Sunsets, flowers, landscapes—these kinds of things don't move me to do anything. I just want to leave them alone. My work comes out of being frustrated about the human condition. And about how people refuse to understand other people. And about how people can be cruel to each other. It's not that I think I can change that, but it's just such a frustrating part of human history.

Recent Videos

JS: Recently, you've returned to video for the first time since the early '70s. In *Violent Incident* (1986), you not only moved from "silent" to "talkies," but you also used actors for the first time. Nevertheless, the video seems to pick right up on issues you've explored from the beginning. The chair is a central element in the action, and the whole tape centers on a cruel joke. Again there is this persistent tension between humor and cruelty.

BN: *Violent Incident* begins with what is supposed to be a joke—but it's a mean joke. A chair is pulled out from under someone who is starting to sit down. It intentionally embarrasses someone and triggers the action. But let me describe how it got into its present form. I started with a scenario, a sequence of events which was this: Two people come to a table that's set for dinner with plates, cocktails, flowers. The man holds the woman's chair for her as she sits down. But as she sits down, he pulls the chair out from under her, and she falls on the floor. He turns around to pick up the chair, and as he bends over, she's standing up, and she gooses him. He turns around and yells at her—calls her names. She grabs the cocktail glass and throws the drink in his face. He slaps her, she knees him in the groin, and as he's doubling over, he grabs a knife from the table. They struggle, and both of them end up on the floor.

Now this action takes all of about 18 seconds. But then it's repeated three more times: the man and woman exchange roles, then the scene is played by two men and then by two women. The images are aggressive; the characters are physically aggressive; the language is abusive. The scripting, having the characters act out these roles and the repetition, all build on that aggressive tension.

JS: Sound is a medium you've explored since your earliest studio performances, films, and audiotapes. The hostile overlaying of angry noises contributes enormously to the tension of *Violent Incident.*

BN: It's similar with the neon pieces that have transformers, buzzing and clicking and whatnot; in some places I've installed them, people are disturbed by these sounds. They want them to be completely quiet. There is an immediacy and an intrusiveness about sound that you can't avoid.

So with *Violent Incident,* which is shown on 12 monitors at the same time, the sound works differently for each installation. At one museum, when it was in the middle of the show, you heard the sound before you actually got to the piece. And the sound followed you around after you left it. It's kind of funny the way *Violent Incident* was installed at the Whitechapel [Art Gallery, London]. Because it was a separate room, the sound was baffled [*sic*]; you only got the higher tones. So the main thing you heard throughout the museum was "Asshole!"

JS: That's sort of the subliminal version of a very aggressive sound piece you used to install invisibly in empty rooms, isn't it?

BN: You mean the piece that said "Get out of the room, get out of my mind"? That piece is still amazingly powerful to me. It's really stuck in my mind. And it's really a frightening piece. I haven't heard it for a few years, but the last time I did, I was impressed with how strong it was. And I think that it is none of those pieces that I can go back to. I don't know where it came from or how I managed to do it because it's so simple and straightforward.

JS: How did that [piece] come about?

BN: Well, I had made a tape of sounds in the studio. And the tape says over and over again, "Get out of the room, get out of my mind." I said it a lot of different ways: I changed my voice and distorted it; I yelled it and growled it and grunted it. Then the piece was installed with the speakers built into the walls, so that when you went into this small room—10 feet square or something—you could hear the sound, but there was no one there. You couldn't see where the sound was coming from. Other times, we just stuck the speakers in the corners of the room and played the tape—like when the walls were too hard to build into. But it seemed to work about as well either way. Either way it was a very powerful piece. It's like a print I did that says, "Pay attention, motherfuckers" (1973). You know, it's so angry it scares people.

JS: Your most recent videotapes feature clowns. I can see a connection to the *Art Make-Up* film we talked about, but why did you use such theatrical clowns?

BN: I got interested in the idea of the clown first of all because there is a mask, and it becomes an abstracted idea of a person. It's not anyone in particular, see; it's just an idea of a person. And for this reason, because clowns are abstract in some sense, they become very disconcerting. You,

I, one, we can't make contact with them. It's hard to make any contact with an idea or an abstraction. Also, when you think about vaudeville clowns or circus clowns, there is a lot of cruelty and meanness. You couldn't get away with that without makeup. People wouldn't put up with it; it's too mean. But in the circus it's okay, it's still funny. Then, there's the history of the unhappy clown: they're anonymous; they lead secret lives. There is a fairly high suicide rate among clowns. Did you know that?

JS: No, I didn't. But it seems that rather than alluding to this melancholic or tragic side of the clown persona, the video emphasizes the different types of mask, the historically specific genres of clowns or clown costumes.

BN: With the clown videotape, there are four different clown costumes; one of them is the Emmett Kelly dumb clown; one is the old French baroque clown (I guess it's French); one is a sort of traditional polka-dot, red-haired, oversize-shoe clown; and one is a jester. The jester and the baroque type are the oldest, but they are pretty recognizable types. They were picked because they have a historical reference, but they are still anonymous. They become masks; they don't become individuals. They don't become anyone you know; they become clowns.

JS: In your tape *Clown Torture* [1987], the clowns don't act like clowns. For one thing, they're not mute. You have the clowns telling stories. Or, I should say, each of the clowns repeats the same story.

BN: Each clown has to tell a story while supporting himself on one leg with the other leg crossed in such a way that it looks like he is imitating sitting down. So there is the physical tension of watching someone balance while trying to do something else—in this case, tell a story. The takes vary because at some point the clown gets tired and falls over. Then I would stop the tape. Each of the four clowns starts from the beginning, tells the story about 15 times or so, falls over, and then the next clown starts.

This circular kind of story, for me, goes back to Warhol films that really have no beginning or end. You could walk in at any time, leave, come back again, and the figure was still asleep or whatever. The circularity is also a lot like La Monte Young's idea about music. The music is always going on. You just happen to come in at the part he's playing

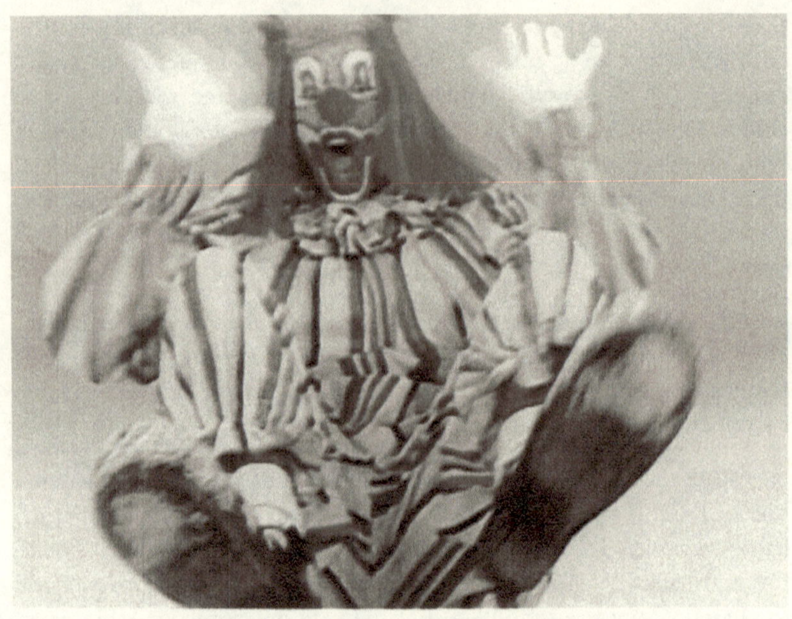

Clown Torture, 1987. Installation: two 20-in. color monitors, two 25-in. color monitors, four speakers, four videotape players, two video projectors, four videotapes (color, sound). Dimensions variable. The Art Institute of Chicago, Watson F. Blair Prize, Wilson L. Mead, and Twentieth-Century Purchase funds; through prior gift of Joseph Winterbotham; gift of the Lannan Foundation. Image courtesy Sperone Westwater, New York.

that day. It's a way of structuring something so that you don't have to make a story.

JS: What's the story the clowns tell?

BN: "It was a dark and stormy night. Three men were sitting around a campfire. One of the men said, 'Tell us a story, Jack.' And Jack said, 'It was a dark and stormy night. Three men were sitting around a campfire. One of the men said, 'Tell us a story, Jack.' And Jack said, 'It was a dark and stormy night. ...'''

Three Statements on the Recent Reception of Bruce Nauman*

John Miller, Pamela M. Lee, and Isabelle Graw

Dada by the Numbers

John Miller

> What, in the end, makes advertisements so superior to criticism? Not what the moving red neon sign says—but the fiery pool reflecting it in the asphalt.
>
> —Walter Benjamin, *One-Way Street*

Although much of the acclaim surrounding Bruce Nauman's recent retrospective at the Museum of Modern Art (MoMA) rests on topical factors (white male rage, a cowboy persona, sensationalism, the endorsement of prominent museums—not the least of which is MoMA itself), the ongoing influence of Nauman's oeuvre pertains almost exclusively to what Walter Benjamin called the modern experience of shock: the impact of technological sensory data on human subjectivity. This kind of shock, which is primarily physiological but which nonetheless always

* The statements given here were written in response to a question posed by the *October* editors about the recent reception of the work of Bruce Nauman, prompted by the retrospective exhibition organized by the Walker Art Center and the Hirshhorn Museum and Sculpture Garden, which traveled to the following institutions from 1993 to 1995: Museo Nacional Centro de Arte Reina Sofía, Madrid; Walker Art Center, Minneapolis; Museum of Contemporary Art, Los Angeles; Hirshhorn Museum and Sculpture Garden, Washington DC; Museum of Modern Art, New York; Kunsthaus, Zurich.

carries a moral charge, results largely from mimetic devices such as the camera, the tape recorder, film, and video—all of which convert the detached contemplation of visual imagery into an immediate, tactile encounter. Insofar as Bruce Nauman's work concerns the receptivity of his audience, his artistic stature is bound up with the momentum of these forces in mass culture. The exact nature of the audience's receptivity develops in relation to these forces. Nauman uses language and architecture within a minimalist rhetorical framework to get at this phenomenological aspect of consciousness.

Whether an audience's response to an artwork ought to be elicited as that artwork's rightful subject has proven to be a point of ideological division, with conservatives inclined to dismiss Nauman's mode of address as mere aggression, as "bad boy" histrionics. But these aesthetic tactics find their precedent in Dadaism. Hilton Kramer, for one, dismisses Nauman as a provocateur, but he has nonetheless accurately identified Nauman's art as "bureaucratic Dada," dependent on large institutions for support and consecrated as an official museum style.[1] Kramer also has typified Nauman's work as academic—which is true to the extent that it concerns questions raised by Benjamin's artwork essay, the preeminent art school text of the past 20 years. But these issues were not so familiar when Nauman began working in the 1960s, and part of the current sense of academicism is attributable to popularization of the neo-Dada impulse—of which Nauman has been the leading proponent. Yet because Nauman's oeuvre focuses on the organization of the senses through technology, it approximates a return—despite (or because of) its iconoclasm—to the classical focus of aesthetics.

Claiming that he wants his work to have the effect of hitting the viewer in the back of the head, Nauman clearly echoes Benjamin's description of the Dadaist artwork as "an instrument of ballistics." Between these two metaphors, the shift from front to back is telling. Benjamin maintained that the role of Dada was to prepare its audience for the effects of film. Nauman, in turn, offers a reconsideration of film and television's a priori.[2]

The logic for the presentation and installation of Nauman's work derives mainly from minimal sculpture.[3] If this style of work, according to Michael Fried, staged a passive-aggressive theater in which the spectator became acutely aware of her or his own presence, Nauman carried this over into direct aggression. His various corridors, video projections, sound installations, holograms, and neon signage all volatilize their exhibition space in a distinctly minimalist fashion but go on to transform so-called minimalist theater into a theater of cruelty, deploying sound, lighting, mirrors, and language to achieve this end.[4] Much has been made of the atmosphere of overstimulation in the MoMA retrospective, but compared to a trip to the amusement park, a night out in a techno club, or even a routine morning's subway commute, the level of excitation is mild. Despite the literal impact of physical stimuli in these works, their significance registers primarily against the norm of contemplation. Nauman offers his audience a chance to sample these stimuli on a seemingly trial basis, but shock remains an inescapable precondition of mass culture. In his *New Yorker* review of the MoMA show, Adam Gopnik reduced this syndrome to annoyance—the "O.K. avant-garde emotion" of the 1990s for viewers with short attention spans. He further characterized annoyance as a late-modern response of viewers "no longer held captive by shock."[5] Distraction, however, is nothing but a function of shock. If Nauman's sensorium vaguely recalls the Kantian awe engendered by a sharp precipice or an erupting volcano, the decisive moment of judgment always comes too late by dint of its being a reasoning process and not an automatic physiological response. This, like mass media, in effect suspends the sublime experience itself.

Nauman self-consciously acknowledges the spectator's fundamental state of apperception in his collage *Please Pay Attention Please*, which is essentially a sign. This sign designates the spectator's behavior (or its own phenomenological relation to that spectator), and, in its so doing, the spectator becomes nominal. In any event, closer scrutiny won't render the work more meaningful; one needs only to register the words subliminally for the sign to function. In this, the form of the work is identical to advertising. Arthur Danto has noted the inadequacy of the term *viewer* in this connection. One becomes, rather, the subject of the work—and a virtual automaton as well.

Directly inspired by Marcel Duchamp, Nauman's puns and figures of speech suggest a resurgent linguistic primitivism in which the gap between signifier and signified is imagined to be closed. This militates against the abstract rationalism afforded by language, a key criterion for the act of judgment. In the photo series including *Drill Team*, *Feet of Clay*, and *Eating My Words*, for example, Nauman mimics—or literalizes—a given saying before the camera. The figure of the artist becomes a witless "figure" … of speech. Puns also deny the Saussurian arbitrariness of the signifier. Every pun expresses the childish desire that phonetic material become one with the referent. Freud accordingly defined the pun as the crudest form of joke: nontendentious, nonsense humor. Both admirers and detractors argue as if the success of Nauman's punworks depends on their sophistication, forgetting that the most a pun ever can hope to elicit is a groan. Rather, Nauman's puns reflect what Benjamin called the Dadaist ambition to produce works resistant to contemplative immersion: "The studied degradation of their material was not the least of their means to achieve this uselessness. Their poems are 'word salad' containing obscenities and every imaginable waste product of language."[6] The neon signs *Violins, Violence, Silence*; *One Hundred Live and Die*; and *Run from Fear/Fun from Rear*, for example, transform words into obdurate objects that discourage rather than invite reflection. The majority of images in Nauman's oeuvre, moreover, come into being through words, be it a linguistic rebus or a talking head on video. Even the mime in *Shit in Your Hat—Head on a Chair* dances to verbal instructions.

Nauman's corridors, his *Yellow Room (Triangular)*, *Get Out of My Mind, Get Out of This Room*, and *Audio-Video Underground Chamber* all play off the rational understanding of architectural space against the felt experience of being inside it. Again Benjamin: "Buildings are appropriated in a twofold manner: by use and by perception—or rather by touch and by sight."[7] Tactile appropriation occurs through habit. One might be able to understand any number of Nauman's constructions from blueprints or pictures, but this differs radically from the experience of being there. One might not linger within these constructions long enough to form any particular habits, but one nonetheless begins to be habitualized by them. *Learned Helplessness in Rats (Rock and Roll Drummer)*, however, works more as a conventional illustration because it makes the viewer an omniscient observer of a rat maze and of videos of a rat ostensibly being tortured by a rock drummer. A tendency observed (and created) by laboratory researchers, "learned helplessness" refers to the "numbing down" that occurs when one is unable to control or alter one's own environment. Several critics have drawn tentative parallels between the rat in the control group and Nauman's own audience, but an analogy between the experience of the rats and the life of the masses would be more compelling. Where one must deliberately seek out

Nauman's work, "advertising delivers the people." Not surprisingly, when Nauman's model of reception reverts to contemplation, the work becomes less convincing. His models for tunnels, for example, are no more architectural than are Peter Halley's cell and conduit paintings. His animal-carcass sculptures *Carousel* and *Animal Pyramid*, through their allusions to totemism and blood sacrifice, read as nostalgia for primitive sacred art.

Dada began as an anarchic cry against the onslaught of modernity, especially warfare. In the 1990s, with widespread institutional support for what has become a broad genre of art production, times have changed. One might blame the messenger for the news. Would celebrating him, then, be an act of perversity? The eagerness of social institutions to acknowledge how the repressive terms of the Debordian spectacle help perpetuate their very existence betokens not only a characteristically liberal admission of false consciousness but also the hubris that the institutional power structure will remain intact despite critical awareness of it. From this perspective, Nauman's work would seem to be more about the way social structures transform people than the other way around. But Michael Taussig frames the problem in a less-totalizing fashion: "With good reason postmodernism has relentlessly instructed us that reality is artifice yet ... not enough surprise has been expressed as to how we nevertheless get on with living, pretending—thanks to the mimetic faculty—that we live facts, not fictions."[8] When Nauman first began exhibiting work, the literalist tendency predominated; certain artists believed they could completely purge their art of metaphor. Now consciousness is seen, via Lacan and others, to be structured through metaphor. Such an understanding prompts not a return to premodernist literary values but rather an awareness of how mimesis operates as a form of "real life." At its best, Nauman's art uncovers these processes in a dramatic fashion—and insight into them may be key to understanding any of the historical forms of consciousness engendered by mass culture, past, present, or future.

Notes

1. Hilton Kramer, "Idiotic Curators Present Wretched Nauman Show," *New York Observer*, March 8, 1995. Drawing the ideological battle lines, Kramer went on to oppose the Dada impulse with "the high artistic purposes" Richard Wagner's music embodied "to such an absolute degree." But, writing about the function of the Wagnerian

Gesamtkunstwerke vis-à-vis the shock of modernity, Susan Buck-Morss describes those purposes as "to hide the alienation and fragmentation, the loneliness and the sensual impoverishment … that was the material out of which it is composed" ("Aesthetics and Anaesthetics: Walter Benjamin's Artwork Essay Reconsidered," *October* 62 [Fall 1992]: 26). Since the early 1970s, in fact, Kramer has observed and lamented Dada's expanding influence. Even so, he refuses to come to terms with what any such latter-day embraces of Dada might mean.

2. A number of conceptualists working at the time of Nauman's emergence also concerned themselves with these issues. Most of John Baldessari's work from this period revolves around the logic of film grammar; William Wegman's videos concern themselves largely with the definition of mise-en-scène; Douglas Huebler's quixotic project to photograph every living person interrogates the value of the camera as a source of information.

3. Early works such as *Henry Moore Bound to Fail* (1967) signaled a rejection of the European tradition of organic composition (which Fried championed in the work of Anthony Caro) as well as an allegiance to minimalist principles.

4. Nauman has remained relatively indifferent to the question of public sculpture—in which, of course, reference to an architectural interior becomes a moot point.

5. Adam Gopnik, "The Nauman Principle," *New Yorker*, March 27, 1995, 106.

6. Walter Benjamin, "The Work of Art in the Age of Mechanical Reproduction," in *Illuminations*, ed. Hannah Arendt, trans. Harry Zohn (New York: Schocken Books, 1969), 237.

7. Ibid.

8. Michael Taussig, "A Report to the Academy," in *Mimesis and Alterity* (New York: Routledge, 1993), xv.

Pater Nauman[1]

Pamela M. Lee

The arid Wittgensteinian, ensnared by his own language games, succumbs to the lurid wink and hiss of neon tubing. Or sometimes he is a latter-day Molloy plodding stiffly on a dimming gray screen. Here, objects echo the human figure, ghostlike and boneless; there, corridors press the body into spaces of disquieting parallax; elsewhere, waxen animals are dragged in circles endlessly, like so many carcasses flayed on a meat rack. And in galleries where noise and video are harnessed as primary media—a virtual *Gesamtkunstwerk* of sensory violence—rats are brutalized and mimes humiliated. The hapless image of a clown shitting stays with us. And so on.

Arcane, bombastic, melancholic, funny: What might this survey of the recent Bruce Nauman retrospective suggest about the artist's heightened status within recent criticism? Compared to the consistent institutional embrace of him in Europe as "arguably the most internationally influential figure of his generation of Americans,"[2] Nauman's reception within the United States has been relatively limited. With greater frequency, however, artists ranging from Kiki Smith to Matthew Barney are claimed as his conceptual progeny.[3] Still, those legions of artists apparently influenced by Nauman remain unnamed, just as much as the specific nature of his timeliness remains unquestioned. One struggles to articulate the peculiar dynamic between his work and that of more recent artists or what might amount to its imagined appeal.

Nauman's formal range is indeed far-flung, and an equally broad sphere of influence might seem the logical outcome of such a protean aesthetic. Process-inspired objects, photography, abstract castings, neon, figurative sculpture, felt, performance pieces, conceptual ruminations, installation-based works, video—save for the exiled genre of painting, it's all there, nearly every material procedure in operation since the mid-sixties. But if such eclecticism appears unwieldy, seemingly resistant to the nominalist drives of the critical marketplace, it has nevertheless been leveled to the category of style, even if rationalized as an antistyle: Nauman's "lack of consistent style and the great diversity of media employed are among his art's most salient characteristics."[4]

There is nothing unique about his spiraling pluralism in itself, particularly when viewed in terms of the mid- to late sixties, a time in which the traditional art object was allegedly "dematerialized." Nauman's example was hardly singular then or in the so-called pluralist era that was soon to follow. Nonetheless, whereas Nauman's diversity is lauded as striking against received conventions of modernist autonomy, Robert Morris's multiple strategies—strategies that both presage and parallel many of Nauman's own—have just as consistently been decried as the worst order of artistic dilettantism.

Its formal disparities and marked humor notwithstanding, the exhibition appears coordinated largely around the seeming antipodes of impotence and violence. In his thematic integration, Nauman is both democratic and pluralistic: the experiences of claustrophobia, frustration, sadism, and humiliation are shared equally among artist, subject viewer, clown, and animal alike and are divided further along the epistemic strata of the phenomenological and the semiotic. This overriding sense of Nauman's inability to master the self's relation to the world is seemingly registered in his almost hysterical proliferation of artistic procedures. Indiscriminately, he makes use of whatever means are available to him, tacitly acknowledging that each is compromised in advance.

What might thus seem a wildly generative impulse is itself born of an inability to produce a total form of representation, a floundering that is strategically entrenched as the artist's project. And, taken as such, there is some insight to be gleaned from a recent discussion between Hilton Kramer and Arthur Danto on contemporary sculpture.[5] Danto suggests that Nauman's interest lies in his internalizing the "plurality" or "disjunctiveness" of the present moment, an observation that extends the model of stylistic eclecticism to the social. As if on cue, Kramer replies that "the questions about Nauman have to be delegated to professional psychiatry, and I wouldn't presume to deal with them."[6] When coupled with Danto's more serious contention that Nauman embodies a generalized social anomie, Kramer's reference to the artist's need for therapy condenses in a profile of an artistic persona that is multiple, an artist whose efforts to rationalize assume the form of frenetic productivity.

If this is the case, what kind of father is Bruce Nauman for the present generation? A father who scatters his energies furiously to no resolution? Or a father of numerous guises, each suggestive of a certain bathos? Harold Bloom provides useful counsel at this point. Reading artistic influence through the Freudian lens of lateness, he reserves a special place for the narrative of the family romance.[7] Here, the anxiety foisted upon all latecomers by the towering figure of the father is partially repressed through the fantasy of either the impotent father or the multiple father. On the one hand, the ephebe's anxiety is mitigated by his belief that the alleged father may not actually exist; on the other hand, his conviction that there are numerous fathers diminishes the monolithic influence of just one. The recent critical assessment of Nauman speaks to the desire for such a Bloomian father. Unconsciously regarding him as at once impotent and multiple, artists who claim him as their antecedent may be placing themselves within his broadly conceptualist sweep, but the need to articulate the specific character of his influence—and therefore acknowledge the degree of their indebtedness—is rendered a nonissue.

For Bloom, the overtaking of the father is accomplished primarily through the mechanics of misprision, the misreadings performed by poets born to lateness; misprision guarantees that the work that came before is willfully misunderstood and thus appropriated for the present moment. "Weaker talents idealize, figures of capable imagination appropriate for themselves," Bloom notes.[8] A strong misreading is precisely that which fails to idealize the model passed down by the previous generation. Nauman's persona as "impotent father" reverses these terms: rather than failing to idealize, it seems to idealize failure. Much recent art, writing, and curating have elevated failure to the status of trope.[9] The dysfunctional, the pathetic, the slacker, the failed body: the past few years have witnessed a proliferation of categories organized around powerlessness as a wide-ranging cultural phenomenon. And although some of these issues have a decidedly critical lineage (notably, the artistic engagement with issues of the failed or abject body is directed toward questions of gender, sexuality, and AIDS), the banalization of such topoi is frequent enough. By a dialectical turn, this work supersedes the virile expressionist artist of the eighties by dressing him down in the persona of loser.

How does Nauman fit into all this? The point, one imagines, is that he doesn't or, better yet, can't. What for Nauman is an exploration of representative means born of a process-minded era has in the nineties hardened into a caricature of impotence. The backward glance by those who would take him as father has seemingly literalized his relationship to this powerlessness; they would make coherent a relationship between present art and Nauman's work, which itself refuses to cohere.

Notes

1. Thanks are due to Matthew Simms for his useful suggestions in the writing of this essay.

2. Robert Storr, "Bruce Nauman," in the gallery guide to the retrospective at the Museum of Modern Art, March 1995.

3. Editor's introduction, "Head Trips," *Artforum* 33, no. 8 (April 1995): 62.

4. Storr, "Bruce Nauman."

5. Suzanne Ramljak, "Summit: Arthur Danto vs. Hilton Kramer," *Sculpture* 14, no. 3 (May–June 1995): 13–14.

6. Ibid., 13.

7. Harold Bloom, *The Anxiety of Influence* (Oxford: Oxford University Press, 1973).

8. Ibid., 5.

9. Artists who might be grouped under this sensibility include Karen Kilimnik, Cary Leibowitz (a.k.a. "Candy Ass"), and Sean Landers, among others. On writing about this phenomenon, see, for example, Jack Bankowsky, "Slackers," *Artforum.* 30, no. 3 (November 1991): 96–100; Sheila Lynch, "Failure as a Medium," *Artweek*, September 13, 1990, 13–14; and Catherine Liu's review of the exhibition *Just Pathetic*, *Artforum* 30, no. 9 (April 1992): 95–96.

Just Being Doesn't Amount to Anything (Some Themes in Bruce Nauman's Work)

Isabelle Graw

Translated by Dorothea von Moltke

My purpose here is to examine the reception of Bruce Nauman's work in order to clarify the interest it generates in its audience.[1] I decided from the outset to regard Nauman as an artist who does not threaten the consciousness of the educated bourgeois individual, who shows psychological abysses that enable that individual to experience the absurdity of his or her own existence. In retrospect, I find this view necessarily self-confirming. Put differently: the liberating quality of Nauman's work and the sense of humor that, according to eyewitnesses, it seemed to possess in the late sixties and early seventies can hardly be reconstructed and understood from this perspective.

Robert Pincus-Witten, for example, spoke in 1972 of the "seminal role" the "untitled rubber, fiberglass, and neon works" played in "redirecting the nature of artistic aspiration in the late '60s."[2] What reorientation is Pincus-Witten alluding to? He is not speaking of the elements of body, video, and performance art in Bruce Nauman's work, which were certainly important points of reference for artists of the seventies. Pincus-Witten is referring explicitly to the fiberglass and rubber works. He shares the view that even the choice of fiberglass itself—a material that appears organic but is of course industrial—disrupts the rigid forms of minimal art. Fiberglass fulfilled the postminimalist desire for tactility. Nauman's early pieces (all "untitled" and most dated 1965) are bent and curved. They wind along the walls and, contrary to minimal art, orient themselves less according to spatial givens than to the bodily measures of the artist. In a work such as *Untitled (Eye-Level Piece)* (1966), participation is taken literally—the piece is mounted at eye level. I nevertheless wonder about a work's achievement if it generates only a slight deviation within a dominant canon, in this case that of minimal art. Or is an engagement with the existing canon indispensable simply because radical statements can sometimes result from deviations?

Pincus-Witten considers the sense of humor, the wordplays, and the wit of these Nauman pieces (the sixties were the time when one began to speak of "pieces" rather than of works of art) to have been a transformative influence, not least because they pointed back to Duchamp. And it is precisely that sense of humor that for me is no longer recuperable—for instance, in the piece *From Hand to Mouth* (1967), in which a figure of speech is taken literally and the bodily distance between mouth and hand is shown. I feel similarly about *Wax Impressions of the Knees of Five Famous Artists* (1966): the title here carries the joke that the hollow forms can't be explained by the knees of famous artists after all.

Viewed today, Nauman's *Henry Moore Bound to Fail* (1967) seems to me to be a better because more contextually specific joke, as it is linked to an acknowledgment of the problem of coming to terms with tradition.[3] But this working through and against older models has always been part of the repertoire of the artist who inhabits the canon. Nauman's work functioned to modify and supplement minimal art: he was included in the canon of "American Sculpture" at a very early point and then reactivated the so-called heritage of Duchamp, evoking an awareness of the absurdity of such a quest.[4]

This was an awareness on the part of both the imaginary and actual viewers who, with a kind of pleased horror, exclaimed, "How absurd!," and considered themselves happily trapped. For absurdity periodically was and is the spice of civilized existence—things that cannot be explained immediately, that make no sense—a play by Beckett, Ionesco, or Albert Camus. But can *Waiting for Godot* be compared to Bruce Nauman's lonely and absurdist studio activities?

Upon further reflection, one could say that every generation of artists goes through the radical chic of alienation. Bruce Nauman says of himself that reading Wittgenstein was a decisive experience for him. Many visual artists are interested in Wittgenstein's skepticism and his critique of reason: his way of thinking in linguistic spaces is appropriated for endgame aesthetics, which can lead to a pessimistic lament over the state of the world. There are many examples of this in Nauman's work. His neon work *RAW/WAR* (1970) represents this arbitrary connection (which Wittgenstein mustn't be held accountable for) of wordplay and a penchant for the apocalyptic.

To insist so explicitly on the idea of wordplay and of the absurd implies a manipulation of reception. Every message reaches its destination. Jean Christophe Ammann, for example, reacted by titling a recent essay "Wittgenstein and Nauman."[5] And as though guided by a hidden hand, he immediately began speaking of the "existential dimension" in Nauman's works. This dimension does indeed exist. One need only scan a few quotes from Nauman, reflecting on the role of the artist in society and on what art in itself is capable of being.[6]

In the works of the sixties, Nauman's alienated relation to himself and to objects was still the central concern. As a fountain (*Self-Portrait as a Fountain* [1966/1970]), he disengaged from the world and yet was able to observe and savor this fact. Meanwhile, the subject—be it Nauman himself or the intended viewer—always remained untouched. Even today, Donald Kuspit raves about the disorienting experience of being in the Nauman corridor, in which one feels as though one were blind and at the mercy of a system.[7]

Existential philosophy's ideology of alienation is an integral part of bourgeois consciousness. Many collectors and curators are enthusiastic about Nauman's 1987 video *Clown Torture* because it is allegedly so relentlessly brutal. Many young existentialists, who claim not to believe that things are as they seem, consider themselves to be just as uncompromising. This does not mean that a feeling of alienation is necessarily accompanied by an enthusiasm for Bruce Nauman. Nauman speaks more to those who have reserved their former alienation in order to see it confirmed in culture. The talk of the harshness of many Nauman videos reveals a fascination with violence and brutality, with a cultural phenomenon that is thought to be loaded with meaning but reveals nothing more than the violence that is omnipresent.

* * *

Nauman always (even in his 1967 neon sign *The True Artist Helps the World by Revealing Mystic Truths*) has attempted to maintain the bourgeois illusion of an artistic position external to society from which it would be possible to describe that society. His corridors and "musical chairs," which are commentaries on such themes as subjective states, the coldness of being, and violence, are examples of this. The fact that these commentaries are made by a distanced but impassioned individual is among their fundamental characteristics. Collectors, I am told, consider Nauman to be a humane artist. They seem to identify with this type of symbolic engagement. Now, as ever, those who vent their outrage are often rewarded with artistic recognition. Artists who symbolically protest the miserable state of the world answer the wishes of a culturally pessimistic, conservative group that reacts simultaneously against what it perceives as violence, progress, and the culture industry.

It is as if at a very early stage Nauman had opted for a political attitude that is currently widely criticized for being nothing more than a passive emotional political engagement. Meanwhile, however, he has always remained within the framework of the individual artist whose lonely studio activities are art. The videos *Playing a Note on the Violin While I Walk around the Studio* (1968) and *Bouncing Two Balls between the Floor and Ceiling with Changing Rhythms* (1968) deal with the studio artist who is occupied with himself. Social relations that are the precondition for the recognition of an artist are screened out.

Nauman reinforces the concept of creativity as the potential of the individual, which need only be persistently developed in order to be recognized. His videos are always the result of an isolated activity. The fact that he acknowledges artistic and other influences in interviews (Moore, de Kooning, Johns, Tuttle, Wittgenstein) complements his construction of himself as an individual artist.

Already in the seventies, Nauman was praised for physically involving the viewer.[8] Yet the body that Nauman involved had neither race nor class nor gender. Perhaps the determinants that constitute identity could not be thought and distinguished in those days as they can be today. In the seventies, it was already considered radical for the white, male, middle-class body to expose itself to experiences of "isolation" and "alienation." Perhaps the integration of the category of the "body" was itself a first step on the way to its ethnic and sexual differentiation.

Nauman's body has a universal claim. This claim is transferred into sculptures such as *Neon Templates of the Left Half of My Body Taken at Ten-Inch Intervals* (1966). He could be given credit retroactively for this universalism if one assumed that Nauman surmised then what Ernesto Laclau today expresses in the following way: every particularism contains a universalism. Applied to Nauman, this would mean that wanting to be generalized is part of Nauman's specific body. It may sound at times as though I am tallying up Nauman's artistic deficits, but this is not my intention. Rather, I want to work my way into the issues raised by his works: existence, absurdity, alienation, wordplay, and, later, engagement and dismay. What sort of dispositions and desires does Nauman count on? What viewer (and respective collectors' desires) does he assume? In a very fundamental way, this raises the question of the extent to which an artist can be held responsible for his reception. If Nauman drops names such as "Beckett" and "Wittgenstein," he thereby directs the way that he is written about. So I would maintain that in Nauman there is a correspondence between artistic presentation and its reception in art criticism.

Notes

1. An expanded version of this essay was originally published in *Texte zur Kunst,* October 1992. It is reprinted here in a revised form as a response to the question posed by *October.*

2. Robert Pincus-Witten, "Bruce Nauman: Another Kind of Reasoning," *Artforum* 10, no. 6 (February 1972): 33 [reprinted in this volume].

3. Nauman, who then tied his arms with a rope in a series of photographs dated 1966–1967 and called *Bound to Fail*, probably wanted to preempt his own failure in a coquettish way.

4. In 1967, he was included in the exhibition *American Sculpture of the Sixties* at the Los Angeles County Museum of Art.

5. Jean-Christophe Ammann, "Wittgenstein and Nauman," in *Bruce Nauman*, exhibition catalog, ed. Nicholas Serota and Joanne Skipwith, 21–29 (London: Whitechapel Art Gallery, 1986).

6. Coosje van Bruggen, *Bruce Nauman: Drawings/ Zeichnungen 1965–1986*, exhibition catalog (Basel: Museum für Gegenwartskunst, 1986), 11–23.

7. Donald Kuspit, "Bruce Nauman," *Artforum* 28, no. 5 (January 1990): 137.

8. Marcia Tucker, "PheNAUMANology," *Artforum* 9, no. 4 (December 1970): 8–44 [reprinted in this volume].

Nauman's Beckett Walk

Kathryn Chiong

> Go on from where you left off, said Mr. Magershon, not from where you began. Or are you like Darwin's caterpillar?[1]

Caterpillar logic provides the model for Samuel Beckett's production, where series upon series go on from where they begin, where "going on" finally takes priority over all ends. And where Beckett leaves off, without having finished, we find Bruce Nauman[2] revolving it all again, leaving us differently at the same spot somewhere in the middle, so that Nauman's work agitates in the same way that the events at Mr. Knott's agitate Watt:

> What distressed Watt in this incident of the Galls father and son, and in subsequent similar incidents, was not so much that he did not know what had happened, for he did not care what had happened, as that nothing had happened, that a thing that was nothing had happened, with the utmost formal distinctness, and that it continued to happen, in his mind, he supposed, though he did not know exactly what that meant, and though it seemed to be outside him, before him, about him, and so on, inexorably to unroll its phases, beginning with the first (the knock that was not a knock) and ending with the last (the door closing that was not a door closing), and omitting none, uninvoked, at the most unexpected moments, and the most inopportune. (*Watt*, 76)

Reading Nauman through Beckett, our discussion can only retrace these lines. Nonetheless, by revisiting "the old thing where it always was, back again" (*Watt*, 44), we find ourselves in hot pursuit of nothing, which is exactly where Beckett and Nauman wanted to place us. It's a little too like running Lewis Carroll's Caucus-race, and we can start and stop where we like (since everybody wins by sheer virtue of having at some point run). As a matter of consistency, however, we could keep pace with Watt, whose first memory of the Galls coming to tune Mr. Knott's piano was a noise.

... beginning with the first (the knock that was not a knock) ...

Think of sound specifically, as the knock that begins an encounter, with Nauman's single-channel video *Wall-Floor Positions* (1968). The work can be seen (without playing the tape) in a succession of photographic stills to reveal Nauman, acting a bad version of the sideshow contortionist. In these closely cropped frames, Nauman assumes every position except for the vertical one, turning the entire body into a single part-object that refuses to produce symmetry. By themselves, the pictures initiate a certain discomfort through an insistence on horizontality. What cannot be guessed without playing the tape, however, is that the crucial aspect of *Wall-Floor Positions* is the first moment, when Nauman enters the frame, falling into focus with a thud. Each subsequent pose is carried off with a similar slam of foot or hand. Each noise, in turn, cocoons itself within what seems an unendurable pause. Such passages "from silence to sound and from sound to silence" (*Watt*, 72) form the incessantly recurring events of Watt's memory, no less than our experience of Nauman's looping videos or Beckett's regressive plays. This passage of sound is what strikes first and hardest in *Wall-Floor Positions*, making similar impact in Beckett's 1966 television play *Eh Joe*.[3] After moments of solitary quiet, paranoid Joe ventures toward the window of his bare room, suddenly drawing apart the curtains with a violent rattle. A lull follows, broken again when Joe approaches the second window and rips the drapes apart once more. The unexpected noise, jolting enough at first, becomes doubly alarming in its reiteration. For now, concentrate on this fact, that the sound must happen, in Beckett as in Nauman, always more than once.

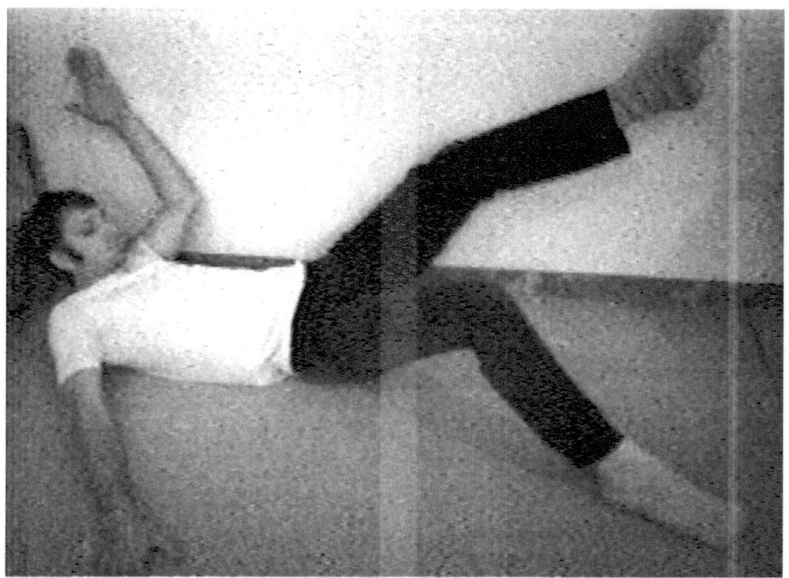

Wall-Floor Positions, 1968. Videotape (black-and-white, sound). 60 min., to be repeated continuously. Distributed by Electronic Arts Intermix. Image courtesy Sperone Westwater, New York.

In order for a knock to be a knock, which might be recognized as "someone at the door," the sound must normally recur, the second proving that the first was not just the banging of a branch but the work of communication. Roman Jakobson identifies this operation in verbal behavior wherein duplication signals "that the uttered sounds do not represent a babble, but a senseful, semantic entity."[4] What if, on the other hand, as *Watt* proposes, the knock is not simply a knock in that it occurs not twice but too many times? What happens, for instance, when a word is repronounced until that senseful semantic entity collapses into a series of too distinct phonemes? The result is not simply babble. Rather, what the excess finally signals is its own presence. The sound, then, not of someone at the door but of *knock-knock-knock-knock*—and this mechanism of repetition.

... in subsequent similar incidents ...

Jacques Derrida describes repetition not as posterior to the origin but as somehow simultaneous with it, "a trace which replaces a presence which has never been present."[5] The notion of an autonomous origin, then, is a kind of lure, a fantasy:

> The first book, the mythic book, the eve prior to all repetition, has lived on the deception that the center was sheltered from play: irreplaceable, withdrawn from metaphor and metonomy, a kind of invariable first name that could be invoked but not repeated. The center of the first book should not have been repeatable in its own representation. Once it lends itself a single time to such a representation—that is to say, once it is written—when one can read a book in the book, an origin in the origin, a center in the center, it is the abyss, is the bottomlessness of infinite redoubling.[6]

Affirming, like Jakobson, that signs are born in their capacity to be repeated, Derrida goes on to venture that at the mystical center where there is no such play of origin, we find death. Repetition is thus conceived not as supplementary accumulation but as an essential operation, as the "bottomlessness" that provides the very grounds for existence. It finds voice in Beckett's and Nauman's production, when a spoken phrase becomes a maddening refrain, when a sound begins to grate in its seeming sameness. Through these repetitions, refusing an isolated origin, Beckett and Nauman show being, so that one might have mentioned to the other, as did Estragon to Vladimir, "We always find something, eh, Didi, to give us the impression we exist?"[7]

And this "something," constantly rehearsed, is often precisely nothing. Nothing but the phrase "lip sync" whispered until the throat dries (Nauman, *Lip Sync* [1969]), nothing but the strum of D, E, A, D on a violin until the arm tires (Nauman, *Violin Tuned D.E.A.D.* [1969]), nothing but the sound of a woman's relentless pacing across the stage (Beckett, *Footfalls* [1976]). These exercises, however, consistently maintain themselves as failed affirmations, as finally only "impressions," which in their patent actuality always ever return to the question "We exist?" For this is also the function of repetition, to unmake the very identity that it seeks to confirm, disrupting the hierarchy of model and copy, as Derrida describes: "We are faced then with mimicry imitating nothing; faced, so to speak, with a double that doubles no simple, a double that nothing anticipates, nothing at least that is not itself already double."[8] Rather than reaffirming the identity of the one, repetition inspires the rabid production of another, from which the one cannot extricate itself, but with which it will never be identical. It is this relationship of nonidentity, somewhere between parasitic and symbiotic, that Beckett and Nauman force their characters to endure with every recurrence.[9]

In Nauman's video installation *Clown Torture* (1987), four different clowns, one after another, tell the same joke while balancing on one leg: "It was a dark and stormy night. Three men were sitting around a campfire. One of the men said, 'Tell us a story, Jack,' and Jack said, 'It was a dark and stormy night. Three men were sitting around a campfire. One of the men said, 'Tell us a story, Jack,' and Jack said, 'It was a dark and

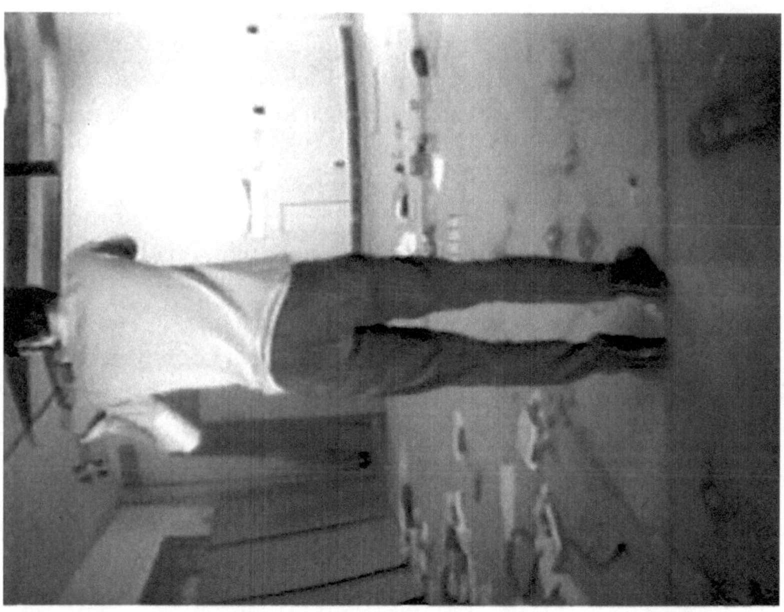

Violin Tuned D.E.A.D., 1969. Videotape (black-and-white, sound). 60 min., to be repeated continuously. Distributed by Electronic Arts Intermix. Image courtesy Sperone Westwater, New York.

stormy night. …'" On its own the joke enacts with marvelous economy the disruptive brand of repetition theorized by Derrida. Around the campfire is spun a tale of "infinite redoubling" in which no origin can be isolated. The joke exists without author and, under Nauman's unfunny direction, is even robbed of its object. The only logic to the joke is one identified by Freud in his famous study, which observes that intrinsic to the "joke-work" is the process of the joke's being told—in other words, of its being repeated.[10] Through each recital, performed now by an Emmett Kelly clown, then by a French baroque type, now by a jester, then by a clown in polka dots and big shoes, the similar incident spins into a series of what Derrida would call "differends," terms in which "difference inscribes itself without any decidable poles, without any independent, irreversible terms."[11] Creating a confusion between two clowns and then four (without there ever having been one in the first place), Nauman's *Clown Torture* enacts this doubling, proving that even in the face of infinite regress,[12] "it's never going to be the same."[13]

Implicated in this specular mechanism is an elimination, partly of narrative and completely of eschatology. Take Nauman's video *Bouncing in the Corner* (1968). Despite dissimilarities among its beats, the stream of thumps produced as Nauman bounces his body into the corner of a studio still engages a continuity, a reassurance that the action is only minimally changing, only repeating. Nauman aptly describes the function of sound, here acting as if "to whistle down a dark space—say cellar stairs—and fill the void to make sure that nothing else is in there."[14] Sound, in other words, assuring us of an absence, so that we can shut our eyes, leave the room, and, because of this thud, be fairly certain that we have missed nothing. The experience is something like listening to the Weather Channel on TV while getting dressed in the morning.

… and that it continued to happen …

In *Clown Torture*, no punchline, no dénouement, just a shaggy-dog tale constantly rewound. As such, I could run the tape as I would run the Caucus-race, start and stop where I like. The order, while perhaps not irrelevant, is certainly changeable in the fashion of *Watt*'s narration: "As Watt told the beginning of his story, not first, but second, so not fourth, but third, now he told its end. Two, one, four, three, that was the order in which Watt told his story" (215). Nauman names such a format "this circular kind of story." It goes back, he says, "to Warhol films that really have no beginning or end. You could walk in at any time, leave, come back again and the figure was still asleep, or whatever. The circularity is also a lot like La Monte Young's idea about music. The music is always going on. ... It's a way of structuring something so that you don't have to make a story."[15]

In order to understand what Nauman means by referring to a story that isn't a story but more like circular music, we might first think of tempo.

In his introductory essay to Alain Robbe-Grillet's pair of novels *Jealousy* and *In the Labyrinth*, Roland Barthes makes a distinction between two concepts of time.[16] The first one, classical, transforms with a reason, an ulterior motive: glory, decay, disappearance. Barthes contrasts this with Robbe-Grillet's temporality, during which "an object, described for the first time at a certain moment in the novel's progress, reappears later on, but with a barely perceptible difference. It is a difference of a situational or spatial order—what was on the right, for example, is now on the left."[17] Transformation here consists of permutation without decay, disappearance, or mystery: "time is never a corruption or even a catastrophe, but merely a change of place, a hideout for data."[18] Nauman often refers to his work as data: "Lack of information input (sensory deprivation). ... Pieces of information which are in 'skew' rather than clearly contradictory, i.e., kinds of information which come from and go to unrelated response mechanism."[19] Using information to take time, using time as a way of structuring information, Nauman's work lends itself to the logic of videotape and television chatter.

Mary Ann Doane describes television as "the textual technology of information theory,"[20] whose effect is rigorous decontextualization and the abolition of narrative. The important distinction Doane makes, however, is that television does not merely transmit this flow of information in its fragmented, multiple form but dramatizes it through catastrophic interruptions. These discontinuities veil the fact that television is a space precisely of no event, disguising machine time in the operations of classical time. Beckett and Nauman expose these theatrics, using them to insist precisely on the uneventful. Laying bare the structure of what Stanley Cavell calls television's "undialectical" serial procedure,[21] Beckett and Nauman harp on noncatastrophic intrusions that fail utterly to destabilize a stable condition, returning always to the show "already in progress." Understanding that TV flow is really "segmentation without closure,"[22] Beckett and Nauman make us watch as events cut through the series without ever successfully leaving their mark. In Beckett's color-television play *Quad I*, four mimes pace around a square, "each following his particular course."[23] Accompanied by a lively percussion, they walk feverishly, dropping in and out of the race in seemingly ordered sequence. To this fifteen-minute play Beckett wrote a five-minute sequel, *Quad II*. The action is essentially the same, but now with only two mimes, shot in black-and-white, without the drums. Like tired ghosts, the mimes continue pacing around the square. "Yes," Beckett said, "marvelous, it's 100,000 years later."[24] Between *Quad I* and *Quad II* lies a space of 100,000 years, but nothing much has changed. Beckett's time remains unperturbed by incident. As Barthes describes, "It is an unwonted time, a time for nothing."[25]

In Nauman's *Violent Incident* (1986), a drama is enacted 12 times simultaneously in a bank of television monitors. Nauman 's proposal for the work is simple: woman pulls chair out from under man, she gooses him, exchange of epithets, scuffling, she gets shot, he gets shot.[26] The scene is replayed in several variations: between two men, between two women, roles reversed, in slow motion, as a rehearsal, using differing color schemes, and so on. In these multiple views, the installation mobilizes Cavell's concept of television as a space of "monitoring" or "simultaneous event reception."[27] The bank of screens, Cavell suggests, provides the best access to television, allowing for a "switching" from one instance to the next, conveniently, in case something were to happen. Necessary to the logic of television's continuance, however, nothing ever does, and we are left in a state of perpetual suspense. The violent incident replays itself over and again, without death ever lending a point to the drama; the gunshot proves to be not at all what we were waiting for. It is just another piece of information, like Beckett's *Quad*, marking an "unwonted time."

Or, to put it differently, in subjugating the event to a constant stream of simultaneity, Nauman has succeeded in mapping spatially what is characteristically conceived linearly, as a timeline. Jean-Luc Nancy describes the appropriateness of line for graphing "pure time": "And so it is with good reason that the line representing it represents the static, unidimensional, nonspatial copresence of its points (a limit of space, not

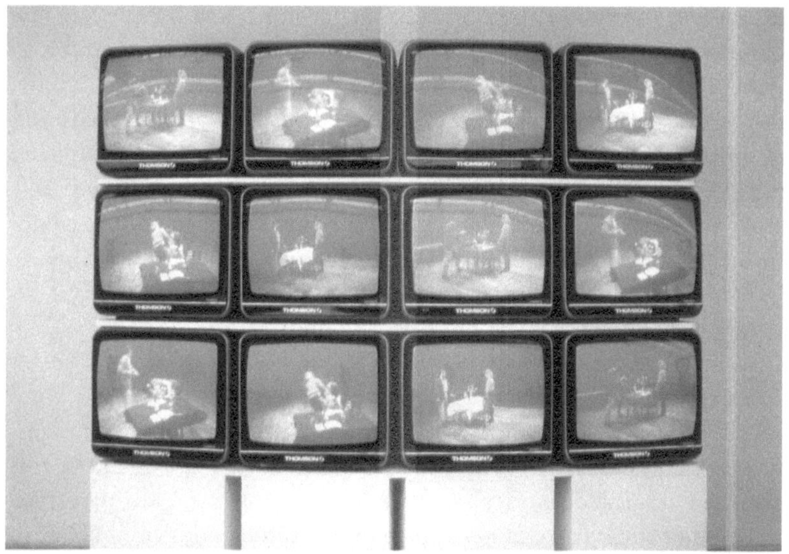

Violent Incident, 1986. Installation, twelve 26-in. color monitors, four videotape players, four videotapes (color, sound). Approx. 102⅛ × 105 × 18½ in. (259.4 × 266.7 × 47 cm). Tate. Purchased 1993. Image courtesy Sperone Westwater, New York.

a space: the limit where space becomes pure time, but where pure time annuls the event)."[28] Pure time annuls the event in being marked not as a thing that itself takes place, that creates and destroys. Rather, pure time exists as a series of "at onces": "It is the altered sameness of the time—the untimeliness of time—and it is thus that it is spacing, or that it is insofar as it spaces itself out."[29] *Violent Incident* produces this "altered sameness": in one take, the man shoots last; in another, the woman (what was once on the right is now on the left). And, as Nancy argues, this undialectical procedure requires a separation, a displacement; but now, instead of dashes on a line, Nauman (and Beckett, too) will tick, like a clock.

As with *Wall-Floor Positions*, even when the viewer leaves the bank of screens, he or she may continue to monitor *Violent Incident* through sound. Nauman describes the audio effect of a particular installation at Whitechapel: "Because it was in a separate room, the sound was baffled; you only got the higher tones. So the main thing you heard throughout the museum was 'Asshole!'"[30] Imagine it, wandering through the exhibition, surrounded by normal, ambient noise, and then, every few minutes or so, a scream—"Asshole!"—reminding you of the fact that in spite of your absence, the incident continues to take place. Significantly, the scream recurs within spaces, between pockets of rest filled with every other sound, giving the false impression of somehow being over. A kind of rhythm is produced then, an oscillation that marks the persistence of goings-on intermittently, within blankets of white noise, punctuated by a high-pitched yell.

... (the door closing that was not a door closing) ...

Consider this rhythm during which, amplified along with the word "Asshole!," is all that comes in between. The white noise, the nonsignifying ground moves forward. It seems in cases to promise a kind of closure and instead delivers a prolongation of suspense, "the perpetual suspense of a tear that can never be entirely formed nor fall."[31] Nauman and Beckett do nothing but point to this almost-shutting that is the sound of *Wall-Floor Positions*, where a slam is always re-marked by a reopening, a silence. The pause is empty, noticeably so, in order to distinguish itself as trap, as that space wherein information, data, stuff accumulates and reformulates irrepressibly. Through Stéphane Mallarmé, Derrida has theorized this blank: "A folding back, once more: the hymen, 'a medium, a pure medium of fiction,' is located between the present acts that don't take place. What takes place is only the *entre*, the place, the spacing, which is nothing, the ideality (as nothingness) of the idea. No act, then, is perpetrated ('Hymen … between perpetration and remembrance'); no act is committed as a crime."[32]

A hymen, figured by the white crease between two pages of a book (or fifteen minutes between two acts of a play).

Waiting for Godot contains an intermission. The curtained stage marks the space of possibility and anticipation, which makes all the more resonant the maddening recurrences on the stage of act 2: "Next day. Same time. Same place," and Vladimir's first words to Estragon, "You again!" (430).[33] What becomes painfully apparent, then, is that the play is precisely this curtained stage, this space of no-event and perpetual waiting. Boasting of their endurance in this place, Vladimir will remark to Estragon, "We are not saints, but we have kept our appointment" (458). Godot, however, will never keep his appointment, and the play brackets nothing but this missed encounter: a meeting that was presumed to occur never does. Thus, the curtain falling at the end of act 2 signals no end but a lingering nonfinality, the suspense of a pause (a tear) hovering between. Not too much unlike the brief switch between monitors or as a video loops back around to the beginning. *Violent Incident* is marked by such hiccups, disturbances that call attention to what seems like the substance, the point, of the work. Again, what one finds is that switch and flicker are all of *Violent Incident*. No crime is committed; nothing is perpetrated. "Asshole!" is only part of the ambient noise after all, signaling nothing, except perhaps an appointment. The incident, it turns out, is about monitoring, waiting in between acts.

At the 1997 Whitney Biennial, Nauman's video installation was called *End of the World* (1996), leading one to expect an apocalypse, only to be met with some sad song perpetually dying. A series of three projected videos replayed differing takes of the same man (whose body is always cropped, so you couldn't precisely tell) playing the same song (too many layers to know for sure) on pedal steel guitars (every one slightly altered from the previous). The videos of each projection were segmented, stopping and starting in a kind of nonthematic orchestration, like entr'acte organ music. Certainly in this constant making and unmaking, there was no cataclysmic explosion then, only a lingering trace, a vestige, which Nancy says is characterized through "its infinite finishing (or infinishing) and not its finite perfection."[34] According to Nancy, art defines itself precisely through the vestigial, "infinishing," nonessential:

> The vestigial is not an essence—and no doubt this is what puts us on the track of "the essence of art." That art is today its own vestige, this is what opens us to it. It is not a degraded presentation of the Idea, nor the presentation of a degraded Idea; it presents what is not "Idea": motion, coming, passage, the going-on of coming-to-presence.[35]

And waiting, too, which Nancy could have mentioned, which both Nauman and Beckett insist on, pointing always to the end, traversing it but never arriving there, a perpetual nonpenetration "without breaking the ice or the mirror."[36] Steven Connor discusses this compulsive

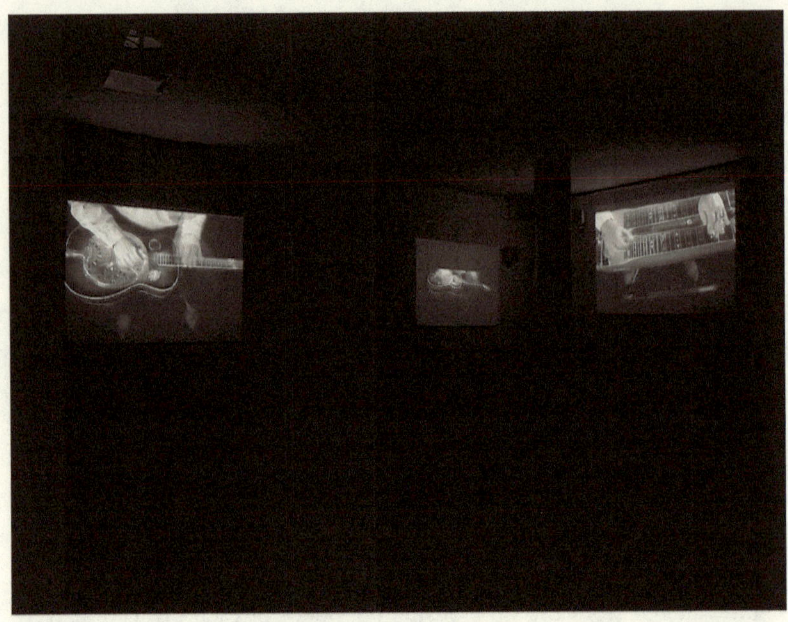

End of the World—Lloyd Maines, 1996. Three video projectors, three video players, three video sources (color, sound). Dimensions variable. Emanuel Hoffmann Foundation, on permanent loan to the Öffentliche Kunstsammlung Basel. Image courtesy Sperone Westwater, New York.

relishing of the ending's immanence in Beckett, quoting the last passage from *Ill Seen, Ill Said*:

> Farewell to farewell. Then in that perfect dark foreknell darling sound pip for end begun. First last moment. Grant only enough remain to devour all. Moment by glutton moment. Sky earth the whole kit and boodle. Not another crumb of carrion left. Lick chops and basta. No. One moment more. One last. Grace to breathe that void. Know happiness.[37]

During *End of the World*, this is the promise of every silence that breaks the stream of pedal steel guitar, the anticipation of "one moment more," of the relishing of space within an "end begun," so that end therefore resides at the unraveled origin.[38]

In his own version of "the end of the world,"[39] Nancy, like Nauman, invokes not a dark apocalypse but a clarity of realization: that there is no "end" in the sense of determinable liquidation with its antipode of birth. In other words, no "'once and for all,' ... but the spacing of all 'onces.'"[40] Brilliantly, Nauman and Beckett engender this finitude, folded within the structure of infinity, the uneventful displacements of "pure time." And through this spacing, which enables a continual surging forth and retreat, enter *End of the World*, like *Violent Incident*, *Quad*, *Footfalls*, *Wall-Floor Positions* ... engaged in a rhythm. Nancy characterizes the perpetual progress (not passage) of the vestige's infinite finishing in just such terms: "This rhythm comprises sequence and syncopation, trajectory and interruption, gait and gap, phase and spasm. It thereby cuts a figure, but this figure is not an image in the sense I have spoken of here. The step of the figure, or the vestige, is its tracing, its spacing."[41]

... and though it seemed to be outside him, before him, about him ...

And what if this spacing were to consist in beating one's entire body against the corner of a wall, as Nauman did in his video *Bouncing in the Corner* (1968)? The knock would signify, once again, not someone at the door but a collision of body and matter. This impact resonates in Nauman and Beckett. Sound produces the difficulty of existing among things, of having sense. In Beckett's radio play *All That Fall* (1957), considerable airtime is given to grunting and groaning, as the heavyset and rickety couple Maddy and Dan Rooney maneuver into cars, up stairs, down roads.[42] Again, what makes the performance exhausting to hear is this strained effort, figured in a rhythm painfully maintained, as the Rooneys inch their way back from the train station toward their home. And prototypically for Beckett, it is precisely this arduous repercussion that proves existence.

In Beckett's 1976 stage play *Footfalls*, the disheveled, aged May speaks with or to an offstage voice accompanied by the sound of her own pacing, to and fro in the dark. While May paces, the single voice recites this schizophrenic narration:

> *The mother*: What do you mean, May, not enough, what can you possibly mean, May, not enough? *May*: I mean, Mother, that I must

> hear the feet, however faint they fall. *The mother*: The motion alone is not enough? *May*: No, Mother, the motion alone is not enough, I must hear the feet, however faint they fall.[43]

Striking the ground, touching it, is not enough. There must be an excess of sense, a vestige of movement that consists in this pulse, however faint, of pacing. Slightly different in dynamic, perhaps, from the slam of *Wall-Floor Positions*, the beat in both is never metronomic but the irregular pulse of a body that falters, accelerates, decelerates. In describing the music of Schumann, Barthes describes such a rhythm of pure violence, invested in the body that "speaks but says nothing."[44] Of Schumann's *Kreisleriana*, Barthes writes, "No, what I hear are blows: I hear what beats in the body, what beats the body, or better: I hear this body that beats."[45] Beating the body into music without the relay of a signifier, this is the power of Schumann's rhythm, which explodes and rages but never expresses. Similarly, if in Nauman's tightly cropped loops of tape a torso is extracted, a head lopped off, if on Beckett's darkened stage only a mouth emerges, a cowled figure scurrying, a hooded lump, what bears the body in to presence is this beating (shuffling, slamming, bouncing) that is at once the sense of touching or hearing something outside the body and the vestige that points to the sense of having touched, stepped, moved.

Barthes describes the effect of Schumann's violent rhythm as madness. Incorporating this pulse, Nauman's installation *Learned Helplessness in Rats (Rock and Roll Drummer)* (1988) is a laboratory for just such destabilization, engaged here by the double accompaniment of a different sort of beat. On one wall, a video projection alternates, clicking regularly from shots of a rat in a Plexiglas maze to live footage from a surveillance camera hovering in the room to a recording of the drum session that produced the installation's obnoxious soundtrack. Madness here, however, is not so much caused by the loudly pounding drum riffs but by the fact that this noise, made somewhere and sometime else by the boy in the video, strikes the body immediately in this small room. What actually sets the viewer reeling is this constant shift, amplified by each mechanical click of the sequencer, switching the projection from prerecorded drummer/rat (then) to live-surveillance footage (now). With every shift Nauman strips away the moorings of past–present, leaving a series of spaced "at onces" that tremble in between.[46]

Engaging this perpetual temporal implosion, Nauman pries apart the seam between now and then, the distance typically screened by the television set. Imposing a remote, other vision on a situated viewer, television creates what Samuel Weber refers to as "undecidability," a condition that the screen itself simultaneously masks and marks.[47] Nauman wants to expose this "undecidability," showing how television's confusion of time also produces a confusion of substance, a sense of being—as Weber notes—"neither fully there, nor entirely here."[48] Appropriately, then, while Nauman's beat attacks before/after, it collapses inside/outside on the way.

... in his mind, he supposed, though he did not know exactly what that meant ...

In Beckett's stage play *Not I* (1972), a disembodied mouth, surrounded by black curtain, is slowly born into light, chattering faster and faster without skipping a beat, slowing only at the intermittent refrain "what? ... who? ... no! ... she!"[49] In *Not I*, constant bafflement about what comes from within the mouth (mind) and what bombards from without. The mouth struggles to keep pace with its own thoughts (which it cannot be sure are its own).[50] Nauman's 60-minute black-and-white video *Lip Sync* (1969) uses the same bodiless orifice, this time suspended upside down by the camera. What is most disturbing about Nauman's mouth is the tempo of repronounced words, "Liiiip ... Sin ... k," which almost seem to come from it, pronounced according to Barthes's definition, wherein pronunciation emerges "from the depths of the body's cavities," manifesting the materiality of signifier-sounds, rubbing against the message in a kind of perverted friction.[51] We hear and see this grating in *Lip Sync* when the mouth closes and swallows after a tiring string of speech, when the throat clears itself of accumulated saliva, when the microphone pops with every force of air from the plosive consonants *p*! and *k*! Most alarming about these sounds, however, is the fact that their synchronization with the mouth on-screen wavers, engendering a perpetual undecidability, as the embodied materiality of voice collides with the absence of a coherent body.

In *Think* (1993), Nauman's head bounces up and down on two television screens, one above the other, the camera tightly focused so that only the top of Nauman's head comes into full view, with the

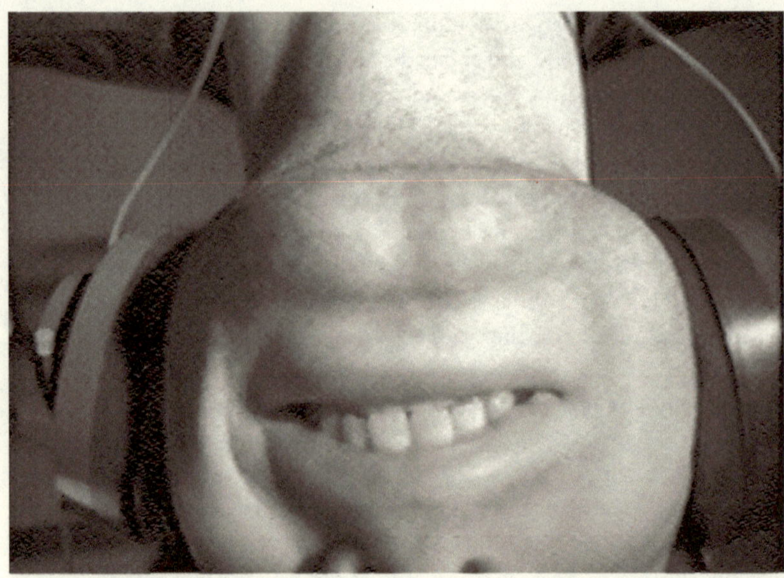

Lip Sync, 1969. Videotape (black-and-white, sound). 60 min., to be repeated continuously. Distributed by Electronic Arts Intermix. Image courtesy Sperone Westwater, New York.

occasional peep of mouth ostensibly chanting as he bounces, "Think! Think! Think!" The laser-disc recordings are twinned but once again not synchronized. The looped segments vary: a snowy image with sound distortion, "Think!" punctuated by clashing cymbals, top screen upside down, bottom screen right side up, vice versa, and so on. What remains constantly clear is the initial impression: that it is difficult to match which voice to which bobbing head, that it is preposterous to follow the imperative "Think! Think! Think!" with so much annoying distraction. The multiple voice, the echo that must yet does not seem to come from the on-screen/onstage fragment is a familiar discombobulating technique, one used in the romantic song:

> What is suggested, what is here vocally put before us, is the anguish of something that threatens to divide, to separate, to dissociate, to dismember the body. The dark voice, voice of Evil or of Death, is a voice without site, a voice without origin: it resonates everywhere. … [I]n every case, it no longer refers to the body, which is distanced in a kind of non-site.[52]

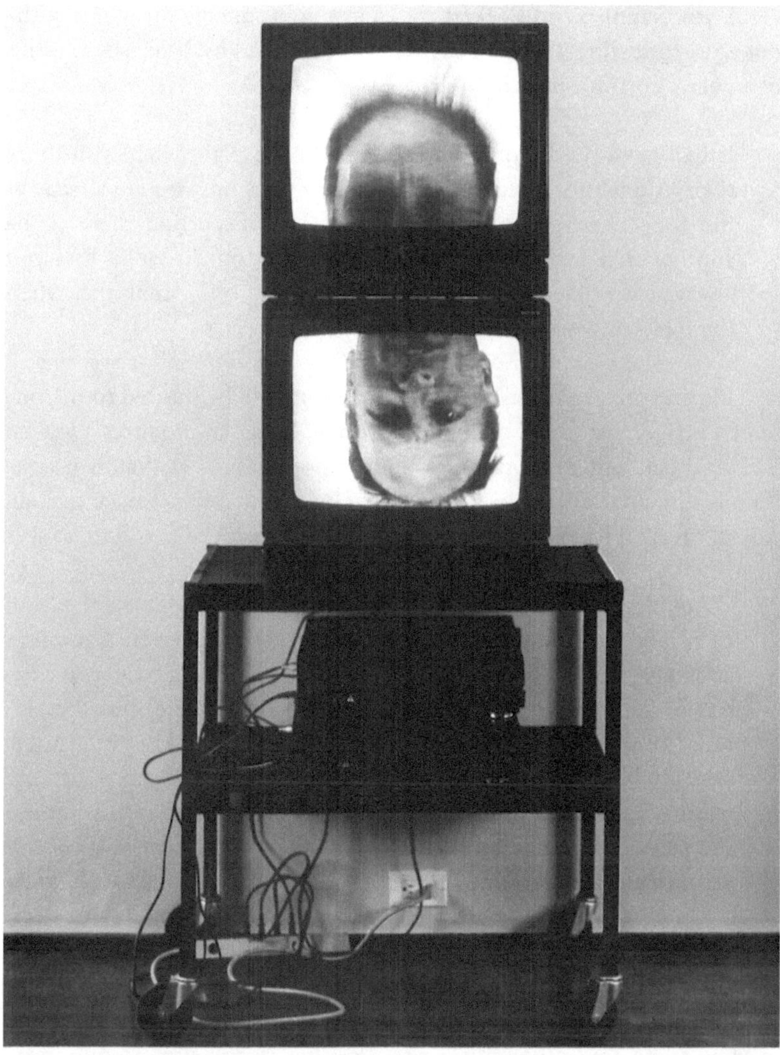

Think, 1993. Two color video monitors, two laser disc players, two laser discs (color, sound), one utility cart. Dimensions variable. The Museum of Modern Art, New York. Gift of Werner and Elaine Dannheisser. Image courtesy Sperone Westwater, New York.

Both Nauman and Beckett are expert in producing this voice without a site, afflicting a kind of sitelessness, described by Nauman in terms of an early corridor piece:

> It had to do with going up the stairs in the dark, when you think there is one more step and you take the step, but you are already at the top ... or going down the stairs and expecting there to be another step, but you are already at the bottom. It seems that you always have that jolt and it really throws you off. I think that when these pieces work they do that too.[53]

Playing on an expectation, that the sound will be sutured to the onscreen image, that it will come from a body, Nauman produces a jolt. In *Think*, shock and frustration are doubly pronounced as Nauman confounds this aural dislocation with an explicit mental sitelessness, making ridiculous the Hegelian notion of thought as a realm of pure interiority:

> Thinking, however, results in thought alone; it evaporates the form of reality into the form of the pure Concept, and even if it grasps and apprehends real things in their particular character and real existence, it nevertheless lifts even this particular sphere into the element of the universal and ideal wherein alone thinking is at home with itself. ... Thinking is only a reconciliation between reality and truth within thinking itself. But poetic creation and formation is a reconciliation in the form of a real phenomenon itself, even if this form be presented only spiritually.[54]

Nancy articulates an interruption in Hegel's model, of art "conceived as the derived, external, and unseeing expression of the internal gaze of pure presence"[55] and consequently of thinking, which could ever be alone "at home with itself." Positing sense before signification, Nancy reverses the dialectic: "thought uses itself to touch (to be touched by) that which is not for it a 'content' but its body: the space of this extension and opening in which and as which it exscribes itself, that is, lets itself be transformed into the concreteness or praxis of sense."[56] For Nauman, like Nancy, to think touches on to jump, to crash cymbals, to scream, to hear. For Nancy, like Beckett, this process (of thought touching its body) is conceived as a step (*Footfalls*, "Suspended Step").

Trekking back to the mind/body problem, which Rosalind Krauss identifies as the snare of Robert Morris's *Box with the Sound of Its Own Making* (1961), we recognize this same fracturing, whereby no substance is integral, whole. Morris's Beckettian construction no doubt opens onto Nauman's, also baffling the notion of founding origin, also tracing the closed circuit of consciousness everywhere to an outside line. The fiction of "internal discourse," as attacked, too, by Derrida in 1969 ("The Double Session"), is left perpetually under siege. Nonetheless, while mobilizing this estrangement, "exscription," sitelessness, Beckett and Nauman still preserve the "concreteness" of sense, the specificities of situation. Their acoustic experiments have little to do with Artaud's, as described by Denis Hollier. If Artaud would open theater to the noises of the street, "to leave the space of representation for that, precisely of the event,"[57] by contrast Nauman and Beckett insist on the theatricality of their works, which only mimic events. For them, sound never breaks into an exterior world of lived experience but bounces incessantly against the framing edges of stage, screen, installation. Their works depend on a relentless specificity[58] in line with Nancy's, in which sense is not indiscriminately dispersed but zoned, discrete.

... with the utmost formal distinctness ...

If film has been theorized as a visual art, menaced by what Hollis Frampton, for instance, would deem the synesthetic "monster" of sound,[59] Beckett's directions for *Film* (1964), consisting mostly of outlines and diagrams, are appropriately headed by the motto "Esse est percipi."[60] Originally titled *The Eye*, *Film* inflicts on Buster Keaton an "anguish of perceivedness" through successive camera angles from which Keaton, designated O (the object), cannot escape: "We're trying to find a ... cinematic equivalent for visual appetite and visual distaste ... a reluctant ... a disgusted vision [O's] and a ferociously voracious one [E's]."[61] As such, the film is silent, but not completely. There is a moment, the slightest threat to visual hegemony, when a woman turns to her companion and "checks him with a gesture and soft 'sssh!'" *Film* reverberates with this quiet exclamation echoing in silence, puncturing the circumference of film's voracious eye with a gaping hole.

Addressing the attempt to stage a theater production of *All That Fall*, Beckett reacted harshly:

> *All That Fall* is a specifically radio play, or rather radio text, for voices, not bodies. I have already refused to have it "staged" and I cannot think of it in such terms. … It is no more theater than *End-Game* is radio and to "act" it is to kill it. Even the reduced visual dimension it will receive from the simplest and most static of readings … will be destructive of whatever quality it may have and which depends on the whole thing's coming out of the dark.[62]

When the transference of the stage play *Act Without Words* to film was proposed to Beckett, he similarly replied, "If we can't keep our genres more or less distinct, or extricate them from the confusion that has them where they are, we might as well go home and lie down."[63] Ironically, however, the very means that Beckett uses in order to keep his genres "more or less distinct" rely on a technique of studied confrontation, if not confusion. Writing about *All That Fall*, Linda Ben-Zvi describes Beckett's method, which constantly thwarts the medium of radio, giving anything but the impression of another world constituted by sound in its entirety. Instead, the listener remains in wondering frustration as Beckett issues cryptic clues, pointing mercilessly to the fact that one is sitting in the dark and wants to see what's going on. Beckett's medium consciousness resides, then, not in forming clear lines of demarcation but in creating constant friction, always implicating "other zones of sensing" in the manner of Nancy's *toucher*:

> Sensing and the sensing-oneself-sense that makes for sensing itself consists always in sensing at the same time that there is some other (which one senses) and that there are other zones of sensing, overlooked by the zone that is sensing at this moment, or else on which this zone touches on all sides but only at the limit where it ceases being the zone that it is.[64]

Beckett's work relentlessly pursues these limits, moving increasingly toward a degree of dissolution. His formalism, therefore, could never be characterized as reductive, but more properly as explosive. As such, *Quad I* and *II* do not produce a distillation, an essence of what it is to be a television play. Indeed, they border so closely on dance that Beckett must plug the spill with a proclamation: the cowled figures are "mimes," he says, "not dancers."[65] In creating this tenuous structure, however,

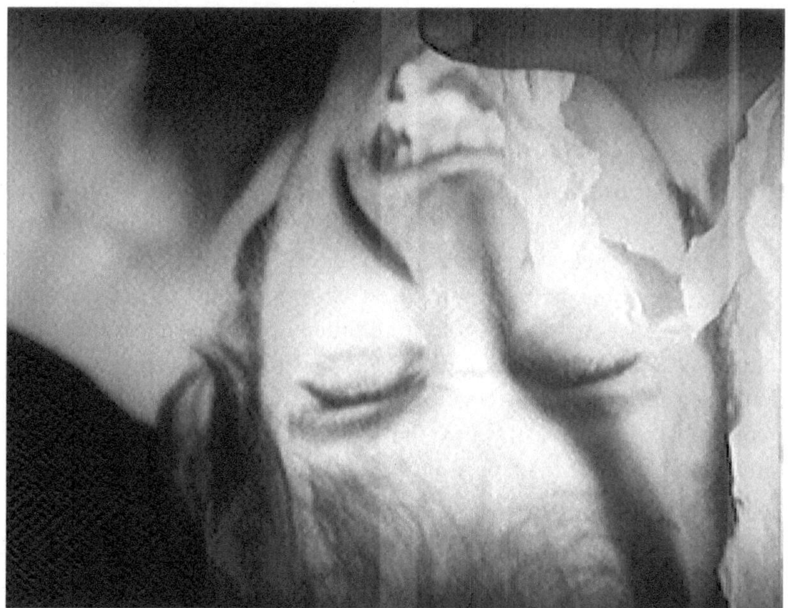

Gauze, 1969. 16-mm film (black-and-white, sound). 8 min. Distributed by Electronic Arts Intermix. Image courtesy Sperone Westwater, New York.

Beckett does not deny the medium's essence. Rather, to use Nancy's terms again, he "entrances" it, seduces it, transverses it.[66]

Like Beckett's *Film*, Nauman's film reels *Art Make-Up: Nos. 1, 2, 3, 4* (1967–1968), the black-and-whites from 1969, *Black Balls*, *Bouncing Balls*, *Gauze*, and *Pulling Mouth*, are silent. Nauman will also agree that "films are about seeing," and as such he, too, will produce an anguish, this time of perceiving, straining vision in his painfully decelerated slow-mos, shot at 1,000 to 4,000 frames per second. His videotapes, on the other hand, will not utilize this form of distortion, profiting instead from the initially accidental effects of a wild track that stretches and tightens, causing sound to go in and out of sync. Nauman himself, of course, will sound far more cavalier about his use of materials:

> But it was simple in that in the '60s you didn't have to pick just one medium. There didn't seem to be any problem with using different kinds of materials, shifting from photographs to dance to performance to videotapes. It seemed very straightforward to use all those

> different ways of expressing ideas or presenting material. You could make neon signs, you could make written pieces, you could make jokes about parts of the body or casting things, or whatever.[67]

Nauman thus refers to working in video, film, speaking as if it were a matter of convenience, not conviction. And his projects are undeniably invested in a kind of plurality without hierarchy: video, photograph, casting, neon sign, whatever. There is, nevertheless, in this seeming "anything goes" approach an obsessively disciplined method, which recognizes as discrete "all those different ways of expressing." As acutely as anyone, Nauman knows what it is to watch a screen, knows the expectations (embodied voices, sutured sound–image), the rhythm (repeated illusion of narrative), the circumstances (somewhat private, somewhat not), the frustrations (endless) that attend a TV viewing. And Nauman, as madly as Beckett, will not desist in unraveling, in making and remaking, until the work resembles a *Violent Incident*: "I liked all this, keep taking it apart, taking it apart."[68]

Obviously, this method of dissection can never produce an autonomous body that one could frame and hang on the wall to look at because it would be dripping, leaking. Neither, on the other hand, does it produce a space of nondifferentiation, of art in general. On this, Nancy writes, "However, there is no 'art' in general: each one indicates the threshold by being itself also the threshold of another art. Each one touches the other without passing into it."[69] Art and sense still intact, defined by thresholds, by spacing. Art that knows itself by rubbing constantly, grating its surface against another "with the utmost formal distinctness."

Notes

1. Samuel Beckett, *Watt* (New York: Grove Press, 1953), 194; all subsequent references are given parenthetically by title and page number in the text. "Darwin's caterpillar" behaved in the following way: when it had completed its cocoon up to the sixth layer and was then placed in a cocoon built to the third layer, the caterpillar would redo the last three stages of the new cocoon. When, however, this same caterpillar was placed in a cocoon already built to the sixth layer, instead of profiting from the work done, it started again at the third stage (see Michael Beausang, "*Watt*: Logic, Insanity, Aphasia," *Style* 30, no. 3 [Fall 1996]: 503–504).

2. While in San Francisco in 1966, Nauman read plays and stories by Beckett, making several references to him in interviews and in work (see *Bruce Nauman*, ed. Joan Simon [Minneapolis: Walker Art Center, 1994]). In 1968, he taped *Slow Angle Walk (Beckett Walk)* and installed at the Fischer Gallery, Düsseldorf, *Six Sound Problems for Konrad*

Fischer, described by Coosje van Bruggen as resembling the stage for Beckett's 1958 play *Krapp's Last Tape* (*Bruce Nauman* [New York: Rizzoli, 1988], 233).

3. *Eh Joe*, produced by BBC television, was first shown on July 4, 1966.

4. Roman Jakobson, "Why Mama and Papa?" in *Selected Writings*, vol. 1 (The Hague: Mouton, 1962), 538–545, and as discussed in Rosalind Krauss, "Yo-Yo," in Yve-Alain Bois and Rosalind Krauss, *Formless: A User's Guide* (New York: Zone Books, 1997), 219–220.

5. Jacques Derrida, *Writing and Difference*, trans. Alan Bass (Chicago: University of Chicago Press, 1978), 295.

6. Ibid., 296.

7. Samuel Beckett, *Waiting for Godot*, reprinted in *I Can't Go On, I'll Go On*, ed. Richard W. Seaver (New York: Grove Press, 1976), 444; all subsequent references are given parenthetically by title and page number in the text.

8. Jacques Derrida, "The Double Session" (1969), reprinted in *Dissemination*, trans. Barbara Johnson (Chicago: University of Chicago Press, 1981), 206.

9. For a comprehensive study of Beckett's use of repetition, see Steven Connor, *Samuel Beckett: Repetition, Theory, and Text* (New York: Blackwell, 1988).

10. Sigmund Freud, *Jokes and Their Relation to the Unconscious* (New York: Norton, 1960), 143.

11. Derrida, "The Double Session," 210.

12. Using the example of *Watt*'s serial manipulations, Rosalind Krauss describes this operation of "infinite regress" wherein logical analysis touches perversely on nonsense ("The Mind/Body Problem: Robert Morris in Series," in *Robert Morris: The Mind/Body Problem* [New York: Guggenheim Museum Foundation, 1994], 2–3). In both *Watt* and the works of Robert Morris, an endless permutational overproduction nullifies the supposed internal coherence of language, body, and mind.

13. Nauman, in Joan Simon, "Breaking the Silence: An Interview with Bruce Nauman," *Art in America* 76, no. 9 (September 1988): 142 [reprinted in this volume].

14. Nauman, in Jane Livingston, "Bruce Nauman," in Jane Livingston and Marcia Tucker, *Bruce Nauman: Work from 1965 to 1972* (Los Angeles: Los Angeles County Museum of Art, 1972), 12.

15. Nauman, in Simon, "Breaking the Silence," 203.

16. Nauman also names Robbe-Grillet as one of his major influences. This connection, also with reference to the essay by Barthes, is mentioned in Kathy Halbreich's essay "Social Life," in *Bruce Nauman*, ed. Simon, 102.

17. Roland Barthes, "Objective Literature: Alain Robbe-Grillet," in Alain Robbe-Grillet, *Two Novels by Alain Robbe-Grillet*, trans. Richard Howard (New York: Grove Press, 1965), 21.

18. Ibid., 22.

19. "Bruce Nauman: Notes and Projects," as printed in Marcia Tucker, "PheNAUMANology," *Artforum* 9, no. 4 (December 1970): 44 [reprinted in this volume].

20. Mary Ann Doane, "Information, Crisis, Catastrophe," in *Logics of Television: Essays in Cultural Criticism*, ed. Patricia Mellencamp (Bloomington: Indiana University Press, 1990), 221–225.

21. Stanley Cavell, "The Fact of Television," in *Video Culture*, ed. John G. Hanhardt (Layton, Utah: G. M. Smith/Peregrine Smith Books, 1986), 210.

22. Jane Feuer, "The Concept of Live Television," in *Regarding Television: Critical Approaches—an Anthology*, ed. E. Ann Kaplan (Frederick, MD: University Publications of America/American Film Institute, 1983), 16.

23. Samuel Beckett, *Quad I*, quoted in Enoch Brater, "Beckett's *Nacht und Traüme* and *Quad*," *Modern Drama* 28, no. 1 (March 1985): 51. The reference is to the production done in Stuttgart by Suddeutscher Rundfunk, aired on October 8, 1981, under the title *Quadrat I + 2*. The text for this play is reduced to a series of mathematical permutations describing the courses, accompanied by a diagram of the stage.

24. Samuel Beckett, *Quad II*, quoted in Brater, "Beckett's *Nacht und Traüme* and *Quad*," 52.

25. Barthes, "Objective Literature," 22.

26. For an exact transcription of *Violent Incident*, see Coosje van Bruggen, "The True Artist Is an Amazing Luminous Fountain," in van Bruggen, *Bruce Nauman*, 119–120.

27. Cavell, "The Fact of Television," 205.

28. Jean-Luc Nancy, "Spanne," in *The Sense of the World*, trans. Jeffrey S. Librett (Minneapolis: University of Minnesota Press, 1997), 65.

29. Ibid., 66.

30. Nauman, in Simon, "Breaking the Silence," 148.

31. Stéphane Mallarmé, quoted in Derrida, "The Double Session," 180.

32. Derrida, "The Double Session," 214.

33. As discussed by Connor in *Samuel Beckett*.

34. Jean-Luc Nancy, "The Vestige of Art," in *The Muses*, trans. Peggy Kamuf (Palo Alto, CA: Stanford University Press, 1996), 98. This discussion relies on Raichel Haidu's work on Nancy's theory of the vestige.

35. Ibid., 98.

36. Mallarmé, quoted in Derrida, "The Double Session," 215.

37. Samuel Beckett, *Ill Seen, Ill Said*, quoted in Connor, *Samuel Beckett*, 10–11.

38. See Jean-Luc Nancy's discussion of finitude in "Infinite Finitude," in *The Sense of the World*, 29–33.

39. Jean-Luc Nancy, "The End of the World," in *The Sense of the World*, 4–9.

40. Nancy, "Spanne," 65.

41. Nancy, "The Vestige of Art," 98.

42. *All That Fall* was first aired by the BBC on January 13, 1957.

43. Samuel Beckett, *Footfalls* (London: Faber and Faber, 1976), 11.

44. Roland Barthes, "Rasch" (1975), in *The Responsibility of Forms*, trans. Richard Howard (Berkeley: University of California Press, 1991), 306.

45. Ibid., 299.

46. Derrida writes:

> The present is no longer a mother-form around which are gathered and differentiated the future (present) and the past (present). What is marked in this hymen

between the future (desire) and the present (fulfillment), between past (remembrance) and the present (perpetration), between the capacity and the act, etc., is only a series of temporal differences without any central present, without a present of which the past and future would be but modifications. ("The Double Session," 210)

47. Samuel Weber, "Television: Set and Screen," in *Mass Mediauras: Form, Technics, Media* (Palo Alto, CA: Stanford University Press, 1996), 108–128.

48. Ibid.

49. Samuel Beckett, *Not I*, reprinted in *I Can't Go On, I'll Go On*, 592–604, and later adapted for television and broadcast by the BBC, around 1977.

50. See Steven Connor, "What? Where? Space and the Body," in *Samuel Beckett*, 140–169.

51. Roland Barthes, "The Grain of the Voice" (1972), in *The Responsibility of Forms*, 270–272.

52. Roland Barthes, "The Romantic Song" (1976), in *The Responsibility of Forms*, 288.

53. Nauman, in Willoughby Sharp, "Bruce Nauman," *Avalanche* 2 (Winter 1971): 30.

54. G. W. F. Hegel, *Aesthetics: Lectures on Fine Arts* (Oxford: Clarendon Press, 1975), 2:976, quoted in Jean-Luc Nancy, "The Girl Who Succeeds the Muses," in *The Muses*, 43.

55. Nancy, "The Girl Who Succeeds the Muses," 54.

56. Jean-Luc Nancy, "Suspended Step," in *The Sense of the World*, 10.

57. Denis Hollier, "The Death of Paper, Part Two: Artaud's Sound System," *October* 80 (Spring 1997): 36.

58. This discussion follows Krauss's work, rethinking the concepts of "medium" and "medium specificity" (see Rosalind Krauss, "' … And Then Turn Away?' An Essay on James Coleman," *October* 81 [Summer 1997]: 5–33).

59. See Hollis Frampton, "The Withering Away of the State of Art," paper delivered at the conference "Open Circuits: The Future of Television," January 23–25, 1974, Museum of Modern Art, New York; reprinted in *Circles of Confusion: Film, Photography, Video; Texts, 1968–1980* (Rochester, NY: Visual Studios Workshop Press, 1983), 161–170.

60. Samuel Beckett, *Film*, in *Eh Joe and Other Writings* (London: Faber and Faber, 1967), 29–44.

61. Beckett, quoted in S. E. Gontarski, *Film and Formal Integrity in Samuel Beckett: Humanistic Perspectives*, ed. Morris Beja, S. E. Gontarski, and Pierre Astier (Columbus: Ohio State University Press, 1983), 135, quoted in Linda Ben-Zvi, "Samuel Beckett's Media Plays," *Modern Drama* 28, no. 1 (March 1985): 30.

62. Beckett, quoted in Thomas F. Van Laan, "*All That Fall* as a 'Play for Radio,'" *Modern Drama* 28, no. 1 (March 1985): 38.

63. Samuel Beckett to his American publisher, August 27, 1957, quoted in Ben-Zvi, "Samuel Beckett's Media Plays," 24. See also Connor, "What? Where? Space and the Body," 150–151.

64. Jean-Luc Nancy, "Why Are There Several Arts and Not Just One?" in *The Muses*, 17.

65. Beckett, quoted in Brater, "Beckett's *Nacht und Traüme* and *Quad*," 51.

66. In "Infinite Finitude," Nancy locates being as anterior to essence. Being neither allows essence to take place nor denies it but instead "entrances" (in the sense both of seduction and of entry) the essence and transverses it. The relationship mirrors the distinction that Nancy wants to make between the sense and signification: "sense comes before all significations, prevents and overtakes them, even as it makes them possible, forming the opening of the general signifyingness [or significance: *significance*] (or the opening of the world) in which and according to which it is first of all possible for significations to come to produce themselves" ("Suspended Step," 10).

67. Nauman, in Simon, "Breaking the Silence,"143.

68. Nauman, in Chris Dercon, "Keep Taking It Apart: A Conversation with Bruce Nauman," *Parkett* 10 (1986): 61.

69. Jean-Luc Nancy, "Painting," in *The Sense of the World*, 83.

Dependent Participation: Bruce Nauman's Environments[1]

Janet Kraynak

> I don't like the idea of free manipulation. … A lot of people had taken a lot of trouble educating the public to participate—If I put this stuff out here you were supposed to participate.
>
> —Bruce Nauman[2]

> A lot of the work is about that, frustration and anger in the, with the social situation, not so much out of specific personal incidents but out of the world or mores or any cultural dissatisfaction, or disjointedness or something, and it doesn't always appear that way in the work, I think. Somehow it generates work. It generates energy from the work.
>
> —Bruce Nauman[3]

Between 1969 and 1974 Bruce Nauman produced a series of hybrid sculptural installations that assertively engage and operate upon the beholder's body, senses, and mind. Erected from temporary walls or permanent rooms, some of the sculptures direct the beholder's passage through space while video monitors play pre-recorded imagery and/or channel live-feed images of the viewer as she circulates the sculptural arena. In others, video is replaced by swaths of inte nse colored lights that illuminate the interiors, performing optical tricks or inducing woozy feelings of nausea. In some, empty space is rendered acoustical through recorded sounds of the artist yelling, laughing, exhaling or through walls lined with thick acoustical materials that invite the viewer to touch and produce sound. In other installations, textual "instructions," in the form of prose writings, are mounted on the walls, serving as directives for the beholder's feelings and actions.

In Nauman's installations the sculptural meets the architectural, the former realized as an environmental arena in which the beholder's role is no longer one of passive witness. Instead, the viewer is directly, physically engaged—"performing" rather than "viewing" the object—and indeed the completion of the object is contingent upon such interactions. As such, they have a long precedent in the pre- and postwar avant-garde, in which methods of artistic production were investigated and transformed as a means of reconsidering the traditional relations between art objects and their audience and as a means of envisioning a different type of subject than the modernist contemplative one. Examples cross the boundaries of time and meaning: from the Russian constructivist doctrine of productivism and Brecht's concept of estrangement to John Cage's incorporation of the audience into the musical composition, minimalism's phenomenological experiments, and conceptual art's rethinking of the networks of artistic distribution, among others.

While the shift toward audience participation historically has been motivated by diverse concerns, frameworks that emphasize its positive attributes as well as its potential for critical transformation dominate the art-historical interpretation. Whether the Marxian model of dealienation (in which the redefinition of object relations leads to a politically emancipated subject) or post-structuralist critiques of authorship (where the activation of the reader dismantles the aura of the individual work and authorial intention) or the ideological mode of collectivism (as an antidote to the passive lull of bourgeois leisure and media), participation is seen as an interventionist gesture that furthers the ambitions of a progressive avant-garde.[4]

But here I want to consider the question of participatory artwork in terms of a more limited art-historical framework of the late 1960s as well as its specific expression in Nauman's early installations. Despite individual differences of materials or design, Nauman's environments consistently figure spectatorial participation as a strange, even alienating, encounter. The viewer is assaulted with sound, frightened with foreboding narrow spaces, and cornered by video cameras recording her every move. Recorded images, moreover, are instantly played back to the viewer, whose body is often reduced to partial fragment or fleeting shadow, resulting in a sense of corporeal dispossession. Physically and psychologically, the viewer continually confronts a collapse of identification between her experience as a body/subject and her image or representation. Technical devices, in conjunction with carefully conceived architectural structures, interrupt passage through space, yielding highly charged environments. In the process, the viewer becomes almost an object—a sculptural element—while external space itself seems to assume agency: overwhelming the spectator not necessarily in terms of scale but as a controlling or disciplining factor.

In short, participation in Nauman's environments emerges as an oppressive concept that is at the *expense* of the viewer: or, at least, while Nauman's installations depend on the viewer's interaction, they are nonetheless ambivalent about the possibilities such involvement affords and, as such, create uncomfortable experiences. Such wariness is echoed in the artist's frequent comments over the years regarding his "mistrust" of audience participation. In the following exchange with Willoughby Sharp, for example, Nauman speaks of his work *Corridor Installation (Nick Wilder Installation)* from 1970:

> **NAUMAN:** The cameras will be set upside down or at some distance from the monitor so that you will only be able to see your back. I have tried to make the situation sufficiently limiting, so that spectators can't display themselves very easily.
>
> **SHARP:** Isn't that rather perverse?
>
> **NAUMAN:** Well, it has more to do with my not allowing people to make their own performance out of my art. Another problem that I worked out was using a single wall, say twenty feet long, that you can walk around. If you put a television camera at one end and the monitor around the corner, when you walk down the wall you can see yourself just as you turn the corner, but only then. You can make a square with the same function—as you turn each corner, you can just see your back going around the corner. It's another way of limiting the situation so that someone else can be a performer, but he can do only what I want him to do. I mistrust audience participation. That's why I try to make these works as limiting as possible.[5]

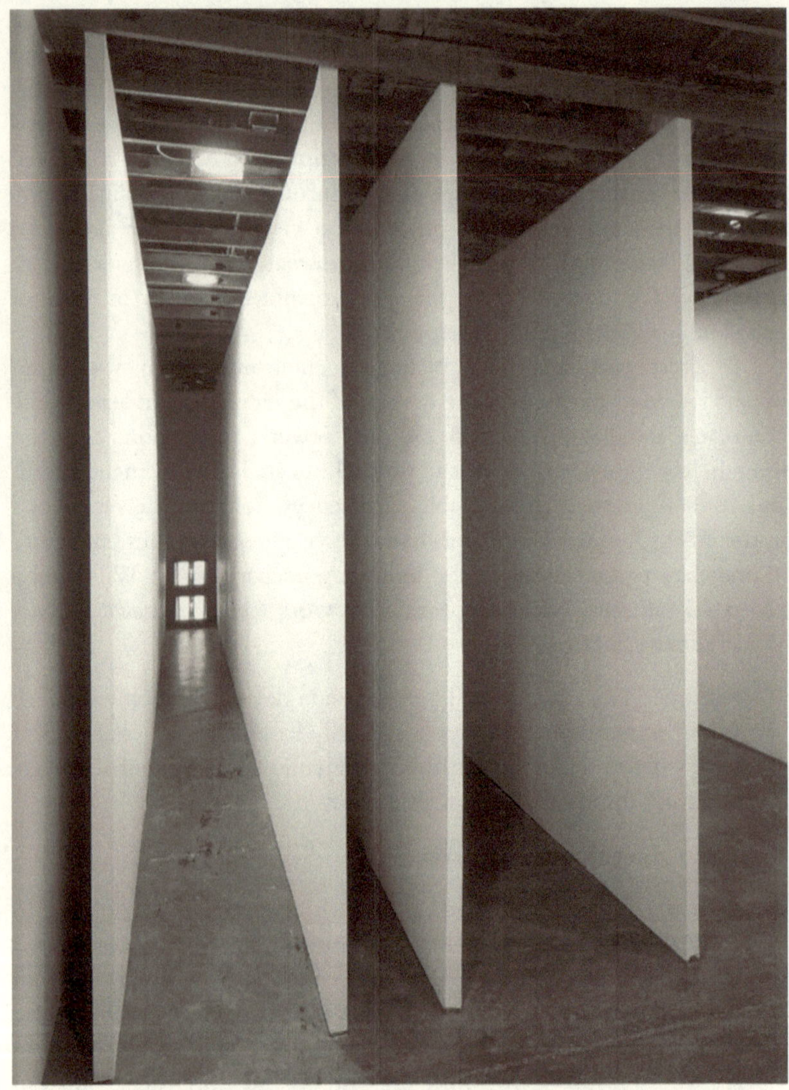

Corridor Installation (Nick Wilder Installation), 1970. Wallboard, three video cameras, scanner and mount, five video monitors, videotape player, videotape (black-and-white, silent). Dimensions variable: 132 × 480 × 360 in. (335.3 × 1219.2 × 914.4 cm) as installed at Nicholas Wilder Gallery, Los Angeles, 1970. Friedrich Christian Flick Collection. Image courtesy Sperone Westwater, New York.

Similarly, in another interview Nauman disdains the creation of open-ended situations, which, he complains, reduce art to a form of "game playing": "I don't like to leave things open so that people feel they are in a situation they can play games with. … I think I am not really interested in game playing. Partly it has to do with control, I guess."[6]

What to make of this apparent tension between the need (or desire) for reciprocal involvement on the part of the viewer and concomitantly a reluctance to allow for it or, at least, to preclude unfettered access? Because of the ways which the spectator is compelled to perform certain tasks and is physically manipulated within the spaces as well as because of the artist's comments (such as those quoted earlier), there has been much speculation regarding not just the nature of Nauman's sculptures but also the artist's perceived relationship with or even personal feelings toward his audience—often with uneasy transpositions being made between Nauman's art and persona.[7] But I want to forgo this tendency to personalize—not the least because the evidence of Nauman's artwork does not support such an approach but also because I am interested in more consequential considerations of historical exigency: specifically how Nauman's environments raise the very question of participation and how this involvement is interpreted.

Participation, this essay suggests, is a historical rather than a static concept, one that bears particular resonance with the emergence of technocratic society in the late 1960s. Characterized not simply by the pace and stuff of technological change (including computers, television, and the familiar trappings of media culture), technocracy also specifically refers to the increasingly administrative order that accompanies these developments. Nauman's environments negotiate this new technocratic space, giving form to the acute anxieties with which it was greeted. The discussion will be guided by a number of contemporary sociological and philosophical writings that attempt to analyze the nature of these changes as well as the conflicts and fears engendered by a social system still in the making. In these writings, what emerges is that participation functions simultaneously as a source of seduction and controversy, touching upon a series of arising social tensions that are part of the larger history of the sixties and its lasting influence on contemporary culture.

Nauman's Environments

Typical of Nauman's production, *Live-Taped Video Corridor* (1970) is an elaboration of an earlier work, in this case the artist's first environmental sculpture, *Performance Corridor* (1969). Employing the same simple structure of a particle board corridor with an entryway open at one end, the later work includes two video monitors placed atop each other on the floor at the closed end of the corridor: a dead-end passage that leads to nowhere. As in *Performance Corridor,* in *Live-Taped Video Corridor,* the beholder performs the simple task of walking in and out of the corridor's interior, enveloped by its narrowly set walls. Here, however, visual and bodily experience is mediated by video: a pre-recorded image of the empty corridor as well as a continuous live feed from a recording camera that is mounted high on the wall near the structure's opening and tracks the viewer's movement through the space. As the viewer works her way toward the corridor's mouth, walking closer to the picture, her body continuously recedes, appearing even smaller. This disconcerting effect is the result of a simple technical detail: because the monitor is placed at the far end of the corridor and the camera at its entry point, as the viewer moves forward, desiring to see and "touch" her image, she is actually traveling farther away from the recording device. Due to the orientation of the camera, moreover, the viewer can see herself only from behind: a perspective of one's body to which one is not normally privy.

In *Live-Taped Video Corridor* a disturbing disjunctive results between vision and experience: I *feel* myself getting closer, yet I *see* myself receding farther away. The two forms of sensorial information do not coordinate but rather contradict each other. Such strangeness is not only unfamiliar but unsettling: an uncomfortable space that welcomes me into its depths yet seems to mock me, subjecting me to its parameters. Concomitantly, it depends on me, however, and I am, technically, a desiring participant.

In subsequent pieces such perceptual effects continue with increasingly elaborate spatial configurations that generate new avenues of audience engagement. In *Corridor Installation (Nick Wilder)* of 1970, the simplicity of the single corridor is multiplied into a sprawling construction consisting of six individual corridors of differing widths, only some of which the beholder can enter, as well as an enclosed, inaccessible room. The corridors are variously lit and unlit; some contain cameras

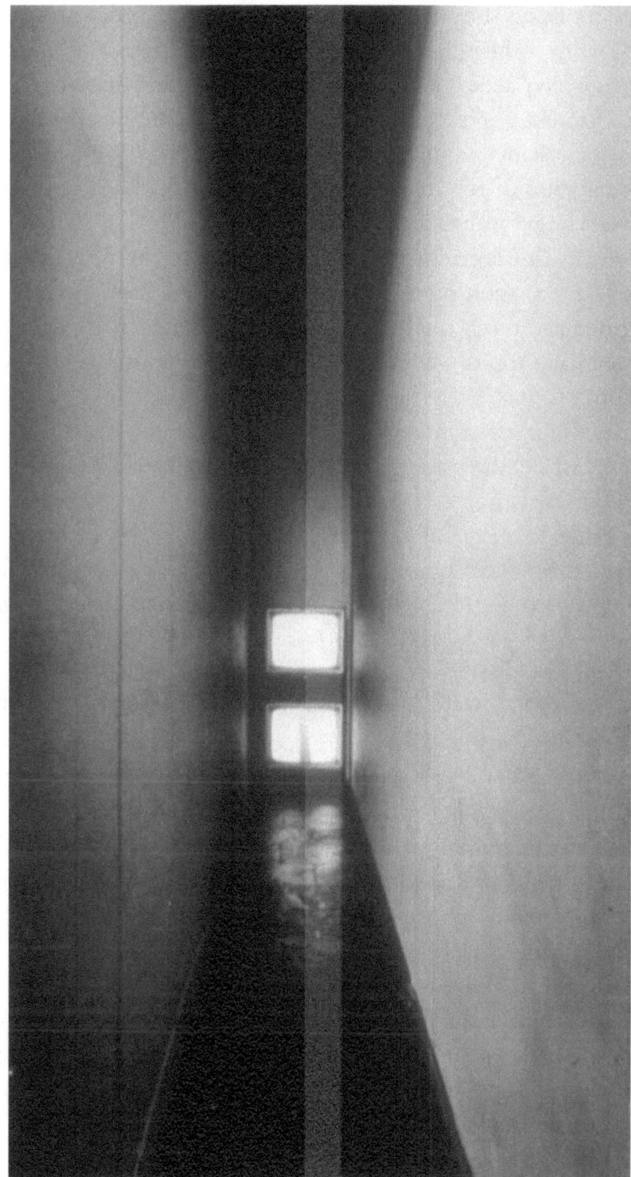

Live-Taped Video Corridor, 1970. Wallboard, video camera, two video monitors, videotape player, videotape. Dimensions vary; approx. 144 × 384 × 20 in. (365.8 × 975.4 × 50.8 cm). Solomon R. Guggenheim Museum, New York. Panza Collection, gift, 1992. Image courtesy Sperone Westwater, New York.

and video monitors showing combinations of pre-recorded and real-time imagery, while others are empty, extremely narrow, and unpassable. Shifting between access and prevention, each individual configuration explores different perceptual and phenomenal conditions. In the fourth corridor, for instance, a monitor sits at the far end of the passage, feeding a live picture of the floor and ceiling of the enclosed, empty room taken by a camera placed in its interior on an oscillating mount. As the beholder exits this corridor, turning a corner into the fifth passage, she encounters a television monitor that captures, for a brief instant, a fleeting, fragmentary image of her back. As if to heighten its destabilizing effect, the image appears sideways, upsetting the viewer's sense of bodily orientation.[8]

If *Corridor Installation* is descriptively confusing, it is experientially unwieldy. The beholder negotiates a maze of intricately designed spaces, arriving at physical impasses, but even when entry is permitted, she finds herself unable to move about freely and subjected to so many weird perceptual tricks. Reinforcing this sense of being "cornered," Nauman shortly afterward created two related installations, *Four Corner Piece* (1970) and *Going Around the Corner Piece* (1970), in which the beholder's passage form one place to another—as seen in the fourth and fifth corridors described earlier—becomes the basis of the sculptural installation. In the latter piece a full-scale square room is constructed and placed in the center of a gallery, like an enlarged minimalist cube. Because it has no entry point, the viewer instead circumnavigates its exterior, at each turn encountering a partial, momentary image of her back going around the corner that plays on a video monitor set upon the floor. Desperate to "capture" the image—to *see* herself properly—the beholder finds herself caught up in an endless cycle of replay, turning around and around and around the corners to no avail. As a result, the viewer is in the awkward—and ultimately frustrating—position of seeming to chase herself from behind, not unlike the proverbial dog hopelessly chasing its tail. (Perhaps, in light of an installation Nauman produced almost two decades later, a more apt analogy is a hapless rat.[9])

The subject's spatial discomfort, of being ill at ease in the external world, is a recurring theme in the literature on modernity: the notion of not belonging tied to both the physical and figurative displacements wrought by industrialization, the architecture of urban life, and the sublime effects of overwhelming space.[10] Yet here I am less interested in

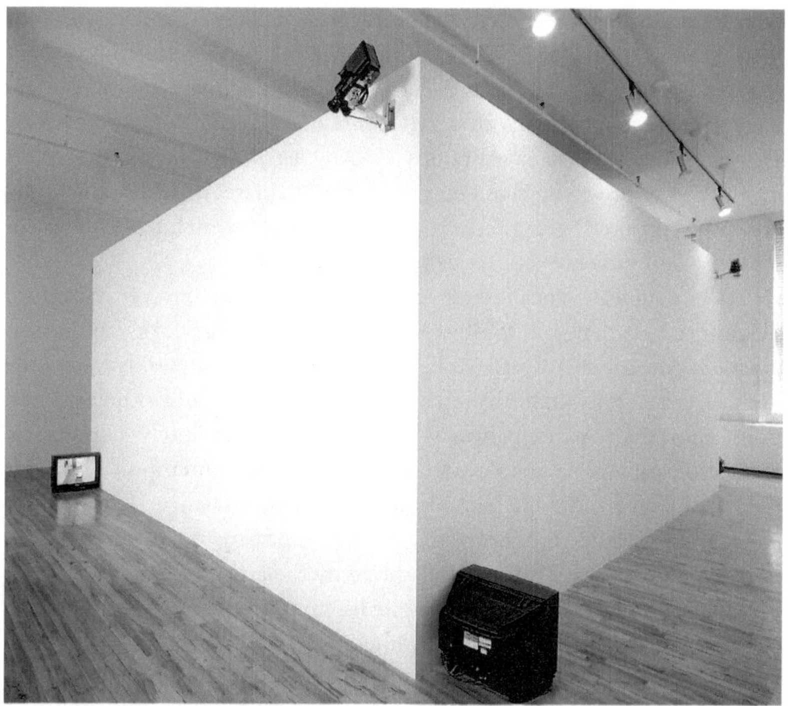

Going Around the Corner Piece, 1970. Wallboard, four video cameras, four video monitors. Walls: 120 × 240 in. (304.8 × 609.6 cm) each. Musée national d'art modern Collection, Centre Pompidou, Paris. Acquisition 1988. Image courtesy Sperone Westwater, New York.

the effects of estrangement than I am in those of solicitation—that is, the simultaneous beseeching and thwarting of the beholder that lies at the center of Nauman's environments.

While, collectively, Nauman's sculptures might be the most systematic in this regard, numerous participatory artworks from the sixties and seventies are similarly characterized by a decidedly confrontational nature, in which the audience is subjected to various forms of manipulation or assault, yielding often unsettling, ambiguous experiences in which the goal of participation is not entirely clear. For example, in Allan Kaprow's *A Spring Happening* (1961) the audience was confined to the darkened interior of a small crate, while various—sometimes frightening—events took place outside, ones that were audible but barely visible to the participants, who, as Judith Rodenbeck maintains, were figured as "objects, collage elements, exchangeable tokens."[11] In Vito Acconci's *Seedbed* (1972) the unsuspecting beholder, walking up a room-size ramp installed in a gallery, is caught off guard by the potentially embarrassing sounds of a private, sexual act. In Yoko Ono's *Cut Piece* (1964) and Marina Abramović's *Rhythm 0* (1974), on the other hand, the gesture to engage takes the form of a dare, in which the audience is confronted with the burden of *how* to act, which has potentially serious—and violent—consequences for the artist.[12]

While such provocative relationships vis-à-vis the viewer constitute a significant tendency in the history of participatory artworks, in current practices the move toward audience involvement frequently manifests itself as a benignly *inclusive* aesthetic. For museums and other institutions, moreover, participation is promoted as a resolutely democratic enterprise, capable of rendering often inaccessible contemporary art less mysterious and more pleasurable for a general audience. The viewer engages in various lighthearted activities: relaxing on a lovely dock installed above a lake, eating food served by the artist, or playing with an inviting mass of sculptural putty while listening to the music of the indie band Stereolab on a Walkman.[13] In these (and other) examples, the once radical premises and potentially destabilizing effects of participation are transmogrified into a user-friendly doctrine of artistic viewing. The artist is no longer producer but caretaker and nurturer who provides sustenance, entertainment, and other pleasures for an audience that can enjoy such spoils without having to purchase anything.[14]

Because these artworks putatively circumvent the commodity system, providing an experiential encounter for the spectator, they are frequently positioned within a genealogy of sixties' practices (such as decommodification, dematerialization, and institutional critique), invoking the language, if not the substance, of radical politics and progressive aesthetics. However, as I have argued elsewhere, such acts of social engagement and benevolence often mask what is in fact an *economic* relationship (i.e., one based on return) that is identifiable if the model of economy is shifted: from the commodity to gift exchange.[15]

While the subject of my earlier discussion focuses on recent artistic practices and develops an alternative theoretical model, it shares with the current essay several key points: first, far from operating *outside* the dominant system, this "gift economy" (as, it will be argued, "participation") is structurally immanent to that system.[16] Second, both propose a reading of *participation as obligation*: a tacit form of control in which reciprocity is all but guaranteed and desires and will are exploited, becoming, in effect, forms of submission—or dependency. Technocratic society, we shall see, is precisely built upon this dynamic: a dialectic of participation and control.

The Programmed Society

The notion of technocracy first widely arose in public discourse in the United States during the twenties and thirties when a group of scientists and social engineers proposed a rationalistic, technological order as a means of curing the social and economic crisis brought on by the Great Depression. For these self-described technocrats, however, faith rested not in technology as an isolated instrument but in its principles of efficiency, which, they believed, could be adapted to the social sphere. As historian William Akin notes, "In the technocrats' minds the ills of the economy were traceable not to the machine per se, but to an *inefficient adjustment of the social order* to modern high-energy technology."[17] For the technocrats, governmental and business institutions—the traditional cornerstones of the capitalist system—were inadequate and inefficient systems that had led the nation to the edge of economic disaster. In their place the technocrats promoted the value of the "technician" (or engineer) and enlisted the scientific management theories of Thorstein Veblen and Frederick W. Taylor, both of whom argued for a broad social application of the principle of technical rationality.[18]

While the technocratic period represents a relatively minor episode in social and political history, debates regarding the emergence of technocracy reached a fever pitch during the sixties.[19] In attempting to grasp the implications of the transformation from an industrial, production-based economy to an informational, service-oriented one, writers such as Daniel Bell speculated that a wholesale reconfiguration of the social structure was under way.[20] While Bell's tome *The Coming of Post-industrial Society: A Venture in Social Forecasting* (whose title reveals the extent to which the future was perceived to be in the present) is one of the most influential on the subject, it ultimately amounts to an apologia for the new system. For Bell, technocracy represents merely one stage in the "progress" of modern society, with the potential to realize the unfettered dreams of capitalism. For others, however, the advent of technocratic society ushers in a moment of profound social crisis. In the sociological writings of Jean Meynaud, Jacques Ellul, and

Alain Touraine, among others, techno-optimism is replaced by skepticism and even anxiety—a dystopic view of technology that recalls the philosophical writings of Heidegger, Adorno, Horkheimer and the contemporary work of Herbert Marcuse, in which technoscientific progress is viewed as inextricably bound to new forms of social domination and oppression.[21]

Technocracy's skeptics draw attention to the increasing value placed on technical "expertise" and the rise of ever more specialized forms of knowledge. As such, they maintain, traditional ideals give way to a relentless (and somewhat blind) pursuit of innovation and technical progress. Despite his otherwise rosy perspective, Bell himself identifies the emergence of technocracy as a historical crux in which modernism's two models of social change—toward "equality" (advocated in the writings of Alexis de Tocqueville) and toward "bureaucracy" (anxiously elaborated by Max Weber)—meet and clash:

> In the last hundred and fifty years, the social tensions of Western society have been framed by these contradictory impulses toward equality and bureaucracy, as these have worked themselves out in the politics and social structure of industrial society. Looking ahead to the next decades, one sees that the desire for greater participation in the decision-making of organizations that control individual lives (schools, hospitals, business firms) and the increasing technical requirements of knowledge (professionalization, meritocracy) form the axes of social conflict in the future.[22]

While Bell does not develop this reading beyond initial speculations, for Alain Touraine the interdependence of equality (i.e., the desire for a more inclusive society) and bureaucracy (i.e., technical, social, and administrative hierarchization) is the central principle of a technocratic society and the main source of its disaccord. Both the tenor and content of Touraine's analysis is more typical of the literature, where the sense of urgency regarding the emergence of technocratic society is seen both in the passionate (and often paranoid) nature of the rhetoric and the extent of its reach.[23] Revealing his dim view, Touraine's study replaces the relatively neutral descriptives "technocratic" or "post-industrial" with the loaded term *programmed*: "the programmed society," he explains, more accurately captures "the nature of production methods and economic organization" of postindustrial culture.[24] For our purposes here, however, it functions as a useful rhetorical shorthand, one that underscores the dual meaning of *programmed*: the technical sense (i.e., computer-language programming, systems logic, game theory) associated with a knowledge-based economy and the social condition of being controlled or managed.

Touraine's book explores the three principle forms of domination, which, he argues, are characteristic of the programmed society: "social integration," "cultural manipulation," and "political aggressiveness." The latter speaks to the development of the technobureaucracy, while the former two relay the push–pull, so to speak, of the new system. Touraine writes: "The individual is pressured into participating—not only in terms of his work but equally in terms of consumption and educations—in the systems of social organizations and power which further the aims of production."[25]

In short, Touraine argues that technocratic society, unlike earlier eras of industrialism, is contingent not upon *exclusion* but upon widespread *inclusion*. Participation is axiomatic to this system, but it is coerced. Moreover, its manipulative power rests upon the relative "success" of the system as well as upon its deviousness: the benefits and pleasures it affords and, as such, the needs it seemingly fulfills, all the while eschewing overt oppression. Whereas in Marxian theory economic exploitation of the workers or working classes results in their social alienation, in the programmed society, Touraine maintains, those of relative affluence—and, as such, with greater "participation" in social, political, and economic life—are nevertheless subject to the lure of propaganda, advertising, and consumption. In short, in addition to the traditional oppressed classes, new ones are formed that cross a broad social strata, all becoming passive participants in their own domination.

Technocratic society, therefore, seems a dramatic shift in which participation leads not to self-determination but, paradoxically, to *alienation*. "Ours is a society of alienation," Touraine writes, "not because it reduces people to misery or because it imposes police restriction, but because it seduces, manipulates, and enforces conformism."[26] In other words, alienation is wrought by complicity and conformity, which ultimately serve to nullify or "manage" dissent. The programmed society, Touraine argues, amounts to an insidious yet potent system of "*dependent participation*."[27]

Weak Participation

To be clear: I am not advocating a deterministic view—that is, that Nauman's controlling environments are a consequence of technocracy or can be "framed" by its context. Rather, I want to suggest that Nauman's environmental sculptures share or are energized from one of the central principles of technocratic society—that of "dependent participation." Art historically, this approach allows for an alternative model of explanation, destabilizing the oppositional logic of contemplative artwork versus participatory artwork and their relative roles within the history of modernism. In contrast, through the model of dependent participation, participation itself represents a form of submission—one not so dissimilar to the slavishness of the seduced viewer that Brechtian distanciation seeks to counter or to the benumbed consumer of mass media that postmodern critiques, embracing semiotic theory, challenge. With this theoretical approach Nauman's environmental sculptures can be seen to question one of the stakes upon which much progressive sculptural work of the sixties turned: namely, the possibility (and benefits) of direct experience.

Central to the notion of "presence" and the phenomenological aspirations of minimalist sculpture (and famously derided by Michael Fried as its problematic "theatricality"[28]), the idea of direct experience was embraced as an antidote to modernism's transcendentalism. Instead, meaning is grounded in the here and now of the temporal, material world, contingent upon the transient situations of encounter. Such forms of lived experience, in the critical thinking of the late sixties, undermined art's rarified (and artificial) aesthetic boundaries and, moreover, questioned the logic of medium specificity that preserved or accommodated this separation. The doctrine of presence reaches its apex in writings on performance, which is not simply insistently temporal but is also heralded as the most immediate and "present" of all forms—given the assumed structure of the copresence of artist and viewer or, in the case of interactive installations, the necessity of the viewer's immediate engagement in order to "see" and ultimately create the work.

But if we consider Nauman's installations, direct experience is insistently, even aggressively, precluded. To recall one of the examples described earlier, *Live-Taped Video Corridor* does not simply disturb phenomenal and perceptual states but seems to insist that experience can be generated *only* through representation and reproduction: a point reinforced in the semantic tethering of the terms "live" (presence) and "taped" (reproduction) in its title.

The effects of media on perception, subjectivity, and reality, of course, have been extensively addressed in the critical literature, particularly in relation to the notion of spectacle culture.[29] In media society, to sum up these arguments, subjective experience and reality are not simply received but also constructed through forms of mediation—such as television, advertising, and other media. In the most extreme readings, this leads to the derealization of the real, its displacement by so much simulacra, as well as the dissolution or "splitting" of the subject herself, who is caught within a mire of imagery and perceptual stimuli. Here, however, I want to leave aside this framework, which has been productively argued in other contexts,[30] as well as its potential focus on the literal presence of technology in Nauman's environmental installations, which is not my concern.[31] Rather, I am interested in a more circumscribed issue: how such mechanisms do not simply filter experience but also render it largely *unmanageable.* In other words, the beholding subject, at the whim of forces that surpass desire or agency, becomes, to borrow Touraine's descriptive, a "*weak participant.*"[32]

Nauman's *Double Steel Cage Piece* (1974) operates on the edge of this premise, in which the possibility of "willing"—but not necessarily free—participation is negotiated. The aspects of authority and control latent in the earlier, abstracted spaces are here thematized into a literal prison. Incarcerating the viewer between two parallel screens of thick wire, the work seems to give concrete form to the Foucauldian nightmare of disciplinary society, in which technology is not simply viewed as a dehumanizing force but also gives rise to potent physical and institutional agents of control.[33] In *Double Steel Cage Piece,* the viewing subject similarly emerges as a disciplined one, who acts—or, rather, behaves—accordingly.

Experience, in short, is not simply mediated and controlled but also *predetermined.* This structure, while characteristic of most all of Nauman's installations, is first and most economically realized in *Performance Corridor.* Without the aid of technical devices but simply due to the physical constraints of its narrow walls (built, moreover, to the measure of the artist's sweeping hips), a succession of like performances results: the "original" one being a video of the artist's performance, which is

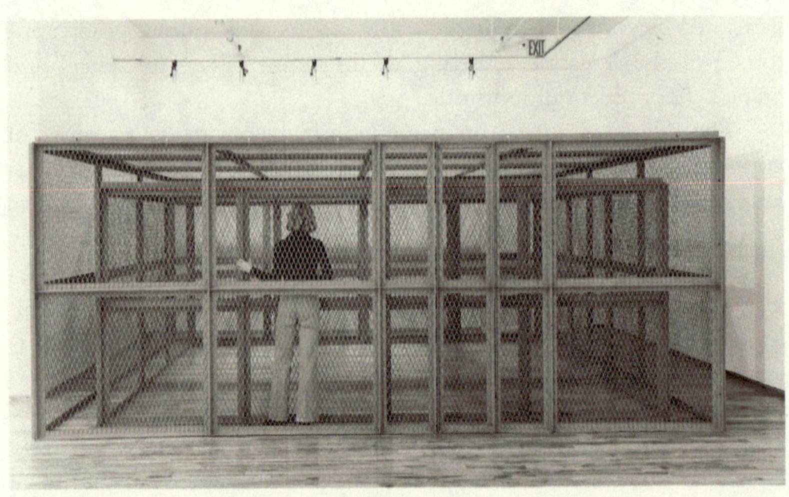

Double Steel Cage Piece, 1974. Steel. 84 × 162 × 198 in. (213.4 × 411.5 × 502.9 cm). Museum Boijmans Van Beuningen, Rotterdam. Image courtesy Sperone Westwater, New York.

subsequently reenacted by the audience, whose autonomy is severely compromised by the nature of the physical structure. What results is a series of *programmed* iterations of the simple act of walking in and out of a corridor.

Heuristically speaking, the curtailing of direct experience—or its management—in Nauman's environments guarantees *repetition*: the outcome is determined largely in advance, and the most effective means of circumscribing the beholder's experience is put into place. All potential variations are carefully considered and reduced through a combination of architectural elements and technical devices so that—in *Going Around the Corner*, for example—the monitors are neatly positioned to face one direction, which, in turn, leads to the audience moving in lockstep, circulating the perimeter in an orderly line, without much interpretive modification. *Floating Room: Lit from Inside* (1972), to give another example, offers an equally guided experience. A square room elevated several inches off the floor is illuminated on the inside by glaring lights. Despite the disorienting nature of its interior space—in which walls fail to reach the floor and the intensity of the lighting induces nothing less than a pulsing headache—the viewer is nonetheless compelled to enter because the only alternative is to remain within the physical unknown of a completely darkened gallery. As critic Jan Butterfield, referring to *Green Light Corridor* (1970), once remarked to the artist, "I think it is a very frightening piece. The manner in which it was structured made it necessary to participate in it your way—and that is frightening."[34]

Through highly prescribed details, Nauman's environments are structured by repetitious interactions. Repetition, however, is central to the principle of *efficiency*, the sine qua non of technological progress. In the sixties a widespread application of the technical notion of efficiency led to the formation or expansion of fields of knowledge, including game or decision theory, in which the ultimate aim (not unlike in Nauman's environments) was to anticipate human responses—and, in so doing, to *manage* them.[35] Through an adaptation of scientific principles of rationality and theories of logic, a means of envisioning and then limiting the range of possible behaviors was found, thereby ensuring a particular outcome.

While their pragmatic uses were numerous (military, scientific, economic, etc.), game theory and decision theory also demonstrate a more generalized characteristic of technocratic culture: its realization of an information- or knowledge-based society, in which "technical" expertise enters into areas hitherto largely immune to it. Information theory, cybernetics, and decision theory (what Daniel Bell aptly terms "intellectual technologies"), for example, operate according to a similar logic in which means and outcome—or input and output, to use the computer terminology—are calculated. Through computation, seemingly unquantifiable variables are parsed into discrete units of analysis, yielding a manageable order. "The goal of the new intellectual technologies is, neither more nor less," Bell exclaims, "to realize the social alchemist's dream: the dream of 'ordering' the mass society. … If the computer is the tool, then *decision theory* is the master."[36]

In short, such knowledge systems, which are central to the sixties' technocratic society, are resolutely goal oriented, working both prescriptively and predictively to ensure the most efficacious and expedient result. As such, they function as an analogue for technocratic culture as a whole—which may be described as a *society of performance*. Whether we are referring to economic activity, educational institutions, or machines such as the computer, the goal of the given system or institution is one and the same: efficiency or a graduated process of improving "performance."

If in his public comments Nauman disdains "games" in the vernacular sense as nonserious "play," his sculptural environments nonetheless incorporate the logic of game theory. Various restraints, both physical and mental, simultaneously anticipate and then circumscribe human response. In the process, uncertainty and interpretive deviation are minimized as much as possible, a dynamic that economists, in an application of game theory, have described as "minimax"—or the minimization of maximum loss.[37] Nauman's installations constitute spaces of "performance"—defined, that is, as *efficient interaction.* To emphasize, the term *performance* here does not simply refer to the viewer creating *a* performance as a *participant*; rather, through the social theory of technology, *performance* acquires a very different meaning, one that concerns the formation of a rationalistic social order.

Whereas the minimalist exploration of phenomenological conditions of perception banked on the ability to assert and engage the direct experience of the beholder, Nauman's installations aim to calculate and determine that experience through laws of probability. This perhaps explains why the artist often describes all aspects of his sculptural work (whether visual, conceptual, or perceptual) as modes of "information": dry language that seems directly at odds with the highly experiential or material qualities of the works themselves.[38] But with this claim and the use of game theory—with its quasi-scientific mapping of responses and mitigation of choice and conflict—as theoretical model for performance (defined now as "efficiency"), it may appear that this essay is proposing that Nauman's installations constitute embodiments of technorationality. Quite to the contrary, I am interested in the point at which the rationalization of society comes under pressure. Rather than speaking to the realization of reason, in other words, Nauman's "performance" environments speak to the moment of reason's collapse, when technological change ushers in an acute crisis of legitimation—a topic of a philosophical debate that arises and is played out against the backdrop of technocratic society.

The Fate of an Idea: Technocracy and Reason

In the late sixties, sociologist Jean Meynaud voiced his fear that "politics" would be displaced by technocracy.[39] What Meynaud means by this is that the pursuit of traditional "political" ideals, including those at the foundation of bourgeois society (i.e., freedom, self-determination, justice), will gradually dwindle away in favor of the singular mission to increase "productivity." Writing a decade later, with the benefit of hindsight and the present realization of developments upon which earlier thinkers could only speculate, Jean-François Lyotard takes the sociological observation one step further, developing a philosophical account of the shifting nature of knowledge and society.[40]

In a not-so-subtle challenge to Jürgen Habermas's theory of communicative reason, Lyotard reflects on what Andrew Feenberg describes as the "technical turn" of contemporary knowledge.[41] Deftly marrying contemporary theory and the social discourse of technology. Lyotard specifically engages with the problematic of "performance." His subject is not simply computer and information technologies but also the reorientation of knowledge itself under the forces of technical change. He writes, "Technology is a game pertaining not to the true, the just, or the beautiful, etc., but to efficiency: a technical 'move' is 'good' when it does better and/or expends less energy than another."[42] Lyotard emphasizes that the "goal" of knowledge has ceased to be the revelation of truth or the realization of human possibility and instead has become the optimizing of "performance." Accordingly, he adapts the linguistic concept of *performativity* (i.e., the performative utterance or language game) as both a methodological model and the fundamental principle of contemporary, technocratic society—which, being knowledge or information based, is "linguistically" oriented. According to the logic of the language game, ever-shifting rules produce a different outcome: hence, Lyotard's now well-known notion of the local or "little" narrative that displaces master or "grand" narratives. But Lyotard argues that knowledge not only is subject to change and competing ideals but with the advent of "language" technologies (problems of communication, cybernetics, computer languages, information storage, to name a few of his examples) is also no longer even a product of individual "knowing." It is, in his words, "exteriorized":

> We must thus expect a thorough exteriorization of knowledge with respect to the "knower," at whatever point he or she may occupy the knowledge process. The old principle that the acquisition of knowledge is indissociable from the training (*Bildung*) of minds, or even of individuals, is becoming obsolete and will become ever

more so. The relationship of the suppliers and users of knowledge to the knowledge they supply and use is now tending, and will increasingly tend, to assume the form already taken by the relationship of commodity producers and consumers to the commodities they produce—that is, the form of value. Knowledge is and will be produced in order to be sold, it is and will be consumed in order to be valorized in a new production: in both cases, the goal is exchange. Knowledge ceases to be an end in itself, it loses its "use-value."[43]

In this passage, not only does Lyotard renounce both subject-centered Hegelianism and the willful humanism of Habermas, but he also emphasizes the commodification of knowledge itself—a subject of earlier speculation, which, he can now assert with some certainty, has come to pass.[44] With the removal of knowledge from the subject's control and the emphasis on "performance" over "truth," however, society loses its bases of legitimation. To recall Lyotard's statement quoted previously, what is "good" is no longer necessarily what is "true." Rather, "goodness" is gauged by productivity, while expending the least possible effort—an acutely passive condition. Due to this reorientation, Lyotard argues, society abdicates any claim to rationality. "The games of scientific language become the games of the rich," Lyotard inveighs, "in which whoever is wealthiest has the best chance of being right. An equation between wealth, efficiency, and truth is thus established."[45]

In this "game"—one of struggle and conflict and precisely *not* the Habermasian dream of trouble-free consensus—Lyotard finds a series of losses: of the possibility of resistance, of the actual fulfillment of human need, and of political idealism. Lyotard's position, however, resists nostalgia, containing no dream of returning to a pretechnical past. Within this system, he counters, the source of domination and resistance are one and the same: the only path for the subject is opened up by an increased access to knowledge that technology affords, while at the same time technology (or, rather, technical society) instills conformity. Hence, the ambivalence of Lyotard's treatise, stuck in the dialectic of participation and control.

The Dream of Interactivity

The equivocality of Lyotard's argument, which distinguishes it from the wholesale technophobia of earlier philosophical accounts, is useful in understanding why we are not simply oppressed but are also seduced by Nauman's environments. What can be irritating lighting, as in the glaring yellow of *Left or Standing, Standing or Left Standing* (1971/1999), is also the source of wondrous optical tricks: the simple juxtaposition of different lighting technologies (fluorescent and incandescent) produces painterly illusions in three-dimensional space.[46] What can be a terrifyingly narrow space in *Live-Taped Video Corridor* also induces a profound pleasure in the game it creates: no matter how much the beholder realizes the futility of the task, she will repeatedly try to "beat the machine" and somehow line up her image to match bodily experience. What can seem to be impossibly manipulative, such as the illuminated cleave of space in *Green Light Corridor* (1970), also reveals "chinks" in the system—or the point where intervention is unable to completely dictate the outcome, as Nauman readily acknowledges.[47]

In Nauman's manipulative yet pleasurable spaces there is also a cautionary tale, one regarding participation as a panacea, a message that resonates perhaps even more intensely in contemporary culture where *dependent participation* is increasingly a reality—and even the operative principle—of a global information society. Advanced information technologies, such as the Internet, afford endless opportunity for interactivity: but hidden—and not so hidden—within them are ever more insidious mechanisms of manipulation (browser tracking, personally targeted marketing, "cookies," etc.). In this system, choice is illusory and participation obligatory: after all, if we don't accept the mechanisms, we cannot purchase a book or a ticket or even view our own private records online. As Alain Touraine observed 40 years ago, to refuse to participate is not a possibility. To be a subject in contemporary culture, one cannot simply reject the cards that historical possibility has dealt. There is little or no choice, which is why perhaps "choice"—and its cousin, "customization"—are now such ubiquitous buzzwords: forms of coercive management sporting a benign guise.

That the body of the spectator in Nauman's environments is the actor through which these dramas and conflicts are played out is not surprising. As a historical agent, the individual is still the cornerstone,

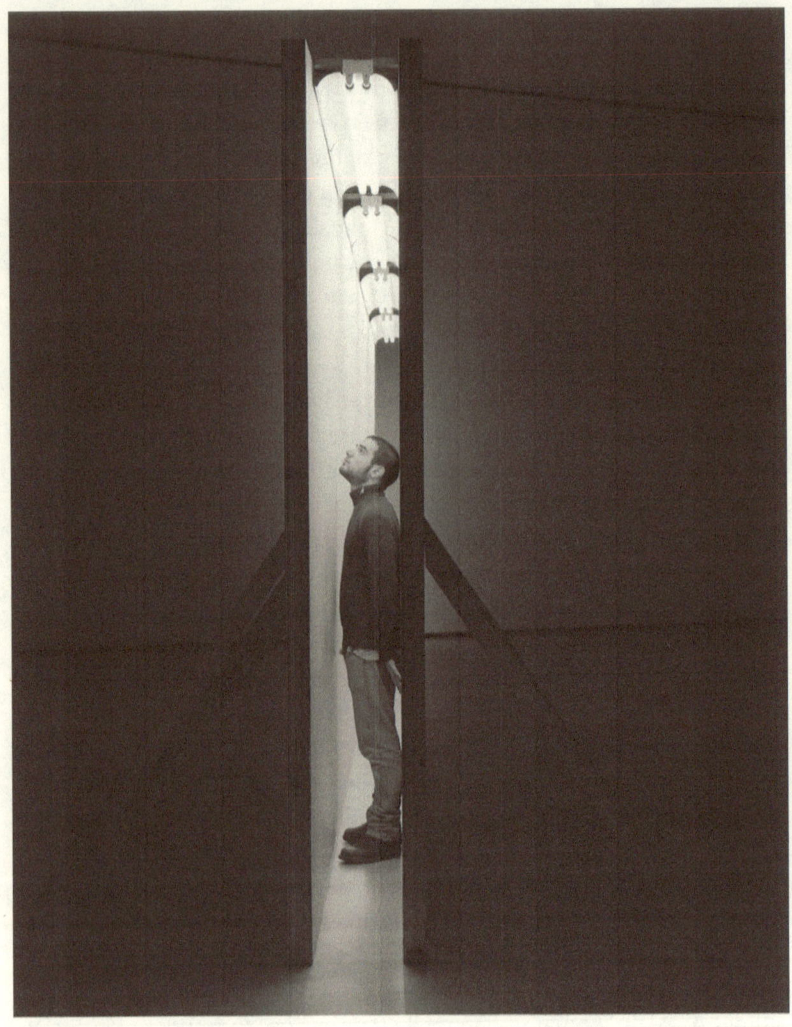

Green Light Corridor, 1970. Wallboard, green fluorescent light fixtures. Dimensions variable: approx. 120 × 480 × 12 in. (304.8 × 1219.2 × 30.5 cm). Solomon R. Guggenheim Museum, New York, Panza Collection, gift, 1992. Image courtesy Sperone Westwater, New York.

the pawn, of a technocratic system that increasingly markets "individual" desire and that, despite providing less autonomy and choice, proffers a fantasy of more and more. Likewise, in Nauman's installations the subject ultimately is the one who must navigate a minefield of participation and control, discovering those small opportunities where conformity breaks down and possibility, even if fleeting and limited, accrues.

Notes

1. © Janet Kraynak (2018). Reprinted with slight amendments from *Grey Room* 39, no. 10 (2003) with permission from the MIT Press and the University of Minnesota Press.

2. Interview by Lorrain Sciarra, 1972, Pomona College, Claremont, CA, 9.

3. Interview by Michele de Angelus, 1980, Smithsonian Institution, Archives of American Art, Washington, DC, 79.

4. Beyond the European/American context, in the South American postwar avant-garde the participant assumed an equal—if not more crucial—role in an explicitly political project: for example, Lygia Clark's interactive "relational objects" and "propositions" produced during the sixties; or Hélio Oiticica's "Quasi-cinema" (a series of interactive, multimedia installations made in the early 1970s) and *Parangolé*, which Oiticica describes as follows: "*Parangolé* is anti-art par excellence; and I intend to extend the practice of appropriation to things of the world which I come across in the streets, vacant lots, fields, and ambient world, things which would not be transportable, but which I would invite the public to participate in. This would be a fatal blow to the concept of the museum, art gallery, etc., and to the very concept of 'exhibition'" (Hélio Oiticica, "Position and Program," in *Conceptual Art: A Critical Anthology*, ed. Alexander Alberro and Blake Stimson [Cambridge, MA: MIT Press, 1999], 9).

5. Willoughby Sharp, "Nauman Interview," *Arts Magazine* 44, no. 5 (March 1970): 23.

6. Jan Butterfield, "Bruce Nauman: The Center of Yourself," *Arts Magazine* 49, no. 46 (February 1975): 55.

7. For example, Paul Schimmel writes, "Throughout Nauman's career he has baited, controlled, bored, infuriated, scared, insulted, angered, imperiled, experimented with, and manipulated us—his viewers—into experiencing his work within his parameters" ("Pay Attention," in *Bruce Nauman*, exhibition catalog and catalog raisonné, ed. Neal Benezra, Kathy Halbreich, and Joan Simon [Minneapolis: Walker Art Center, 1994], 69). A more extreme biographical leap is evidenced in the following observation by Andrew Solomon, from an article that profiles the artist on the occasion of the opening of his 1995 retrospective at the Museum of Modern Art in New York: "Looking at Nauman's retrospective is like walking through someone else's psychoanalysis: it's full of patterns and recurring wishes, anxieties and obsessions; it's sometimes rather comical and often hostile; it keeps turning out to be about something other than what's apparently being said. Like someone else's psychoanalysis, Nauman's work is often boring and repetitive. … I had seen Nauman's work for years and had never wanted to meet him. I had thought he was probably sadistic and controlling and brilliant and unforgiving and cold" ("Bruce Nauman: Complex Cowboy," *New York Times Magazine*, March 5, 1995).

8. For further description of *Corridor Installation (Nick Wilder)*, see entry 172 in *Bruce Nauman*, ed. Benezra, Halbreich, and Simon, 241.

9. Referenced here are Nauman's two related pieces *Learned Helplessness in Rats (Rock and Roll Drummer)* (1988) and *Rats and Bats (Learned Helplessness in Rats II)* (1988). In both, a rat navigates the interior space of a Plexiglas maze placed on the floor of a darkened gallery, while a combination of closed-circuit and pre-recorded imagery is projected onto the walls of the gallery. The rat essentially performs the same role as the beholder in the earlier corridor installations described previously.

10. For example, architectural historian Anthony Vidler theorizes modern space through the Freudian notion of the *unheimlich*. He writes, "The labyrinthine spaces of the modern city have been constructed as the sources of modern anxiety, from revolution and epidemic to phobia and alienation" (*The Architectural Uncanny: Essays in the Modern Unhomely* [Cambridge, MA: MIT Press, 1992], ix).

11. Judith Rodenbeck, "Crash: Happenings (as) the Black Box of Experience, 1958–1966," PhD diss., Columbia University, 2002, 105. Rodenbeck further observes: "This piece is often discussed in relation to the notion of 'rebirth'—a mythic, even epiphanic reading … [but] attendees recall the smell of fear—Kaprow himself admits he was interested in this as an element. The imagery—no, the actuality—of confinement as well as the assaultive violence of the audience's 'liberation' by a roaring lawnmower has as much to do with the historically specific imagery of the Holocaust or of behaviorist experiments as it does with any mythical notion of 'rebirth'" (105–106).

12. Frazer Ward has written compellingly about the issues of performance and audience involvement through a theory of ethics exploring the nature of "acts" rather than simply the entreaty "to act" ("Marina Abramović's *Rhythm 0*: Performance, Audience, Ethics," paper presented at the College Art Association Annual Conference, Philadelphia, February 2002).

13. The works referred to here include Jorge Pardo's *Pier* (1997), installed in situ for the *Sculpture Projects* exhibition, Münster, Germany 1997; Rirkrit Tiravanija's *Untitled (Free)* (1992) as well as the artist's many other performances/installations in which he prepares and serves food; and Charles Long's *Bubble Gum Station* (1995), an installation (which is part of a series of sculptures collectively titled *The Amorphous Body Study Center*) consisting of a central pedestal holding a large blob of bright pink clay, which viewers are encouraged to manipulate while listening to music through headphones attached to the sculptural mass. Of course, not all contemporary works interpret audience participation in such terms: for example, Andrea Zittel's *A–Z Carpet Furniture* (1993; part of her *A–Z Designs for Living* series), among other works, touches upon the more oppressive or sinister aspects of design, controlling the viewer/inhabitant through domestic objects and spaces. Other pieces by the artist, however, such as *Escape Vehicles*, more readily approach the "user-friendly" doctrine of participation. In *Escape Vehicles*, the collector customizes the interior of a small unit (the shell of which is designed by Zittel), creating a private space of personal taste and objects. Even this work, however, tarries between pleasure and oppression: as Stefano Basilico mentioned to me, in *Escape Vehicle* one basically designs one's own coffin, a decidedly morbid task.

14. Miwon Kwon, in an important study of the historical and theoretical transformations of "site-specific" practices, discusses this relatively recent phenomenon of the "artist as service-provider." Drawing upon—and inverting—Benjamin Buchloh's construct of the "aesthetics of administration," which he developed in relationship to conceptual art,

Kwon theorizes the "administration of aesthetics" in the art of the 1980s and 1990s (*One Place after Another: Site-Specific Art and Locational Identity* [Cambridge, MA: MIT Press, 2002], 51).

15. The argument was developed in relation to the work of Rirkrit Tiravanija, whose various projects entail serving food and drink, performing live music, re-creating a full-scale model of the interior of his apartment in a gallery, and so on—all of which generate spaces for social exchange. The "generosity" often attributed to these works is, however, misleading in that, according to the structural logic of the gift, it demands reciprocity and fosters social contracts of obligation. See Janet Kraynak, "Rirkrit Tiravanija's Liability," *Documents* 13 (Fall 1998): 26–40.

16. In the essay on Rirkrit Tiravanija's work cited in the previous note, I draw upon Pierre Bourdieu's concept of symbolic "capital," which represents an intangible yet powerful source of economic and political wealth, and contend that "the gift" in fact constitutes a central economic force in late-capitalist society.

17. William Akin, *Technocracy and the American Dream: The Technocratic Movement 1900–41* (Berkeley: University of California Press, 1977), x, emphasis added.

18. In *The Theory of Business Enterprise* (New Brunswick, NJ: Transaction, 1904), Thorstein Veblen maintains that the rationality and objectivity of the scientist (or the engineer) were an antidote to the uncontainable self-centeredness of the capitalist businessman, who, rather than aiding the economy, was detrimental to its smooth functioning. Frederick Taylor, whose theory of scientific management has been widely discussed, was similarly committed to scientific principles of rationality, which, he argued, could be applied to generate increasingly efficient models of work, the factory, and, by extension, social life (*The Principles of Scientific Management* [New York: Norton, 1911]).

19. Referring to the sixties as an important turning point, Andrew Feenberg, in his study on the philosophy of technology, writes: "It is not easy to explain the dramatic shift in attitudes towards technology that occurred in the 1960s. By the end of the decade early enthusiasm for nuclear energy and the space program gave way to technophobic reaction. But it was not so much technology itself and the rising technocracy that provoked public hostility" (*Questioning Technology* [New York: Routledge, 1999], 4).

20. Daniel Bell, *The Coming of Post-industrial Society: A Venture in Social Forecasting* (New York: Basic Books, 1973).

21. Jean Meynaud, *Technocracy*, trans. Paul Barnes (New York: Free Press, 1968); Jacques Ellul, *The Technological Society*, trans. John Wilkinson (New York: Knopf, 1967); Alain Touraine, *The Post-industrial Society: Tomorrow's Social History: Classes, Conflicts, and Culture in the Programmed Society*, trans. Leonard F. X. Mayhew (New York: Random House, 1971); Martin Heidegger, *The Question Concerning Technology*, trans W. Lovitt (New York: Harper and Row, 1977); Max Horkheimer and Theodor W. Adorno, *The Dialectic of Enlightenment*, trans. John Cumming (New York: Herder & Herder, 1972); Herbert Marcuse, *One-Dimensional Man: Studies in the Ideology of Advanced Industrial Society* (Boston: Beacon Press, 1964).

22. Bell, *The Coming of Post-industrial Society*, 8.

23. For example, Theodore Roszak, in *The Making of a Counter Culture: Reflections on the Technocratic Society and Its Youthful Opposition* (New York: Anchor Books, 1969), argues that "counterculture" in the United States arose as a specific reaction to technocratic society. Similarly, Andrew Feenberg explores the relationship between the student

revolts of May 1968 in France and technocracy, including the students' protest against the transformation of the university into a "knowledge factory" (*Questioning Technology*, 21–43).

24. Touraine, *The Post-industrial Society*.

25. Ibid., 7.

26. Ibid., 9.

27. Ibid. The complete quote is, "Alienation means canceling out social conflict by creating dependent participation."

28. In his essay (now equally as famous for the accuracy of its reading of minimalist sculpture as for its decidedly negative assessment), Michael Fried posits an opposition between minimalist "presence" (defined as material and temporal) and modernist "presentness," the latter an essentially atemporal construct in which time exists in an ideal, arrested state ("Art and Objecthood," *Artforum* 5, no. 10 [June 1967]: 12–23).

29. Guy Debord, *The Society of the Spectacle* (Detroit: Black and Red, 1970), first English translation. Debord writes, "The spectacle is not a collection of images, but a social relation among people mediated by images." Later on, Jean Baudrillard radicalized Debord's notion of spectacle, claiming that the "real" itself no longer exists but rather is atomized into an endlessly self-referential chain of signifiers ("Simulacra and Simulation," in *Selected Writings*, ed. Mark Poster [Stanford, CA: Stanford University Press, 1988], 166–184).

30. See Jonathan Crary, *Suspensions of Perception: Attention, Spectacle, and Modern Culture* (Cambridge, MA: MIT Press, 1999). For some recent studies that develop such themes in relation to television, technology, and postwar media culture more specifically, see Anna McCarthy, "From Screen to Site: Television's Material Culture, and Its Place," *October* 98 (Fall 2001): 93–111; Pamela M. Lee, "Bridget Riley's Eye/Body Problem," *October* 98 (Fall 2001): 27–46; David Joselit, "The Video Public Sphere," *Art Journal* 59, no. 2 (Summer 2000): 46–53; Branden W. Joseph, "'My Mind Split Open': Andy Warhol's Exploding Plastic Inevitable," *Grey Room* 8 (Summer 2002): 80–107; and David Joselit, "Yippie Pop: Abbie Hoffman, Andy Warhol, and Sixties Media Politics," *Grey Room* 8 (Summer 2002): 62–79.

31. One danger this approach poses is of lapsing into technofetishism, which, given Nauman's complicated relationship to new technologies, is highly suspect. Despite continually experimenting with different techniques and media, the artist often utilizes outdated or outmoded techniques—such as neon, which in the 1960s, as Brenda Richardson notes, was already tainted by obsolescence ("Bruce Nauman: Neons," in *Bruce Nauman: Neons*, exhibition catalog [Baltimore: Baltimore Museum of Art, 1982], 13–39). Furthermore, when Nauman employs newer technologies—such as the Sony Portapak video camera in the late sixties and, most recently, infrared digital photography—he often subjects the medium to extreme forms of manipulation, harnessing it for decidedly dated visual effects, such as filmic graininess. The futuristic and the retro are thus continuously inverted.

32. Furthermore, Touraine writes, "A choice between returning to traditional cultural themes and memberships or the passive consumption of the mass media does not exist. These are two closely connected manifestations of cultural under-development, which is itself *bound to the weak participation of the masses* in the values and products of technical civilization and social democracy" (*The Post-industrial Society*, 203, emphasis added).

33. Michel Foucault, *Discipline and Punish: The Birth of the Prison*, trans. Alan Sheridan (New York: Vintage Books, 1979).

34. Butterfield, "Bruce Nauman," 54.

35. Game theory has a long history, but two key postwar texts are H. W. Kuhn and A. W. Tucker, eds., *Contributions to the Theory of Games*, vol. 1 of *Annals of Mathematics Studies* (Princeton, NJ: Princeton University Press, 1950), and John Charles McKinsey, *Introduction to the Theory of Games* (New York: McGraw Hill, 1952).

36. Bell, *The Coming of Post-industrial Society*, 33.

37. As cited in Bell (ibid., 31), the economic application of the principle of "minimax" appears in John von Neumann and Oskar Morgenstern, *Theory of Games and Economic Behavior* (Princeton, NJ: Princeton University Press, 1944).

38. For example, in the following comment Nauman refers to two early sculptures: *A Cast of the Space under My Chair* (1965–1968), a somewhat battered cubic form, and *Shelf Sinking into the Wall with Copper-Painted Plaster Casts of the Spaces Underneath* (1966), both of which are largely unreadable in the absence of their titles: "I think, in a sense, a lot of the titles … where there were titles like *Shelves Sinking into the Wall*, and all that, were sort of trying to give two pieces of information. … And probably what I found out from that is that you can give two pieces of information and the piece is finally about that. It's about the tension of not being able to put them together" (interview by de Angelus, 73–74).

39. "Let us suppose that in a world in which the profit motive becomes more and more paramount," Jean Meynaud writes, "the political authorities (as is already partly true) failed to keep a close watch on the activities of technologists, who do not all have the public interest at heart; in the end, the effect would be a barely perceptible evolution towards a régime which would be democratic only on the surface. The elected representatives would be deprived of the substance of their power. … The democratic principle would then be nothing more than the 'front' … behind which the true leaders of the country would justify or disguise their domination" (*Technocracy*, 15–16).

40. Jean-François Lyotard, *The Postmodern Condition: A Report on Knowledge*, trans. Geoff Bennington and Brian Massumi (Minneapolis: University of Minnesota Press, 1984).

41. Andrew Feenberg, *Alternative Modernity: The Technical Turn in Philosophy and Social Thinking* (Berkeley: University of California Press, 1995).

42. Lyotard, *The Postmodern Condition*, 44.

43. Ibid., 4–5.

44. And perhaps it has come to pass even more so in contemporary culture, where, for example, in educational institutions the drive for "efficiency" is equated with tangible evidence such as test scores rather than the acquisition of knowledge and where the reward is not the creation of an educated or enlightened population but money—in the form of additional school funding or salary incentives. Such outcomes of technocracy, only feared by earlier writers, are increasingly the rule of contemporary society.

45. Lyotard, *The Postmodern Condition*, 45.

46. Formerly called *Installation with Yellow Lights*, the piece *Left or Standing, Standing or Left Standing*—named for the accompanying text written by the artist—consists of a trapezoidal room whose walls do not extend to the ceiling and that is illuminated with bright, yellow fluorescent lights. Two corridors on either side of the central room are lit with

incandescent lights; as a result, when the viewer looks up to the gap between the wall and ceiling, the two forms of light blend, yielding a purple afterimage.

47. In response to an inquiry by Jan Butterfield regarding whether he "queries people afterwards" to check if the participant's reaction to any given installation is similar to his own, Nauman comments: "People will tell me that they tried it and it didn't do what I said it would for them; or that they read a great deal about a given piece, but didn't have the response they were 'supposed to'; or, conversely that they did not seem to relate at all to what I had written in the instructions. For example, I will say at some point that the exercise will become very sensual, or very sexual, and people will tell me that it didn't for them" (Butterfield, "Bruce Nauman," 55).

Nauman's Body of Sculpture

Anne M. Wagner

The year was 1966. In May, Bruce Nauman earned a master's degree in art with an emphasis on sculpture from the University of California at Davis. That fall he moved to San Francisco, laid claim to the seedy premises of what had once been the California Grocery, and put his training to work teaching sculpture at the San Francisco Art Institute. Eighteen months later, he was still there, directing three studios for a total of ten contact hours per week, a class load that nowadays would amount to more or less a full-time job. It saw him putting beginners in touch with the most basic sculptural materials—clay, plaster, wood—and expected him to have sufficient maturity, as the course catalog phrased it, "to present material from his experience, convictions, and technical knowledge in the order and at the rate which, in his judgment, will be best related to the needs of the individual student."[1]

1966, in other words, is the year that Bruce Nauman went professional, the year that, at age twenty-four, he got a job. And it is also, for all intents and purposes, the moment when Nauman *became* Nauman—when the Nauman name, as the subpsychedelic lettering with which his friend Jack Fulton framed a photo (from 1966) of studio-plus-occupant testified, emerged as a real substantive, stood for something to which its bearer could now lay proper claim. Fulton records but does not reveal where that transformation happened: in the California Grocery, behind grubby windows that had once promised simple pleasures: a bag of candy, a bottle of wine. These are the same windows whose plate-glass surfaces Nauman (formerly the artist) soon washed, then lined with a

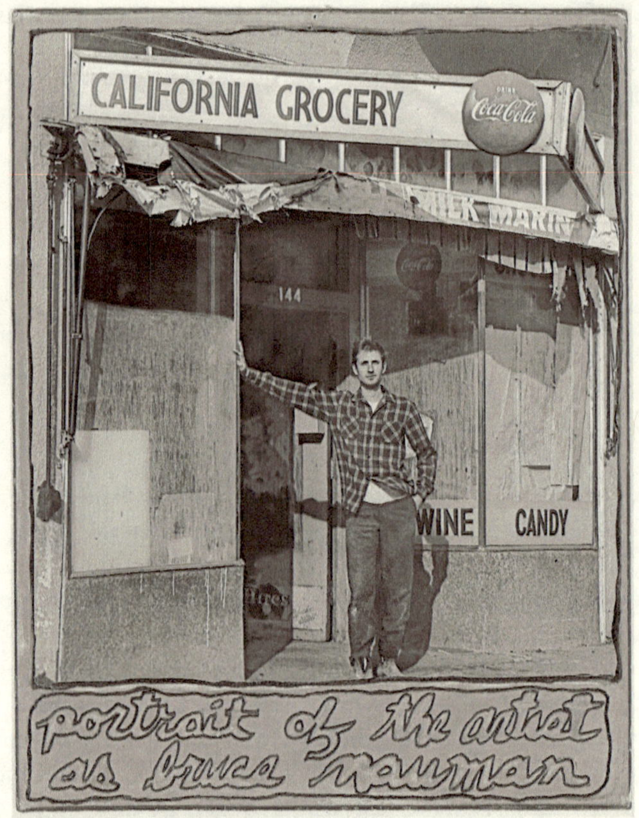

Jack Fulton, *Portrait of the Artist as Bruce Nauman*, 1966. Black-and-white photograph on cardboard with gold and silver paint. 10 × 8 in. © 2018 Jack Fulton / Artists Rights Society (ARS), New York. Photograph courtesy Jack Fulton / Art Resource, NY.

Mylar window shade, its blocked-out legend—"The true artist is an amazing luminous fountain"—assertively framing whatever was (or was not) going on inside.

Does the significance of this year need further emphasis? In 1966 Nauman emerged from the university as a professional sculptor in the making (or so his Davis diploma promised), and it was as an instructor of sculpture (what the Art Institute rather pompously termed a "master artist-teacher") that he first found work that paid. These are the facts in the case. Yet we might be inclined to dismiss them, not least because they are so hard to square with how we customarily understand this particular artist's coming of age. For years now, since the artist became Nauman, his art has seemed unclassifiable according to standard media distinctions. Instead, as his window shade insisted, it relied on other skills. Its antimagic embraced whatever went on inside the grocery, whether it involved writing, drawing, casting, pacing, filming, or stomping, whether it deployed fat or flour or makeup, a violin, or just a squared-off guideline taped directly onto the floor. All these things happened and were used in the studio. The space was a petri dish. Activity was all.

How did this come about? Why move not just from medium to media but from art making to art-as-making? As Nauman tells it, his new context was the key. By now, the story, which dates to a 1970 interview with Willoughby Sharp, has assumed something of the status of a myth of origins. "The first real change came when I had a studio. I was working very little, teaching a class one night a week ... and I didn't know what to do with all that time. ... There was nothing in the studio because I didn't have much money for materials. So I was forced to examine myself and what I was doing there."[2] What this narrative tells us is that "real change" involved what we might term spatial self-scrutiny: with no materials around him, the artist was freed from their inbuilt limitations to focus on his own limits: what he was doing *there*, how his actions and motives had meaning as those of a substantive body and mutable self.

Like many myths, this one speaks, retrospectively, to past circumstance, to a decisive event: Nauman's art had left behind the limits and allegiances built into devotion to a single discipline. And as myths often do, it seems quite persuasive if taken on its own peculiar terms. Hanging out in the studio *is* what made Nauman into Nauman. It was there that he left his erstwhile "artist's" persona behind. It was there, for example, that he famously made *Failing to Levitate in the Studio* (1966), that quasi-forensic effort to prove that artists, like ghosts and spirits, do not exist. Faced with the photographic evidence, who could possibly demur? Of course, art cannot achieve transcendence; or if transcendence is in the offing, it will take someone other than a Nauman to bring it off. As he will later put it, he is bound to fail. Unless, that is, he restricts his art to the basics, himself, a body at work in a studio space. Surely Nauman did his utmost to take the measure of this fundamental set of facts.

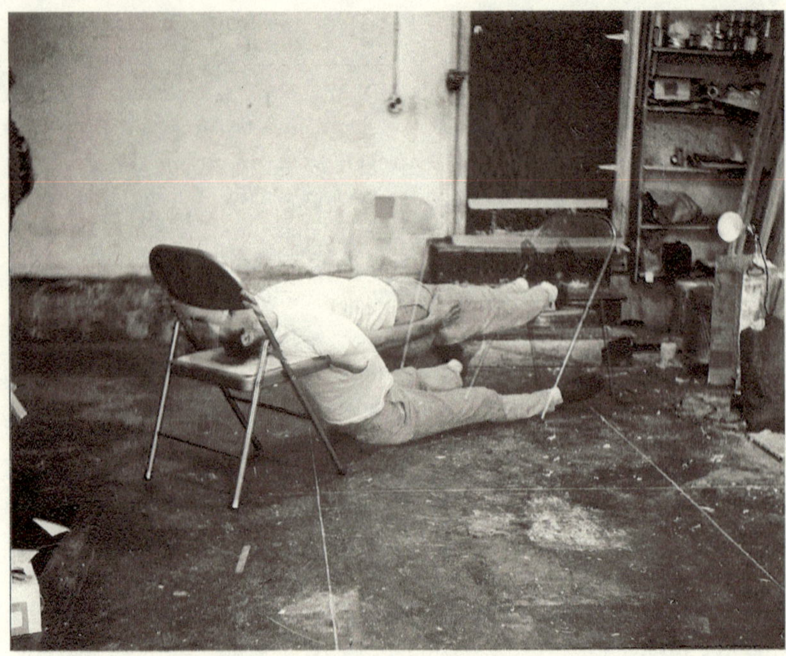

Failing to Levitate in the Studio, 1966. Black-and-white photograph. 20 × 24 in. (50.8 × 60.9 cm). Collection of the artist. Image courtesy Sperone Westwater, New York.

What would happen if we were to follow Nauman's lead? If we, too, considered him as a situated body—took stock of the spatial and bodily situations he was able to register or concretize as form? And what if we also aimed to grasp what it was in Art that Nauman's actions were working against? What might they have been devised to reject? If these questions motivate this essay, this is because there is still so much to understand about what is sometimes termed the "postmedium" condition, for which read the end to the artist's professional allegiance to the tangible or the optical, to painting or sculpture—as if such loyalty were ever a hard-and-fast rule. Something did happen in Nauman's studio, and understanding it does not merely involve grasping what, in supplanting *medium* by *mediums* (as well as *media*), he hoped to accomplish.[3] Equally relevant is how that transformation came about. It did not happen overnight. Sculpture—a traditional activity long identified with a specific set of techniques and materials—first had to be decisively conquered and then aggressively destroyed. That inevitably violent process, of a kind endemic in the 1960s, could not help but demonstrate, however obliquely, what the art attacked understood the enemy's strengths and weaknesses to be. The result, accordingly, is not mere destruction. The new media artists *gave an account* of the "old" medium, be it painting or sculpture, they aimed to put aside. Forced superannuation is a form of dependency, if not quite a tribute, and it is only through such back-handed reliance that the non- or anti-art practices so characteristic of the moment could have prevailed.

Let us return, then, to Nauman as the sculptor that, as he completed his schooling in the mid-1960s, he was training to become. What did he actually know about his future specialty? As might be expected, answers are circumstantial at best. On the one hand, art at Davis in the early 1960s was a young and experimental department, and its master's degree program, established in 1961, was still working out the kinks. New professors, including those inventive object makers Robert Arneson, William T. Wiley, and Manuel Neri, were arriving nearly every year, and at least some of their efforts—works such as Arneson's 1965 *Self-Portrait of the Artist Losing His Marbles*—come close in their ambivalent tone and feeling toward traditional sculptural formats (the bust, in this case) to Nauman, to *Myself as a Marble Fountain* (1967), say. Whether cracked open to expose a man's inner marbles or to spew out his inner waters, both enact dramas—or melodramas—of bodily emission and loss. And in each case, a time-honored medium—sculpture—is both the vehicle and the butt of the joke. On the other hand, the real centerpiece of sculpture at Davis was not its innovative faculty but rather the metal-casting foundry and curriculum set up by Professor Tio Giambruni, who in buying and installing the necessary equipment created one of the first such facilities to be established at any West Coast university. Given this emphasis on bronze and the monument, the Davis program in sculpture hardly seems modern: on the contrary, with its molten metals and crowds of assistants, it is remembered for its distinctly Renaissance methods and feel. We might imagine that such a context was inimical to Nauman, yet Giambruni's casting course was one in which he, along with all the other sculpture students, was expected to enroll.[4]

It is typical of Nauman in the 1960s that his time in the foundry promptly sparked perverse uses of the lessons Giambruni had aimed to impart. Process not product was still the issue, but in a notably low-tech

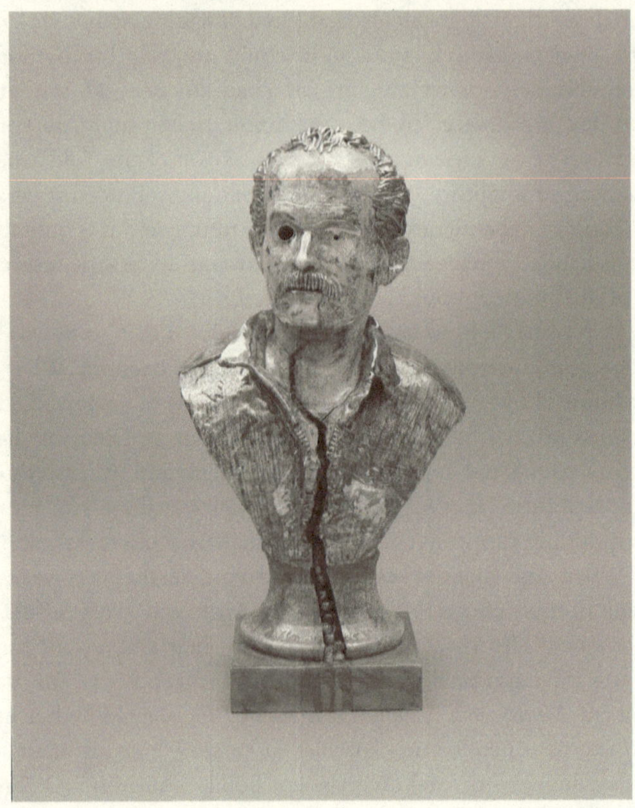

Robert Arneson, *Self-Portrait of the Artist Losing His Marbles*, 1965. Glazed earthenware, Luster glaze, marbles, pigments; hand built. 31 × 17½ × 9½ in. (78.7 × 44.5 × 24.1 cm). Museum of Art and Design. Gift of the Johnson Wax Company, through the American Craft Council, 1977. Art © Estate of Robert Arneson/Licensed by VAGA, New York. Photograph: Ed Watkins, 2007.

way. As Neal Benezra phrases it, Nauman's work now "focused on the process of *making* itself by analyzing the venerable tradition of casting."[5] No one should be misled by this reference to analysis: less intellectual than practical, its results were rudimentary at best. Turning his back on the finely tuned operations of the caster, Nauman employed an anti-technology that was distinctly, even aggressively, deskilled. If, like any foundry worker, he relied on plaster molds and models, his were based on lumpy clay originals quickly massed as rough-and-ready forms.[6] Long loaves and large lozenges were his specialty; "soft-shape" forms, he called them, as if avoiding other more colorful turns of phrase. Such abject shapes were promptly joined by stiffer, perkier molds and models put together from cardboard and wood. Both formal categories—the hard and the soft—served to generate a whole series of resin and polyester pieces, yet the results have the feel less of authentic originals than of comic replicants. "Same mold" declares one drawing of two twinned uprights: Nauman soon realized, as did Rodin before him, that more than one cast could be taken from any molded matrix and its identical products joined together to form a strangely palindromic whole.[7] It is as if "Madam, I'm Adam" had been reformulated as sculpture. The result was a physical pun, the physical here looking distinctly exhausted:

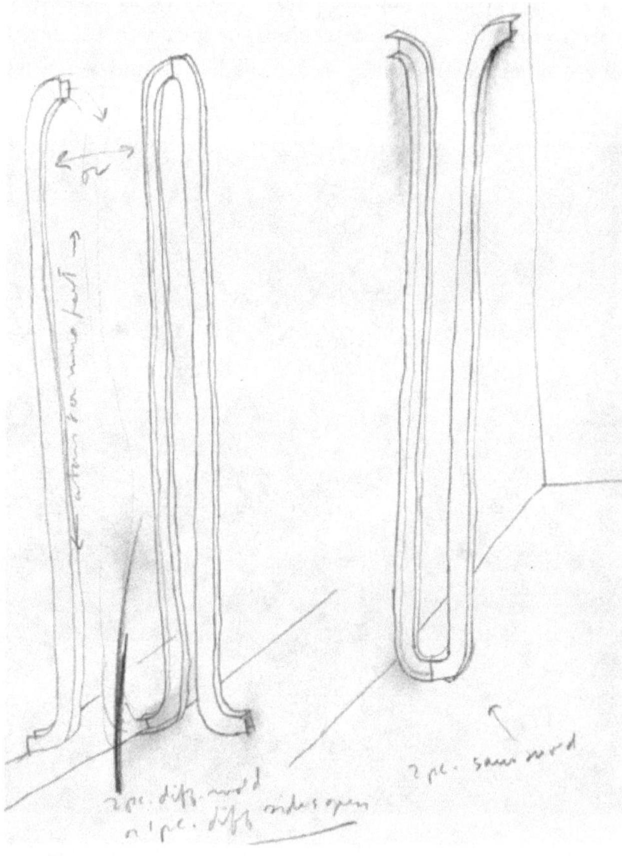

Untitled (2 pc. different mold, 2 pc. same mold …), c. 1965. Felt-tip pen on verso of ditto paper. 11 × 8½ in. (28 × 21.6 cm). Image courtesy Sperone Westwater, New York.

something tells me that Giambruni would have failed to get the joke that speaks so directly to and of the essence of the cast.

The stuttering of internal replication is not all these strange works are after. Made as mere skins painted onto then lifted off of the mold's surface (which is how resin and polyester are frequently worked with), the sculptures look like remainders (and reminders) of some absent form. What kind of form, however, is hard to say. When the critic Fidel A. Danieli calls such pieces "end or waste products," the reference seems more industrial than natural, as befits their look as hollow repetitious oddments of workaday stuff. In his next breath, however, Danieli changes register. Nature triumphs, he declares, with Nauman's "molds" (particularly his fiberglass sculptures) now emerging as versions of some "static frozen chrysalis."[8] The new phrasing speaks to the brittle presence of these objects as remainders, castoffs left behind, even while the

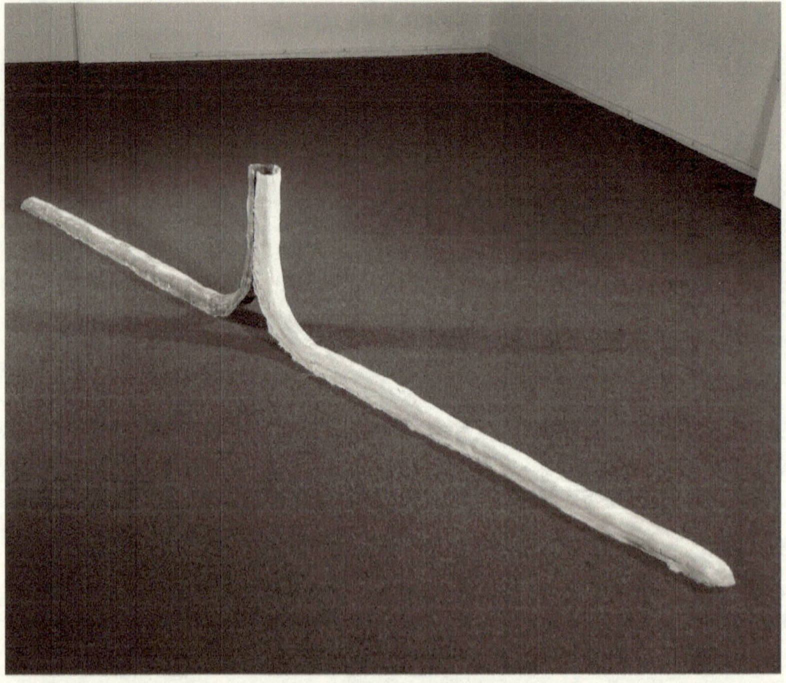

Untitled, 1965. Fiberglass, polyester resin. 24 × 132 × 5 in. (61 × 335.3 × 12.7 cm). Collezione Prada, Milano. Image courtesy Sperone Westwater, New York.

words reach (desperately?) for a naturalism that Nauman's castings do their best to disallow.

Danieli was responding not only to Nauman's first solo exhibition (a selection of fiberglass works was shown at the Nicholas Wilder Gallery, Los Angeles, in May 1966) but also to whatever he, as a local critic, had seen in the studio. Its contents would soon become more widely known. In the fall of 1966, Lucy R. Lippard included Nauman's work in *Eccentric Abstraction*, the notorious exhibition staged at the Fischbach Gallery, New York.[9] What is salient—perhaps even epochal—about that context is its effort to define what Lippard announced as a new "non-sculptural style." As she presents it, its deconstructive tenets move beyond the nature/culture duality that Danieli insists on, yet basic contradictions still remain in play. Imaginative, sensual, nonspatial, antiformal, the new work was decisively bodily, though in a wholly new way. It combined deathly passivity with vital presence. Now opposites ally: form and content elide. "The future of sculpture," Lippard hopefully concluded, "may very well lie in such non-sculptural styles."[10]

What needs emphasizing in the case of Nauman, however, is how decidedly that nonsculptural future sets itself against the example of an all-too-sculptural past. Lippard's view of Nauman is her clearest case in point. "Nauman's pieces," she declares, speaking again of the contents of the studio, "are carelessly surfaced, somewhat aged, blurred and repellent, wholly non-sculptural and deceptively inconsequential at first sight."[11] Why does she trot out this laundry list of quasi-faults? The answer seems clear: behind each of Nauman's apparent failings stands a shadow antithesis, a bygone practice of sculpture that the artist has coolly trumped. Real sculpture is not a careless art. It is supposed to be timeless; it wants to be looked at; it has something to convey. Its meticulous surfaces are made to last. Not Nauman's. And that is not all. The negations continue. When Lippard asserts that the fragility of Nauman's works "suggests fragmentation," that his pieces are "disturbingly self-sufficient," and that this quality has the "toughness of lost, leftover function and a total lack of elegance,"[12] the outworn ethos of monolith and monument haunts every word. While it has no function, Nauman's sculpture still seems purposive, even declarative: the residue of self-sufficiency, even monumentality, still clings to it, even though it has retained nothing very substantive to say.

Lippard, as always, was in pitch-perfect tune with the changing times. Well before 1966, Robert Morris and Donald Judd had laid down the commandments of the new minimalist aesthetic: the contents of the *Primary Structures* show, which was held in April at the Jewish Museum, New York, showed clearly how far the creed had spread.[13] But with Richard Tuttle's having already begun to exhibit his hand-shaped wall pieces (including two in San Francisco, which Nauman saw and promptly adapted[14]), the gamut of postminimalist apostasy was well under way. There is no doubt that Nauman, too, was instantly ready to depart from minimalism, via an "early" focus, as Marcia Tucker put it six years later, "on certain physical properties without reference to the object as such." In place of objecthood are actions: "leaning, hanging, bending, rearing, folding, propping"—this is Tucker's chosen list.[15] What is striking about these postures and movements is how most court real confusion between the artist and his objects. Who does what? Is the one a surrogate for the other, or are they comrades at arms? When Mel Bochner complains, "Nauman's work is really not-work," a similar problem looms. When "work" merely "looks like a lot of rags thrown on the ground or draped on the wall," the failure can be traced back only to the artist's aggressively inept actions: in 1966, throwing and draping are not yet bona fide artistic moves. Of course "not-work" results. Likewise if "not-work" looks tired ("The tiredness of it is unusual"), it follows that its maker is worn out, too.[16]

Or so Bochner seems to suspect. He is wrong. Nauman was actually only at the beginning of a process of dismantling an entire system of representation once impervious to exhaustion, a system deeply bound up with solidity, presence, coherence, thingness, and embodiment. I do not think this catalog of qualities exaggerates the cast. If sculpture's age-old resources are materiality and bodiliness, then these same characteristics could not help but bear the brunt of Nauman's attack. Sculpture relied on physical presence; thus, sculpture's physicality was the enemy, and a formidable one.

The blow could be struck only at sculpture as both body and thing. Already late in 1966, Nauman had measured (or claimed to measure) the right rear quarter of his own body, somewhere about buttock height. The curved line that resulted was then used, in triplicate, as a template to design a quasi-geometrical container made from galvanized iron and standing, like the artist, precisely six feet tall. The receptacle looks a bit like a fluted column, or at least a section of one—even more so in Nauman's drawing for the work—except, of course, for the opening along the frontal edge. This slit declares a practical purpose: it is a working object, one that claims its readiness for (horrifying) use.[17] Designated *Storage Capsule for the Right Rear Quarter of My Body* (1966), this object imagines nothing less than the meticulous butchering of the artist's carcass, even while it prepares a ship-shape casket ready to seal away the result. Next to this ghoulish concept, Robert Morris's 1961 *Column*—the work he designed as a "costume" to be "worn" on stage until the chosen moment, when, with the artist inside it, it would topple—seems both emotionally and formally contained. Nauman's piece, by contrast, hyperbolizes sculpture as a bodily object by figuring a body part—the right rear quarter—we can feel as part of ourselves but never look at directly. Feel painfully, thanks to a process of careful excision: now we begin to realize why Nick Wilder, the LA dealer, was subjected to two months of nightmares after encountering his first Nauman—nightmares that meant, Wilder soon realized, that here was an artist worth a solo show.[18]

In the mid-1960s, Nauman devised a variety of methods to do away with sculptural objects as bodies and physical things. A perverse tactility is the frequent result. Like *Storage Capsule*, the new works summon the body in absentia, replacing it by some tangible token that tries, however incompetently, to reference a fleshly part. Or sometimes to mime the role of flesh itself. Take, for example, the notorious untitled 1967 work that combines a folded pair of wax-and-plaster arms with a knotted length of a ship's hawser, the only grade of rope with bodily presence and heft that is truly bodily in size. Nauman uses it to suggest the innards (bones, muscles, arteries, ligaments) that are contained in or lie beneath a corporeal shell. The conjunction is deeply distressing, not least because of the materials in play. The arms themselves, which are vividly present, not only mine the meticulous naturalism traditionally achievable in wax but also back it with the illusion of solidity supplied by a plaster cast. Above the elbows, however, naturalism screeches to a halt. This is a body, we soon realize, that has no insides; its subtle surfaces conceal only twisted hanks of hemp on which the arms are strung. It is up to us to decide what the knot suggests. Perhaps it is merely material, although its asymmetry makes it seem more purposeful than that. Rope and arms form a unit or circuit that summons a particular posture or stance: part bravado, part wariness, they conjure the studio, the place where the twentieth-century

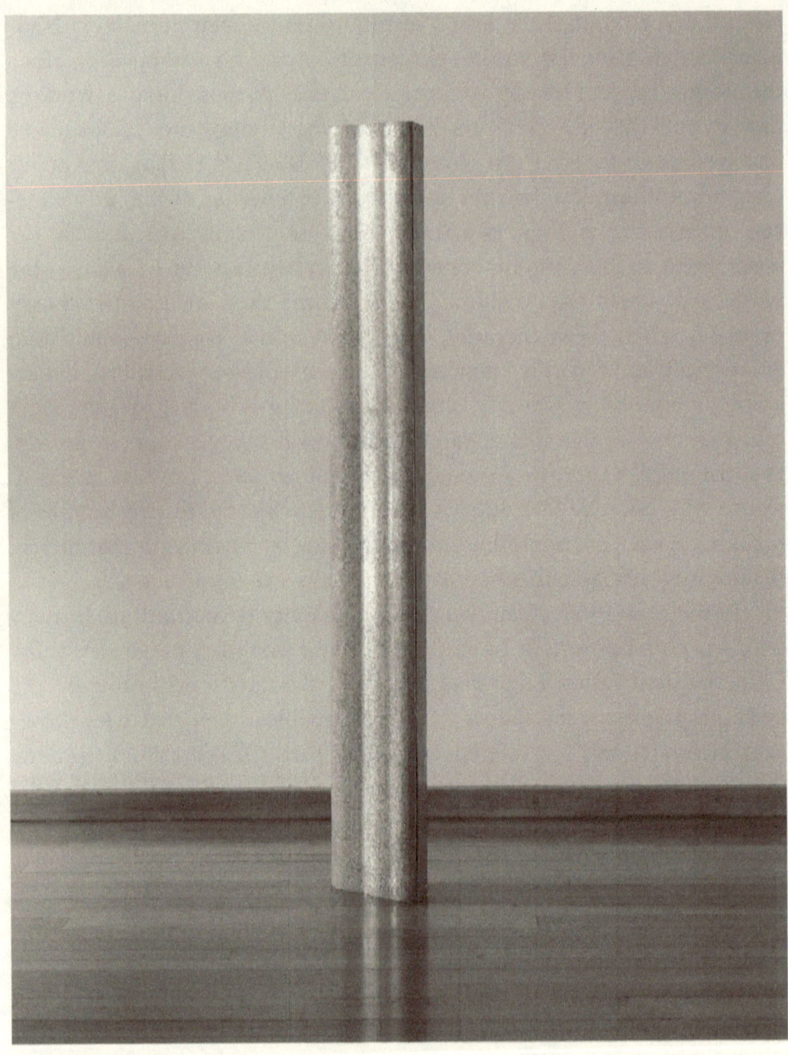

Storage Capsule for the Right Rear Quarter of My Body, 1966. Galvanized iron. 72 × 9½ × 6 in. (182.9 × 24.1 × 15.2 cm). Kunstmuseum Basel. Photograph: Martin P. Bühler.

artist (think of Jackson Pollock and Willem de Kooning) most often—occasionally bare-chestedly—strikes a pose. But this is only one possible reading: Might not they stand in for the psychic makeup of a subject belonging more typically, more generally, to the year in which the sculpture got done?[19] Is this the sixties itself, nightmares and all? Such an empathic or historical reading, of course, would be entirely consistent with traditional responses to sculpture—a realization that insists only on how difficult it is to make something be *non*sculptural. Sculpture—for which read bodily presence, bodily expression—will out.

One solution would be to dispense with the body entirely, which of course Nauman also did. In a whole series of works that also began in 1966, he imagined various "devices," as some are labeled, to serve as supplements to a body that otherwise would be lost or wayward or, in some cases, simply incomplete. Such phrases describe *Device for a Left Armpit* (1967) as well as *Neon Templates of the Left Half of My Body Taken at Ten-Inch Intervals* (1966), both of which claim not only to register the body in its absence but also to give it a truly rudimentary shape—think topography or contour, maybe arm or armpit, but not much more. In fact, the question in both cases is precisely what manner of corporeal being—how shapeless or shapely, how much marked by these descriptive processes—these works imply. What kind of a body could actually risk being fitted back into—or initially used to generate—such strange constraints? What would be the cost to life and limb? Are life and limb even needed anymore?

Nauman's other devices seem less threatening, though even more (anti)sculptural. Chief among them are two works, each called *Device to Stand In* (both 1966), though their effects are fleshed out, so to speak, by assorted other pieces, mostly destroyed, which operated in similar ways. Each aims to limit or fix the body in a spatial surrounding by giving it somewhere to stand. In the case of each *Device*, the job is done by a simple but efficient contraption, a brass or steel wedge with a foot slot. (Two destroyed *Devices* used a rubber mat with left and right footprints and a slotted cardboard box.[20]) On the one hand, each of these experiments awaits an occupant: it needs a human presence to seem complete. On the other, its integrity as a work means it should remain empty so that the viewer will conjure a phantom figure to stand within the empty slot. But what would it actually be like to assume that position? A sacrifice, no doubt. Fixed in place like a column or statue, anyone standing

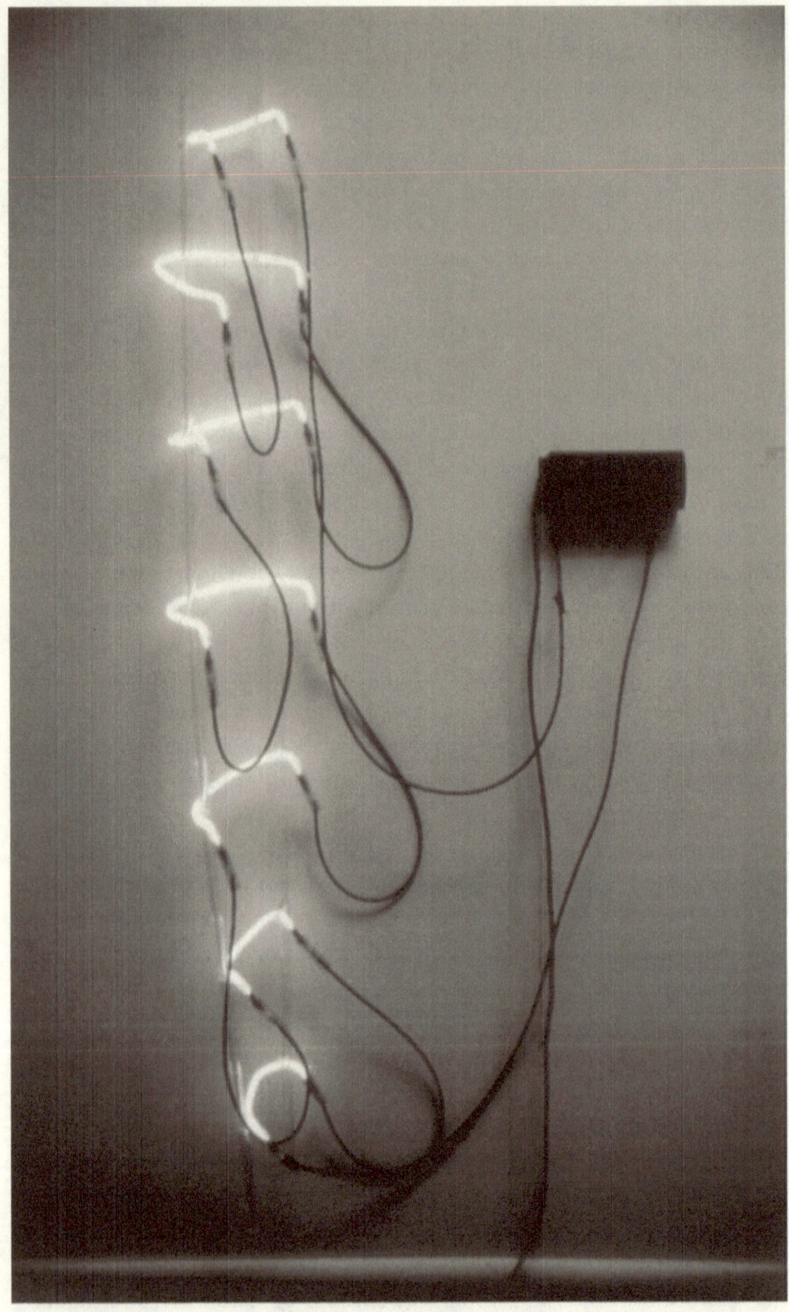

Neon Templates of the Left Half of My Body Taken at Ten-Inch Intervals, 1966. Neon tubing with clear-glass suspension frame. 70 × 9 × 6 in. (177.8 × 22.9 × 15.2 cm). Philip Johnson Glass House Collection, National Trust for Historic Preservation. Image courtesy Sperone Westwater, New York.

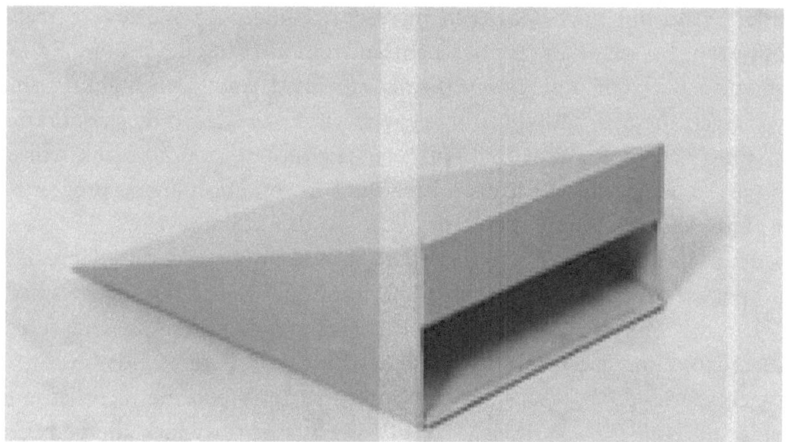

Device to Stand In, 1966. Steel, blue lacquer. 8¾ × 27¼ × 17¼ in. (27.2 × 69.2 × 43.8 cm). San Francisco Museum of Modern Art, the Panza Collection. Purchased, by exchange, through the bequest of J. D. Zellerbach and gift of Mrs. Charles DeYoung Elkus, Mr. and Mrs. William C. Janss, Mr. and Mrs. Alfred Jaretzki Jr., Harriet Lane Levy, and anonymous donors as well as through the Accessions Committee Fund. Image courtesy Sperone Westwater, New York.

there could not avoid taking the place of sculpture, in a substitution that is also a loss. For if the *Devices* allow sculpture to feed itself on the body's aliveness, they extract a high price. Thus commandeered, the victim would be frozen on the spot. The result would be a body turned into sculpture, standing upright within the confines of a room. Would that body be a Nauman? Of course. With works like these, he takes the role of Pygmalion's negative alter ego, while the frozen viewer plays Galatea in reverse.

What all this goes to show is not only how much sculpture needs a body. Nauman's antisculpture needs, one too, but differently, and those differences are precisely what these works seem designed to show: flesh, not stone; animation, not petrification; absence, not presence, ladies and gentlemen, all this by means of a simple device. What the *Device* works also demonstrate, however, is that how sculpture and space come together was for Nauman a major issue. Only consider the title of his first artist's book, which he eloquently, prosaically dubbed *Pictures of Sculpture in a Room*. Privately published in 1966 while its author was still a student at Davis, the brief pamphlet (just three folded pages) presents small-scale photographs of four different sculptures, one per page. Each shows a single work in isolation in the generic room of the pamphlet's title.[21] And not only does each represent a different sculptural format, but each, by virtue of its placement and action (hanging, leaning), also adopts a different post. None is truly animated, and none nightmarish, yet given the four individuating characterizations offered by the photographs (they look a little like portraits, carefully isolated on blank white pages), it seems clear that even here the anthropomorphizing process is well under way. Along these lines, it is worth recalling Marcia Tucker's remark apropos of the sculpture that "a change in position affects the properties of volume, shape, size, and location." What Tucker does not say in this quite orthodox minimalist reading is that, like his sculpture, Nauman himself had already begun taking "positions," notably in a twice-repeated performance that two years later would be recorded on video as *Wall-Floor Positions* (1968). It is not that this work allowed the artist to become a sculpture or that his changing positions transformed his identity: he stays Nauman the whole way through. Yet the man and his works are still thoroughly and self-consciously analogized: only consider the brief catalog of the eponymous positions offered to an interviewer ("standing with my back to the wall for about forty-five seconds or a minute, leaning out from the wall, then bending at the waist, squatting, sitting, then finally standing up") and then the question that ensued: "Willoughby Sharp: 'Did the performance relate to sculptural problems that you were thinking about then?' Nauman: 'Yes.'"[22]

As this exchange reminds us, it will not do to exaggerate the violence implied by Nauman's artworks: some were as mundane as the actions just described. Yet no one can overlook his absurdist propensity for macabre play. His interests leaned toward the body in extremis: frozen still or trapped in meaningless motion; absented, fragmented, reduced to elements or parts—for example, wax and fat. This was the gambit of a strange work attempted and photographed sometime in 1967 and later destroyed.[23] Seven wax slabs, each again termed a template of the left side of the artist's body, were stacked in a makeshift tower, whose six-foot height was provided by seven stacked cans of grease. The arrangement makes both more bodily and more prosaic a related study for a wax-template composition also dated 1967, this one a drawing that vertiginously imagines an "abstracted sculpture." Here, too, abstraction goes only so far. Nauman has peppered the drawing with the names of body parts: head, shoulder, chest, waist, thigh, knee, and calf. In the end, the final, more figural arrangement relies instead on a canonical principle

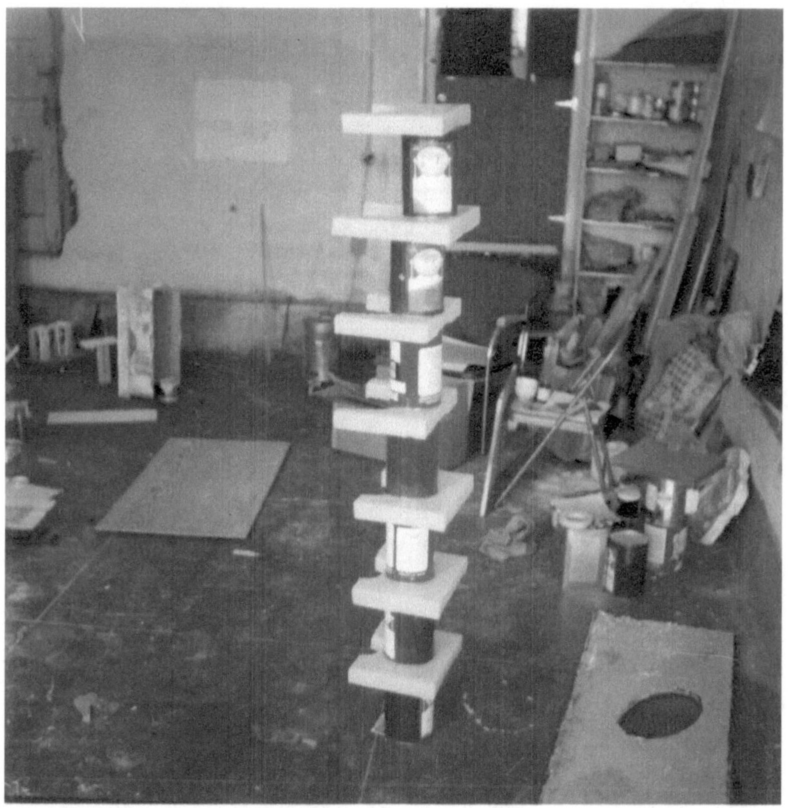

Wax Templates of the Left Half of My Body Separated by Cans of Grease, c. 1967. Wax, seven metal cans. Height approx. 72 in. (182.9 cm). Destroyed by the artist. Image courtesy Sperone Westwater, New York.

of classical proportion, which dictates that the beautiful body should be seven heads tall. Or if not heads, then cans, with templates added, mime a makeshift spine.[24] The result (inevitably titled *Wax Templates of the Left Half of My Body Separated by Cans of Grease* [1967]) is just bodily enough to make its anticanonical point. And to suggest something much more ghoulish, a knacker's nightmare of the body as remainder, boiled down to a greasy residue, then packaged for sale. As a motif for sculpture, the idea harks back to Joseph Beuys's 1964 *Fettstuhl (Fat Chair)*—which likewise replaces a body with a sloping deposit of fat.[25] Carefully planed and measured, the slab sits on its chair like a proxy or substitute; it is left to us to wonder where its parent body went.

The answer that Nauman himself would give to that question is now familiar: to the studio. If it was there that the figural body was banished from his sculptural practice, it was also there that he used performance to lay claim to some of the principal qualities of figurative sculptural form. The guiding wish behind many of the performances taped in the grocery seems to have been to approach the simultaneous aliveness and deadness of the sculpted work of art. Not only do such exercises have him declaring his "thereness" as a mere physical property or activity—a condition of the various ways (walking, stamping, stomping, bouncing, slowly, quickly, exaggeratedly, at an angle) he takes up space—but in two instances his scenarios imagine a body assuming basic geometries—sphere and cylinder—in animate approximation of a minimalist work of art.[26] How might this be done? To make a cylinder, for example, the performer is to lie "along the wall/floor junction of the room, face into the corner." Not only is it easy to identify this location as one much frequented by Nauman's objects, but it is also clear that, once established there, every fiber of the performer's body is to concentrate on behaving as cylindrically as it possibly can. How? "Concentrate on straightening and lengthening the body along a line which passes through the center of the body parallel to the corner of the room in which you lie. At the same time attempt to draw the body in around the line. Then attempt to push that line into the corner of the room." It should be clear that this exercise pits utter immobility against extreme bodily concentration, even exertion. And it is likewise obvious that for a body to approach a sculptural minimalism, every fiber of its being must be kept on red alert. Once again, it is sculpture—in its most uncanny version—that is calling the shots. One of the tenets—even clichés—of minimalism is that it puts the viewer in mind of his or her body. In Nauman, by contrast, the body minimalism was content merely to gesture toward is somehow actively immobilized—disanimated—by the sculpture that invokes it; through that process, body and sculpture are meant to become quite scarily alike.

* * *

This essay departs from the claim that Nauman's assault on sculpture inevitably gives an account of the very medium it worked to take apart. What better way to conclude, then, by asking once more what Nauman took sculpture to be? Two major points stand out. First of all is his sense of sculpture's terse concreteness (as opposed to painting, which he mistrusted as "lush"). Of course, that physicality seems an obvious quality, but what precisely does it mean? Nauman's investigations of the 1960s take that question to heart. His answer goes like this. As an object, sculpture offers a means of description, even delimitation. It deals in edges, backs, and sides. It separates itself from its surround. One reason this seems invaluable to an artist like Nauman is that those same limits cannot help but raise the question of what it might mean to exceed them. Sculpture, in its defining claim to presence, inevitably evokes such excesses, just as its surfaces summon sensations of both inside and out. Yet traditional sculpture does not really like to dwell on these conditions, however inescapable they are. It does not always assert them as *the* defining fact. For Nauman, by contrast, no ontological distinction could be more salient. "Both what's inside and what's outside determine our physical, physiological and psychological responses—how we look at an object," he declares.[27] If such a statement declares the end of mere surface as the register of sculptural meaning, it also puts paid to the sensory urgencies lodged in a purely phenomenological stance. Both what is inside and what is outside are determinant (what is seen and what is invisible), and to demonstrate those determinations is a further purpose not only of the early fiberglass pieces but also of works such as *Platform Made Up of the Space between Two Rectilinear Boxes on the Floor* (1966) and *A Cast of the Space under My Chair* (1965–1968).[28] Pieces like these point to a fascination with *edges*, above all, which emerge uncannily where none can actually be perceived. In casting, Nauman says, "I always like the parting lines and the seams." These, he continues, "help to locate the structure of an object, but in the finished sculpture usually get removed." The implication seems to be that through a project of recovering once-invisible links and edges, new and more accurate structures can be revealed.[29] Finish does not matter a jot: instead, Nauman's objects aim to do away with perimeters by the contradictory tactic of bringing them to light. Perhaps the issue is that without edges we could not trust ourselves to tell the difference between bodies and objects or know how and where they sit within their larger envelope of space. For Nauman, *structure* seems to mean all this and more.

Which is to say that in the mid-1960s Nauman took limits seriously and followed where they led him: toward the vagaries of domestic objects and interior space. It is there that he envisions the body, one object among many, but possessing a fragile aliveness that cannot quite be quelled. This is my second major point. Nauman used sculpture, as well as his responses to it, to measure that aliveness and to push aliveness to a crux. His work holds the body hostage to the threat (and the necessity) of an encounter with sculpture as a frozen corpse. I say "necessity" advisedly. Nauman, alone of all his contemporaries, took the complex bodiliness of the medium profoundly to heart. This is why we can do no better in concluding than to remember his attentions to a figure both beloved and reviled in the 1960s, sculpture's elder statesman Henry Moore. A series of works—among them a wax-coated relief sculpture promptly editioned in iron, several elaborate drawings, and two large-scale photographs—do their best to enter the debate, with Nauman speaking for both sides. In one image, Moore is symbolically enshrined: a tomb-cum-storage capsule preserves him, as if cryogenically frozen, for some future age. In another, one of the two photographs, a strange whirling spiral—a light trap, Nauman calls it—is set going, as if such sizzling electrification could catch Moore's essence in its coils. In still another, "Moore" (with Nauman as Moore's stand-in) is imaged (to quote the work's title) as if "bound to fail." His arms tied behind him, Moore looks like Nauman's hostage, until we remember that with Nauman himself having served as the model for the role of the elder sculptor, the younger, for all intents and purposes, becomes hostage to himself. As so often with Nauman, the sadism is playful, up to a point. The masochism, too. But neither should obscure the issues that Nauman is contesting with his British mentor: what Nauman laid waste to—though at the same time wishing to hold on to—are the surface and substance, the tactility and presence, of the sculptural work of art.

"A point in space is a place for an argument," Wittgenstein declared.[30] In Nauman's case, the quarrel is considerably expanded to take in nearly every aspect of sculpture's materiality—its expressive form. It is staged, moreover, by sustained recourse to a medium to which he owes everything yet is fully resolved to leave physically and analytically exhausted—as indeed he does. This may well be why Alex Potts finds Nauman's "object-like works" "pretty unremarkable." They engage too closely with the problem of what the sculptural object is: they are so single-mindedly aimed at taking sculpture apart. Potts does not concede that Nauman later arrives at "an emphatic negation of sculptural values"—though only when he turns to installation as his

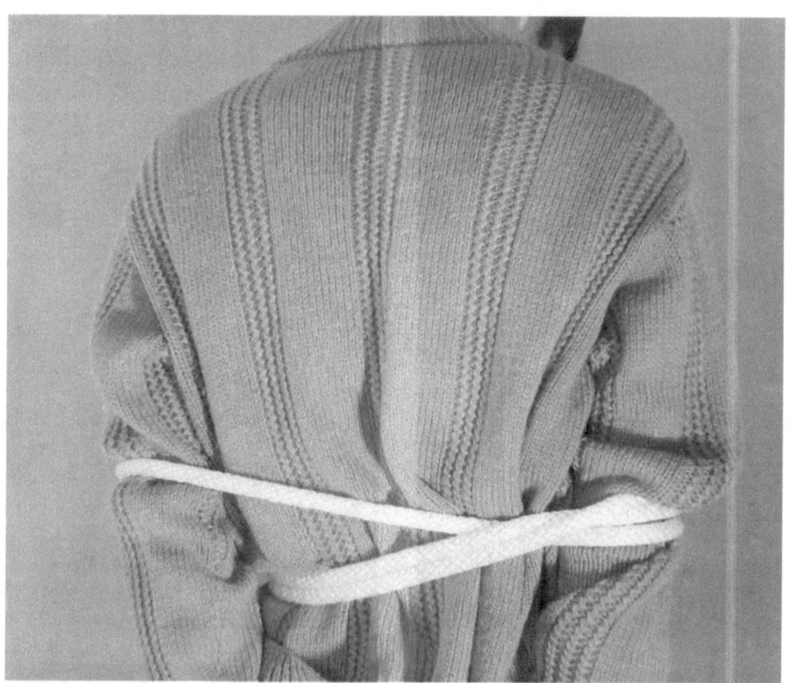

Bound to Fail, 1967, from *Eleven Color Photographs*, 1966–1967/1970.
Portfolio of 11 color photographs. Various sizes, approx. 19¾ × 23 in. (50.2 × 58.4 cm) each. Published by the Leo Castelli Gallery, New York. Edition of eight. Image courtesy Sperone Westwater, New York.

means.[31] Here I disagree. I think the negation happens earlier, through the elaborate dialectics I have described. It is as if the autocritical practices once assumed to be paradigmatic of modernism have been taken to the nth degree—all the better to subject the paradigm itself to lethal assault. Of course, I am not claiming that there can be no more sculpture after Nauman. Yet the sensory past with which sculpture was for so long connected—which it aimed to embody—surely cannot continue. Instead, Nauman's work turns inward, not in pursuit of introspection but to turn the very idea of inwardness inside out. And his work simultaneously turns outward, toward mere surface or mere solidity, so as to forsake the privacy, the discreteness, of our sense of bodies and things. This new congress of inside and outside strikes sculpture at its heart.[32] Both a hectic animation and a dead disanimation are its weapons—so much so that I cannot help believing that Nauman must somewhere have preserved a longing for a bit of stability, some solid yet animate form, anything other than this endless backing and forthing of objects and bodies, neither of which can be properly alive or finally dead. And if it is animate form you yearn for, Moore *is* the answer—hence, Nauman's prudence in storing him so carefully away.

Notes

1. *College of San Francisco Art Institute*, catalog (San Francisco: San Francisco Art Institute, 1967–1968), 38.

2. Nauman, in Willoughby Sharp, "Nauman Interview, 1970," in Bruce Nauman, *Please Pay Attention Please: Bruce Nauman's Words*, ed. Janet Kraynak (Cambridge, MA: MIT Press, 2003), 117–118.

3. In using both *mediums* and *media* here, I am invoking the practice followed and explained by Rosalind Krauss in *"A Voyage on the North Sea": Art in the Age of the Post-medium Condition* (London: Thames and Hudson, 1999), 5–7.

4. See "University of California: In Memoriam, 1974," memo to Tio Giambruni, signed by fellow Davis professors R. M. Johnson, M. C. Reagan, and D. Schapiro, Online Archive of the University of California, http://texts.cdlib.org/view?docId=hb6h4nb3q7;NAAN=13030. In later comments to Michele de Angelus ("Interview with Bruce Nauman, May 27 and 30, 1980," in Nauman, *Please Pay Attention*, 225–226), Nauman makes clear that he saw the Davis sculpture program, with its devotion to clay or casting and total neglect of welding, as distinctly outmoded. The focus on bronzes seems to have sent his mind back to the faux "bronzes" that he, while an undergraduate at the University of Wisconsin, had seen made of tinted fiberglass.

5. Neal Benezra, "Surveying Nauman," in *Bruce Nauman: Exhibition Catalogue and Catalogue Raisonné*, ed. Joan Simon (Minneapolis: Walker Art Center, 1994), 19. This catalog is hereafter cited with the abbreviation *CR*.

6. Judging from the evidence offered by the list of destroyed works presented by the catalogue raisonné, Nauman seems to have initially believed it possible to sidestep the use of a plaster mold taken from the initial clay "soft-shape." His first attempt in fiberglass and resin, based directly on a clay model and now documented only by a photograph, did not have the desired effect. See *CR* D-1.

7. Such works include *CR* 17–23, seven untitled pieces from 1965.

8. Fidel A Danieli, "The Art of Bruce Nauman," *Artforum* 6, no. 4 (December 1967): 16 [reprinted in this volume].

9. The show apparently included only a few works by Nauman, among them *CR* 59. Though installed horizontally at the Fischbach Gallery, it is most often treated as a vertical work.

10. Lucy R. Lippard, "Eccentric Abstraction," *Art International*, November 1966, reprinted in *The New Sculpture 1965–1975*, exhibition catalog, ed. Richard Armstrong and Richard Marshall (New York: Whitney Museum of American Art, 1990), 58.

11. Ibid., 57.

12. Ibid.

13. On *Primary Structures*, see James Meyer, *Minimalism: Art and Polemics in the Sixties* (New Haven, CT: Yale University Press, 2001), 13–24.

14. De Angelus, "Interview with Bruce Nauman," 226–227. The works by Tuttle that Nauman had encountered were shown at *The 7th Selection for the Encouragement of Contemporary Art: A New York Collector Selects*, San Francisco Museum of Modern Art, January 22–February 14, 1965, and are identified in the exhibition checklist as *Abstract Picture*, oil on canvas and wood, and *Silver Abstract*, plywood construction. The second of these, now known as *Silver Picture* or *Silver Abstraction*, dates from 1964.

15. Marcia Tucker, "Bruce Nauman," in Jane Livingston and Marcia Tucker, *Bruce Nauman: Work from 1965 to 1972* (Los Angeles: Los Angeles County Museum of Art, 1972), 32. It is worth noting that Tucker's list, rather more than Nauman's sculpture, bears a relation to Richard Serra's *Verb List* of 1967–1968. The comparison is telling because Serra's list, which is composed of 37 infinitives (beginning with "to scatter, to arrange, to repair, to discard" and ending with "to continue") and 17 prepositional phrases ("of waves, of electromagnetic, of inertia … of tides, of reflection … of time, of carbonization"), insists on intentions and reference, while Tucker, as noticed earlier, is concerned with action or process. See Richard Serra, *Writings/Interviews* (Chicago: University of Chicago Press, 1994), 4.

16. Mel Bochner, "Eccentric Abstraction," *Arts Magazine* 41 (November 1966): 58, quoted in Richard Armstrong, "Between Geometry and Gesture," in *The New Sculpture 1965–1975*, ed. Armstrong and Marshall, 14.

17. In an interview with Joe Raffaele (1966), Nauman is asked to comment on the importance he places on process versus conception: What matters more, the actual doing or the idea itself? Nauman replies, "A little of each—although it should be O.K. if someone else made it. The problem is, you can't get someone else to make it right. I've had that problem. I think I make the plans as well as they can be made, and then I bring them to somebody. And they make the piece wrong. Or they can make it stronger and do it another way" (Joe Raffaele and Elizabeth Baker, "The Way-Out West: Interviews with Four San Francisco Artists, 1967 [1966]," in Nauman, *Please Pay Attention*, 106).

18. This story is told by Nauman in the course of his long 1980 interview by Michele de Angelus ("Interview with Bruce Nauman," 242). Described only as a "low plastic piece," the work was then in the possession of Tony De Lap but has since deteriorated and no longer exists.

19. Robert Morris has also used rope to summon bodily sensations. See *Untitled (Knots)* (1963), a painted-wood and hemp rope piece now at the Detroit Institute of Arts. Not only is this piece certainly part of the pedigree of Nauman's piece, but it also invokes another important precedent for Nauman: Jasper Johns's *Target with Plaster Casts* (1955).

20. These are *CR* D-9 and D-17. Danieli refers to "a recent green and red rubber pad to be stood upon," which may well be D-9 ("The Art of Bruce Nauman," 18).

21. See *CR* 48, which provides identifications of each work. My thanks to Anne Byrd for viewing the Museum of Modern Art copy of this book as my proxy and for providing me with scans of its images.

22. The Davis performance is identified in the catalog raisonné as *CR* 5; its video version is *CR* 138. For Nauman's exchange with Willoughby Sharp in 1970, see Sharp, "Nauman Interview," 122.

23. The work is *CR* D-21. My discussion relies on the information provided by the catalog.

24. Oddly and comically, the cans defer even further to sculptural tradition in that all seven bear a brand label with a funny little head, a sign that insists that the figure be understood as seven heads high.

25. Although Nauman did not see Beuys's work until a trip to Düsseldorf in 1968, he had heard tell of it some years earlier. In the 1980 interview conducted by Michele de Angelus, he recalls that in about 1965 or 1966 he met the curator Kasper König, who "told [him] some things about Joseph Beuys" (de Angelus, "Interview with Bruce Nauman," 251). Nauman's own chair work, *A Cast of the Space under My Chair* (1965–1968), though produced in its definitive concrete version during the German trip, dates in conception to three years earlier. It is possible that as a spatial concretization, the piece also responds to Beuys's rendering of human presence as fat.

26. Nauman's instructions for "Body as Cylinder" and "Body as a Sphere" seem to have been formulated by 1969. See Bruce Nauman, "Notes and Projects, 1970," in Nauman, *Please Pay Attention Please*, 57. The quotations given subsequently in the text are likewise taken from that source.

27. Nauman, in Joan Simon, "Breaking the Silence: An Interview with Bruce Nauman, 1988," in Nauman, *Please Pay Attention*, 324 [reprinted in this volume].

28. For *Platform Made Up of the Space between Two Rectilinear Boxes on the Floor*, see *CR* 50; for *A Cast of the Space under My Chair*, see note 25.

29. Nauman, in Simon, "Breaking the Silence."

30. Ludwig Wittgenstein, *Tractus Logico-Philosophicus*, 2.0131, quoted in Ann Wilson Lloyd, "Casting about with Bruce Nauman," *Sculpture* 13, no. 4 (July–August 1994): 20–27.

31. Alex Potts, *The Sculptural Imagination: Figurative, Modernist, Minimalist* (New Haven, CT: Yale University Press, 2001), 370.

32. This formulation arises from discussions with Jeremy Melius, to whom I am grateful.

Video Promenades: Nauman Taking Architecture for a Walk

Rosalind Krauss

Within the development of modern architecture, one of the problems posed by larger and larger buildings was that of circulation: how to move ever greater numbers of people through the taller and longer spaces of skyscrapers, shopping malls, and giant hotels while making such trajectories pleasantly habitable and not disorienting to their milling crowds. Gradually, architects made circulation itself into an autonomous form—think of Frank Lloyd Wright's solution to the Guggenheim Museum, where the spiral ramp-as-pure-circulation is also the space of exhibition, the advantage of combining the two being the phenomenological payoff that from the moment one moves onto the ramp one can see the endpoint of the trajectory, so that circulation and its goal are combined with brilliant efficiency. All the ramps and spiral staircases of modernist architecture—Le Corbusier has to be included here—have this drive behind them, and the term used by archi-speak to mark the autonomously conceived axis of circulation was *promenade. Promenade* signaled the independent focus of the design as the specificity of architecture itself. In his early videos, Bruce Nauman recorded his search for an idea by showing himself "bouncing in a corner" or "turning upside-down." Such pacing within his studio was, I realize, a form of *promenade.* The corridors he devised to mark this activity were continuous, then, with the most modernist and highest forms of architecture. But with the video monitors added to them, they descended from the heights of *promenade* to the depths of surveillance—becoming the antiarchitecture of the merely anonymous hallways of office buildings or

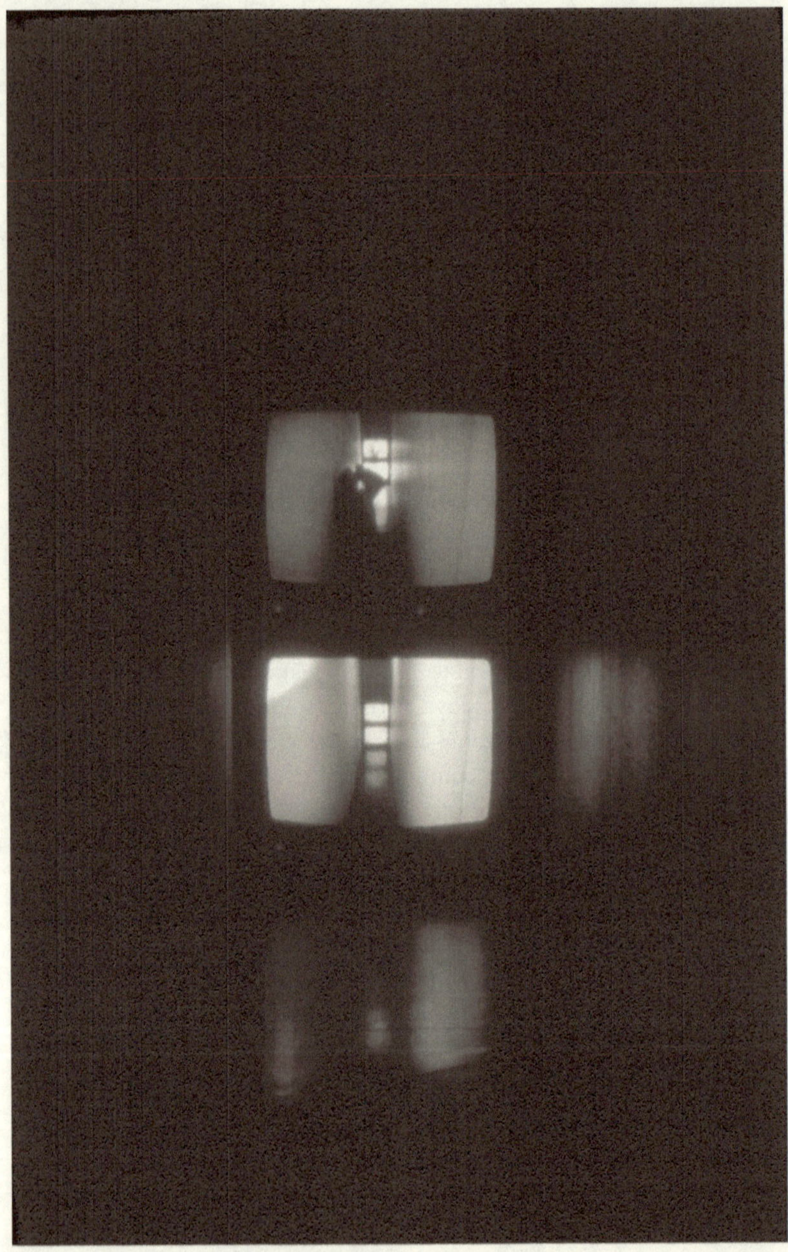

Live-Taped Video Corridor, 1970 (detail). Wallboard, video camera, two video monitors, videotape player, videotape. Dimensions vary; approx. 144 × 384 × 20 in. (365.8 × 975.4 × 50.8 cm). Solomon R. Guggenheim Museum, New York. Panza Collection, gift, 1992. Image courtesy Sperone Westwater, New York.

apartment complexes, within which televisual security measures are on constant alert.

By 1986 and Nauman's work *Violent Incident*, the bank of monitors, through which the viewer oversees the onset and development of the altercation between two characters who eventually shoot one another, switches one's perspective from being the object monitored in the apartment corridors to that of the subject of surveillance—that is, from watched to watcher. And with this switch, Nauman seemed to have entered the uncertain terrain of locating the specificity of video as a medium.

Not only had video no specificity as an aesthetic support, but it also seemed to avoid the whole modernist project of keying the meaning of a work to the revelation of the specific nature of its material form. This conceptual lacuna attracted attention during the '60s and '70s as critics and theorists took up the problem of video's elusive essence.

Fred Jameson's response was to deal video into the dominant aesthetic form of late capital, which for him was postmodernism. Adopting Raymond Williams's designation for television ("total flow"), Jameson was intent as well to characterize the internal workings and structures of such continuous but uninflected sensory stimulation, a continuousness most theorists simply reduced to the epithet "boredom."[1]

Postmodernism, Jameson retorts, is not boring. Rather, it generates the stimulating form of a constant sampling of tiny quotations, each of which beams the signal of a narrative as a kind of emblem or logo—the looming monolith in the landscape, for example, announcing in a flash the whole unfolding of Kubrick's *2001*. Postmodernism is a collage of such fragmentary quotes, each become a signifier without any referent in the field of the Real. If video is the exemplary medium of postmodernism, Jameson concludes, it is because it has the capacity to stage such ceaseless reshuffling of the fragments of preexistent texts.

For Stanley Cavell, television is also essentialized around the idea of "total flow." He renames this, however, calling it "a current of simultaneous event reception."[2] Such a current, he argues, is not perceived through what we ordinarily understand as viewing but rather through the more passive activity of monitoring. It is surveillance, then, that essentializes television's technical support in video. Nauman's activity in video has consistently developed within the terms of this argument, although I am sure it is not an analysis with which he is familiar. I would say instead that he was instinctively attracted to the ubiquitously placed surveillance monitors, and this is why he used them consistently in his video corridors and in the later work *Mapping the Studio*.

Since neither surveillance nor total flow captures the essence of video, I turn to yet another theorization of this medium so resistant to notions of essence. This is Sam Weber's brilliant essay "Television: Set and Screen," which engages less with artists' video than it does with broadcast television. Weber moves in on the question of ontology by refusing it on the grounds that one must always respect what he calls television's "constitutive heterogeneity." Television's defining condition, he argues, is difference. It is different from film as well as being different from what is generally known as visual perception. "Above all," he concludes, "television differs from itself."[3] This is because with the phenomenon signaled by the singular noun *television* there are secreted three different operations: production, transmission (broadcast), and reception. If television means seeing at a distance, it can also be said that it transports vision itself, placing it directly before the viewer. But no single body could perceive this vision since it takes place, Weber argues, in three different places at once: the place of recording, the place of reception, and the place of transmission. Thus, to watch television is to watch the invisible separation of the visual datum, split between its three places of habitation, and what the television screen does is to take this invisible separation and turn it into the singular, visual logo of a gestalt. Weber's conclusion is that television has to be characterized through the term *differential specificity*, which, though it sounds like a paradox,[4] is necessary in order to respect the complexity of this form.

Mapping the Studio continues Nauman's investigations of video as a form of monitoring. The seven cameras within his studio were mounted to record continuously the invasion of the space by a horde of mice, who are attacked from time to time by Nauman's cat. The mice, a shade of gray matching the concrete floor exactly, seem to explode into our field of vision only through their motion, like little furry blurs within the darkness. Barely visible, they are the support for a vision that is itself split between its site of recording and its site of reception. The projection screen—as Weber had seen it—is precisely the field on which this invisible separation surfaces as gestalt.

Mapping the Studio brings us into contact with Jameson's notion of television's specificity as well as with those of Cavell and Weber. For as

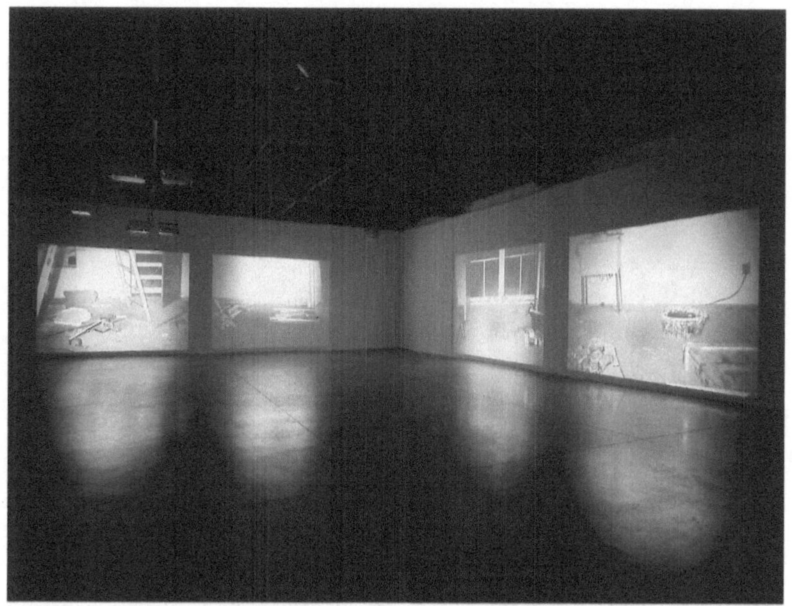

Mapping the Studio I (Fat Chance John Cage), 2001. DVD projections (color, sound). 5 hr., 45 min. Dia Art Foundation; partial gift, Lannan Foundation, 2013. Image courtesy Sperone Westwater, New York.

we ourselves patiently watch for the appearance of the mice, we transform ourselves into so many cats poised like Tom waiting for the appearance of little Jerry. Memories of Saturday afternoon cartoons flood us with bursts of narrativity in the Jamesonian sense of postmodern citation. And this brings us to yet another issue of specificity—namely, the type of perception that reenacts the bodiless form of vision of the unmanned camera mindlessly watching its portion of the terrain. As we now watch our own portion, focused on this or that patch of wall, we feel ourselves embodying the recording device, thus splitting our own perceptual field into a having-been-there of past-time recording and a being-there-now of present reception. Nauman's video corridors avoid this differential perception by staging both the simultaneity of recording and reception and the synonymy of watcher and watched, as the participant monitors himself moving down the corridor toward a view of his own body growing steadily smaller.

To become the subject of surveillance as one experiences *Mapping the Studio* is to reverse the conditions Michel Foucault outlines in *Discipline and Punish*,[5] where the panopticon's structure produces the disciplinary subject through a constant surveillance in which the warden in the watchtower remains invisible, thus forcing the watched subject to internalize the surveillant authority and to become his or her own watcher: the obedient schoolfellow or the regimented soldier. The only experience we can have as the object of this gaze is when, sitting on our rolling desk chairs and scooting through the space like so many mice, we become the doubles of the little furry schmoos suddenly erupting into vision on the screens.

Fastidious in his use of language, Nauman subtitled this work *Fat Chance John Cage*, which demands consideration. I decide it is an elegant reference to the masterpiece of the master of the modernist notion of the poetic medium: Stéphane Mallarmé's *A Roll of the Dice Will Never Abolish Chance*. John Cage was the great apostle of chance as a form of composing that voided every possibility of reflection on the medium—making all sound, ambient as well as recorded, into music. Mallarmé held onto the magical specificity of poetic language, particularly its placement on the pages of a book, black against white, disappearing and reappearing as it crosses the gutter of the book's binding. By signaling chance, Nauman's subtitle focuses on the disembodiment of the gaze and its reembodiment by the work's viewers. Thus it names, I would argue, its own commitment to the specificity of video, even if that were Weber's paradoxical concept of self-difference. Even if the seven projectors and their surrounding walls appear to stage *Mapping the Studio* as the currently ubiquitous installation art, it seems to me that the work disdains this fashion.

If this is so, Nauman must be added to the little group of knights working in the service of the medium, from his earliest video corridors to his works such as *World Peace* and finally to *Mapping the Studio*. "Fat chance," indeed, John Cage.

Notes

1. Frederic Jameson, *Postmodernism, or, The Cultural Logic of Late Capitalism* (Durham, NC: Duke University Press, 1991), 70.

2. Stanley Cavell, "The Fact of Television," in *Video Culture: A Critical Investigation*, ed. John G. Hanhardt (New York: Visual Studies Workshop, 1986), 212.

3. Samuel Weber, "Television: Set and Screen," in *Mass Mediauras: Form, Technics, Media* (Stanford, CA: Stanford University Press, 1996), 110.

4. The paradox can be read off of the Derridean *différance*, meant to deconstruct the very possibility of "specificity" of the constancy of the "self" by showing it always-already divided and thus self-differing.

5. Michel Foucault, *Discipline and Punish: The Birth of the Prison*, trans. Alan Sheridan (New York: Random House, 1977).

Bruce Nauman Going Solo[1]

Robert Slifkin

Like many of the artist's sculptures from the 1960s, Bruce Nauman's *John Coltrane Piece* (1968) couples intransigent materiality with willful inscrutability to produce a mysterious, if not melancholic, effect. Created the year after the celebrated saxophonist's death, the three-foot-square sheet of aluminum, rising only three inches off the ground, stands—however lowly and unassumingly—as a portable cenotaph. The work's mirrored base, invisible to the naked eye yet intelligible through the work's written description, keenly literalizes its appeal to nonexistence. Partaking in the artist's penchant for punning titles, the work concretizes Coltrane's composition "Peace on Earth." With its lack of a traditional pedestal and its level, horizontal alignment on the gallery floor, Nauman's sculpture is, literally, a "piece" on earth.

Like its minimalist contemporaries, and in particular the floor works of Carl Andre assembled out of square metal tiles, the specific objective of Nauman's *John Coltrane Piece*—manifested most visibly in its geometric austerity and industrial materiality—invites a degree of subjective projection from the viewer. Without a discernable focal point, let alone compositional order or figural referent, the work (again, like a great deal of minimalist art of the time) diminishes signs of artistic authority, in turn increasing the participatory aesthetic possibilities for the viewer. Yet if Andre's works similarly do away with conventional markers of aesthetic autonomy (such as pedestals) in order to expand their engagement with the space in which they are situated, Nauman's piece, through its hidden mirror, paradoxically makes the dark and slender

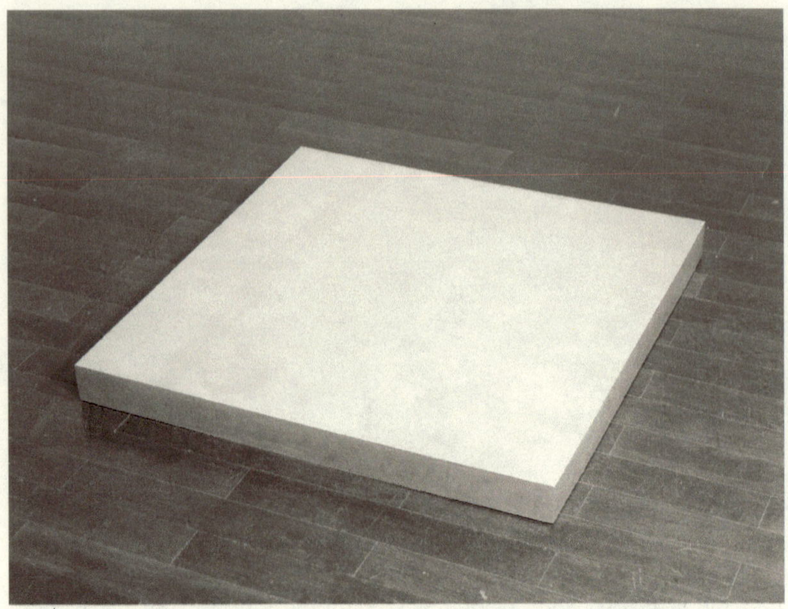

John Coltrane Piece, 1968. Aluminum with mirror-finish bottom face. 3 × 36 × 36 in. (7.6 × 91.4 × 91.4 cm). Sammlung Ludwig, Ludwig Forum für Internationale Kunst Aachen.

space between the sculpture and the floor its primary site of focus. That is to say, while minimalist works such as Andre's effectively blurred the boundary between art and life, Nauman's piece claimed that boundary as a space worth examining in and of itself.

If mirrors are conventionally used as means for seeing oneself or the world outside of oneself as a representation, in Nauman's *John Coltrane Piece* any such self-identification is rendered impossible. Nothing can be reflected without light or distance, both of which are denied in the work. (Nauman would explicitly explore the necessary condition of light in a related sculpture, *Dark*, also from 1968. In *Dark*, the work's title is written underneath a similarly large and flat square steel panel placed directly on the ground.) Repeatedly in Nauman's work from the 1960s, this space—where art meets life, where the artificial meets the natural, where the figurative meets the literal—is shown to be a site of darkness, of indeterminacy, of illegibility, and of privacy, a place where meaning breaks down and becomes solely a personal matter and messages become intransmissible.

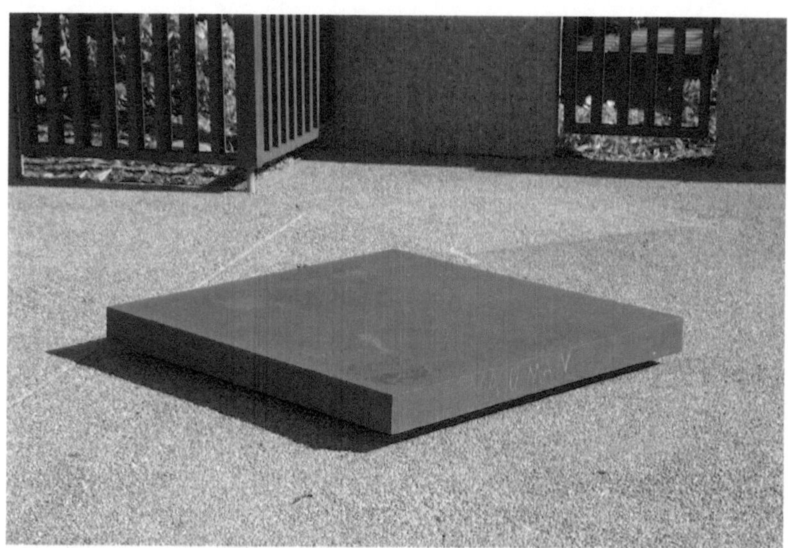

Dark, 1968. Steel. 4 × 48 × 48 in. (10.2 × 121.9 × 121.9 cm). Southwestern College Art Gallery. Image courtesy Sperone Westwater, New York.

In a 1970 conversation with curator and critic Willoughby Sharp, Nauman commented on this aspect of *Coltrane Piece*, noting that the work and his art in general "tend[] to fall in the private category."[2] In many ways the related themes of privacy and concealment (and their antipodes of communication and clarity) have been central concerns throughout the artist's lengthy career. In a 1972 interview, Nauman acknowledged that his preoccupation with the subject of privacy entailed the danger of hermeticism, noting that "if you make work that's just too private, nobody can understand it."[3] The tension between the desire for communication—and, as a possible analogue, community—and, as Nauman put it, the "personal fear of exposing myself" runs through much of the artist's oeuvre. In many ways, it would become the central theme of the remarkable body of work that Nauman produced between 1967 and 1973, in which the artist began to use film and video—media that, because of their capacity to automatically mirror the world back to the artist and correspondingly project or transmit it to a distant audience, serve as ideal formats through which to explore the agnostic duality between the appeal for an intimate, if not private, experience and the acknowledgment that any successful artistic statement entails a degree of publicness that must transcend the boundaries of the individual subject.[4]

The exploration of private and public meaning established materially and spatially in sculptures such as *John Coltrane Piece* and *Dark* was particularly "humanized" in a pair of nearly hour-long videos created by Nauman in 1973, in which two actors attempt to meld their bodies into the floor of a television studio. Nauman provided the actors with explicit instructions and allowed them to practice the exercise before the recording began. As evinced by the titles of the two videos—*Elke Allowing the Floor to Rise Up over Her, Face Up* and *Tony Sinking into the Floor, Face Up and Face Down*—once again it is the thin space between body and floor that becomes the crucial site of Nauman's artistic investigation. While the action in both videos is generally quite uneventful (depicting the actors gradually getting their bodies comfortable in a horizontal position and then holding the position for a long period of time), in both cases the participants had to stop midexercise due to the disturbing intensity of the experience. Elke suffered from what Nauman called "a violent reaction," and Tony coughed and choked, succumbing to the fear that the molecules of his skin might be torn from the surface of the ground.[5] Like the space between Nauman's *Coltrane Piece* and the gallery floor, the space between the actors' bodies and the floor of the television studio becomes both the focus of the viewer's attention and a site that suggests a certain impossibility, whether of metaphysical transcendence, meaning, or simply visibility.

Nauman's interest in the meditative, if not quasi-therapeutic, practices enacted in these two videos from 1973 was, in part, influenced by his reading of the book *Gestalt Therapy* (1951) by Frederick Perls, Ralph F. Hefferline, and Paul Goodman. The book, whose first sentence invited readers to "invade your own privacy," espoused ways to establish a sense of psychic cohesiveness, or what the authors called a "strong gestalt," through a series of attention-focusing exercises that examined the interplay between the "organism and the environment."[6] According to the authors, due to the dulling effects of modern life with its various forms of distraction, most individuals cast off parts of themselves in the name of efficiency only to ultimately render themselves less psychically effective because of these losses. "Attention, concentration, interest, concern, excitement and grace are representative of healthy figure–ground formation, while confusion, boredom, fixations, anxiety,

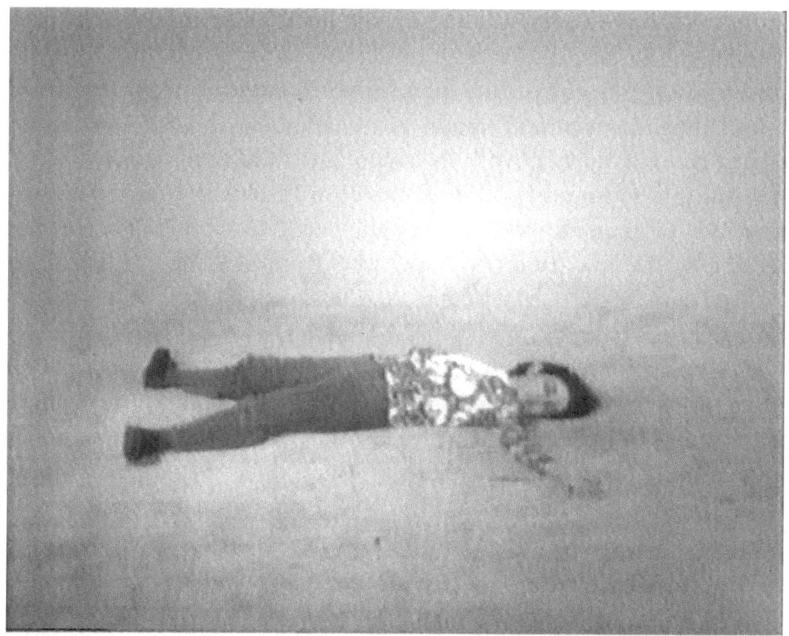

Elke Allowing the Floor to Rise Up over Her, Face Up, 1973. Videotape (color, sound). 40 min., to be repeated continuously. Distributed by Electronic Arts Intermix. Image courtesy Sperone Westwater, New York.

amnesias, stagnation and self-consciousness are indicative of figure–ground formation which is disturbed."[7]

It is quite understandable why the book's diagnosis of the blurred boundaries between the self and the external world resonated with Nauman. The artist's first major body of sculptures consisted of fiberglass molds that were split such that their interiors were as visible and sculpturally important as their exteriors. This interest in making interiority visible—and converting "ground" into "figure"—was perhaps most famously explored in the artist's concrete sculpture *A Cast of the Space under My Chair* (1965–1968). That said, Nauman's work hardly suggests a wholesale adoption of the tenets of *Gestalt Therapy* (which would promote the strong articulation of such boundaries). Insofar as Perls and his collaborators provided various exercises to help demarcate one's gestalt, Nauman drew upon these attention-focusing practices and turned them into methodologies for examining moments of what might be called *gestalt incohesion*—situations in which the body might meld into its surroundings.[8] In fact, the artist created a series of works that, in their instructional character, appear like perverted exercises from the book, but Nauman's "exercises" appear to be less about the cohesion of the ego or its fluid interplay with its environment and more about its dilution into its surroundings. For instance, in "Instructions for a Mental Exercise," written in 1969 but not published until 1974 (and apparently serving as the foundation for the two "floor melding" videos from 1973), Nauman encouraged the participant to attempt just such a physical amalgamation with his or her surroundings.[9]

Nauman continued this line of investigation in another instruction-based piece entitled *Body Pressure*. First exhibited at the Konrad Fischer Gallery in 1974, the work entailed nothing more than a free-standing wall and a set of instructions, printed in German and English, and similar to the earlier *Mental Exercise*. In *Body Pressure*, the participant was instructed to press his or her body against the wall and, according to the accompanying text, "form an image of yourself (suppose you had just stepped forward) on the opposite side of the wall pressing back against the wall very hard."[10] Like the pair of "floor melding" videos from 1973 and the two floor sculptures from 1968 already discussed in this essay, *Body Pressure* utilized a flat surface—in this case a vertical one—as the focal site of the work. Yet in this instance rather than the incorporation of the body into a resistant surface, a bodily double is projected on the other side of the wall. Nauman notes in the final line of the instructions: "This may become a very erotic exercise."

The distinctly erotic potential of *Body Pressure* may be best understood in relation to a work by Dan Graham from two years earlier, entitled *Body Press*. (The titular similarity suggests the possibility of direct influence.) At once a sculpture, a performance, and a film, *Body Press* encompassed a cylinder with a mirrored interior in which a naked man and woman, both holding 16-millimeter cameras, were instructed to record their skin—both in the distorted reflection of the curved, mirrored interior and by directly filming their bodies—changing cameras midway through the exercise. The two films were then projected on opposite ends of the gallery space so that, in a sense, the mirrored surface of the cylinder served as a literal prefiguration of the performance's subsequent projection.

The cinematic component of *Body Press* makes explicit the way in which the wall functions in Nauman's *Body Pressure* as both a barrier that the self should literally internalize and a screen upon which the self is virtually projected.[11] With its enactment of bodily projection across a flat screen, in many regards the situation proposed in *Body Pressure* resembles that of the respective transmission and projection of video and film. As art historian Rosalind Krauss recognized in a seminal essay from 1976, the use of mirroring, whether literal or imaginary, was a central component of a wide array of early video art practices. Repeatedly, artists such as Nauman, Graham, and Vito Acconci placed themselves between the video camera and the monitor so that "the self [was] split and doubled by the mirror reflections of synchronous feedback."[12] For Krauss, this technique of "self-encapsulation" revealed the medium of video art to be not so much a material substrate (as it was in traditional artistic formats such as painting or sculpture) but rather a psychological condition—namely, narcissism. Placing their bodies between the recording input of the video camera and the receiving output of the monitor, early video artists entered into a literal situation whose virtual compression of time and space found a material correlate not only in the flat horizontal planes of Nauman's *John Coltrane Piece* and *Dark* but perhaps even more explicitly in the series of corridors that Nauman constructed between 1969 and 1974.

Like much minimalist art of the period, Nauman's corridor works emphasized the viewer's bodily engagement with the work of art, activating the space in and around the object and, in turn, like the dispersed apparatus of video, complicated and expanded conventional notions of autonomous and pure artistic media. In fact, many of the ostensibly sculptural corridors had material connections to video. The first one Nauman constructed, *Performance Corridor* (1969), consisted of nothing more than two parallel 12-foot-long unadorned walls set 20 inches apart from one another and was originally created as a prop for his video *Walk with Contrapposto* (1968). Several of the structures utilized actual mirrors, sometimes placed at the end of the corridor at an angle, which presented confusing views to approaching spectators. In other instances, Nauman placed video monitors at the end of passageways, further substantiating the connection not only between mirror and monitor but also between the corridors and the dynamics of the video apparatus.[13] For instance, in Nauman's *Live-Taped Video Corridor* (1970) two monitors stacked vertically were placed at the end of a walkway. The top monitor showed a closed-circuit image of the narrow space between the walls, taken from above the entrance so that as a person approached the monitor, she confronted an image of herself from behind, producing an unnerving effect in which her body diminished in size the closer it came to the monitor; the lower monitor displayed a previously recorded image of the corridor empty. Like many of the works already discussed, *Live-Taped Video Corridor* presented a situation in which a body enters a physical space only to have its materiality seem to diminish and ultimately disappear within it.

Nauman has stated that the corridor pieces were "about the connection between public and private experience," going on to add that "the video helps the private part even though it's a public situation. The way you watch television is a private kind of experience."[14] Repeatedly in his published interviews the artist describes his use of video and film in terms of his interest in examining "the connection between public and private experience." Describing how he began making videos after producing a series of short films, the artist stated, "Video is a much more 'private' kind of communication" than film. "You sit and have contact with a television set, as opposed to film, where generally a lot of people go and the image is very large; it's more of a common experience."[15]

If in the 1960s and 1970s Nauman associated privacy with the medium of video, this motif found a degree of overdetermination in his chosen locale for almost all of the video works—namely, his studio. Unlike many 1960s artists who radically undermined the romantic vision of the solitary artist working in seclusion in the studio—through managerial models (Warhol), physical displacement (Smithson), or dematerialization (conceptual art)—Nauman's artistic practice, while hardly traditional, was resolutely studio based.[16] At precisely the same moment of art's apparent displacement, dematerialization, and expansion beyond traditional media and modes of production, Nauman used the studio as a means to determine the ontology of the work of art and his identity as an artist. As he recollected about this crucial moment in his early career, "[Because] I was an artist and I was in the studio, then whatever it was I was doing in the studio must be art. And what I was in fact doing was drinking coffee and pacing the floor. It became a question of how to structure those activities into being art, or some kind of cohesive unit that could be available to people. At this point art became more of an activity and less of a product."[17] Nauman's solution to this crisis of artistic identity and, as he notes, communication with a public was to document his activities—first through film and then, after obtaining the necessary equipment from his dealer Leo Castelli, through videotape. In works such as *Stamping in the Studio* and *Slow Angle Walk (Beckett Walk)* (both 1968) Nauman literally videotaped himself pacing around the studio for 60 minutes, albeit with a rigorous intensity that invested his actions with a sense of artistic intentionality that was reiterated in the oftentimes skewed or even inverted camera angles.[18]

The video apparatus of camera and monitor thus became a structuring boundary that could demarcate artistic production just as categorically as more conventional markers of aesthetic significance such as frames and pedestals. By simply being recorded as an event, even drinking coffee and pacing the floor could be discerned as art. And by performing acts that entailed a certain degree of rigor and endurance, Nauman sought to engender a model of communication with his audience. As he noted to Sharp, "If you really believe in what you're doing and do it was well as you can … if you are honestly getting tired … there has to be a certain sympathetic response in someone who is watching you."[19] The medium of video with its divided modes of recording and transmission allowed Nauman to invest his intensely private actions with a degree of public communication and through its durational component, which the artist took to its material limit in the form of a 60-minute tape, with even expressive potential.

Yet the aesthetic boundary of video was one in which the self could not only be recorded and transmitted but, as in *Body Pressure* and to a lesser extent in *John Coltrane Piece,* also incorporated, albeit virtually. And as in other works that employed actual sculptural elements to figure this merger of body and artistic medium, the process intimated a sense of privacy. If a central strategy of Nauman's art has been to "give two kinds of information that don't line up" in an effort to forge a productively thought-provoking confusion, the artist's use of video, specifically, has aligned this approach with his equally strong interest in examining the dichotomy between public and private experience.[20] As David Joselit has noted, "Television is the first major public medium experienced in private."[21] The intimacy of the format was enhanced by its low-grade resolution (especially in its formative years), which promoted the use of close-ups and more intimate modes of reception, typically in the viewer's living room and bedroom. While the video apparatus offered a means for defeating the privacy of experience through a model of mass reproduction and distribution, it nonetheless encouraged a private mode of viewership. Nauman would figure the fundamental intimacy of the medium by documenting himself performing a series of hermetically intense actions alone in his unadorned and nearly vacant studio. Yet by recording and exhibiting these actions, the artist made public—publicized—this privacy. "You work alone in the studio," he stated, "and then the work goes out into a public situation."[22] If, for Nauman, the studio was a site of privacy and the gallery a "public situation," video made the fundamental, if rarely considered, dynamic of privacy and publicness underlying any artistic utterance an essential condition of its medium. In fact, the artist would describe the nature of television as "opaque," going on to add that "it only gives to you, you can't give back. You can't participate. I like that."[23] That is to say, the video apparatus—with its split formats of recording and transmission—made explicit the ultimate public reception that haunts even the most solitary moments of artistic production as well as the possibility of a private experience of a work in its public exhibition. In Nauman's video works, an intimate symmetry is established between the solitary artist and an (imagined) isolated viewer.

This aspect of the medium of video was powerfully reinforced by its use of monitors, the very same material substrate required in the medium of broadcast television. Some of the artists who first explored the potential of video art also considered the possibilities of public broadcasting, albeit frequently perverting the dominant understanding of its mass-communication potential by producing willfully recalcitrant and boring programs. In 1967, Nauman participated in a televised video project by his friend and previous teacher at UC Davis, William Allan. In the program broadcast on KQED (the public-television channel for the San Francisco Bay Area where Allan was an artist-in-residence at the Experimental Television Project), Nauman opened five 10-pound bags of white flour and proceeded to make "flour arrangements" with his limbs. As Nauman went about his task, Allan and the painter Peter Saul sat on a raised platform (and notably behind a real flower arrangement) and discussed various topics in the casually confident demeanor characteristic of television talk-show hosts. A camera mounted directly above Nauman recorded aerial shots of his work in progress that were then interspersed

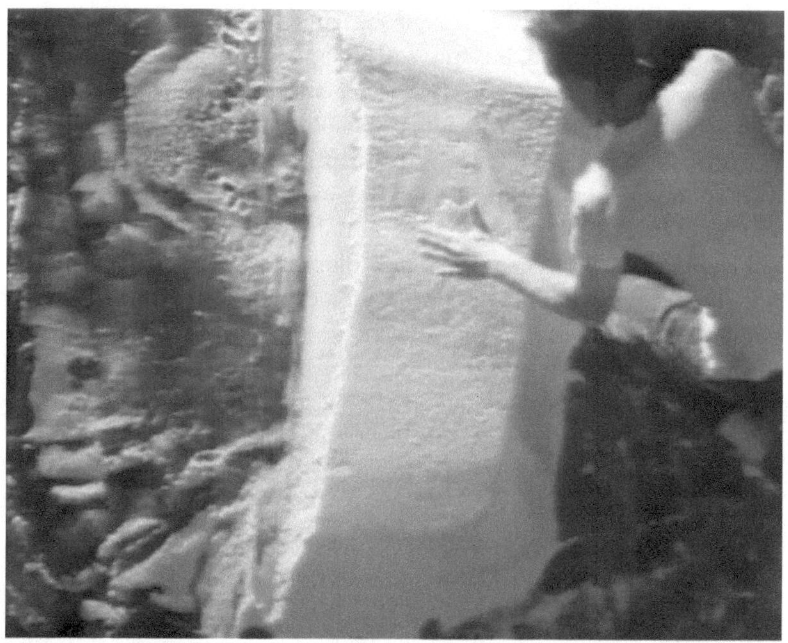

Untitled [*Flour Arrangements*], made with William Allan and Peter Saul for the National Center for Experiments in Television Project, KQED, San Francisco, 1967. Single-channel video (black-and-white, sound). 24 min., 9 sec. Image courtesy University of California, Berkeley, Art Museum and Pacific Film Archive.

between Allan and Saul's commentary and occasionally projected behind the two interlocutors.

Nauman's performance on Allan's program expanded upon a series of seven color photographs of similar "flour arrangements" that the artist produced the same year. According to Nauman, the *Flour Arrangements* series came out of the same central problem of determining the essence of artistic identity. Trying to produce an intentionally "unfamiliar situation," Nauman emptied his studio and worked exclusively on these arrangements "for about a month." If Allan's program offered a release from the hothouse environment of the artist's studio, turning a sculptural "unfamiliar situation" into a decidedly public one (via its broadcast from a television studio), it nonetheless partook in a decidedly indifferent, if not antagonistic, attitude toward public, let alone mass-media, communication.[24]

Nauman's indifference to reaching large audiences was related to what he described as his "mistrust [of] audience participation." Speaking about the already mentioned *Performance Corridor*, Nauman noted that "the piece is important because it gave me the idea that you could make a participation piece without the participants being able to alter your work."[25] Such control—literalized in the extremely narrow passageways of most of his corridors that allowed for only one body at a time to enter and experience them—ensured, according to the artist, that "people were bound to have more or less the same experience I had."[26] Like the instruction pieces, the corridors were predicated on the idea of re-creating a sensation that the artist himself had already personally experienced through a strategy of making the work "as limiting as possible."[27] As such, these works engaged in a dialectic between privacy and publicness, at once demanding an intimate, singular experience in the name of communion, if on the interpersonal rather than collective level, breaking down the barriers of privacy, albeit through techniques that destabilized, if not destroyed, the stable figure or ego of the participant. This paradox encapsulates the challenge that Nauman's artistic project faced in terms of privacy and publicness. Like many artists working in the 1960s, Nauman was wary of facile and fallacious models of communication, such as expressionism, that promised universal comprehension. Yet he was also suspicious of the phenomenologically inflected reception of minimalist art that ostensibly offered infinitely unique subjective experience. Against the two extremes of tenuous universality and incommunicable individuality, Nauman sought to produce situations and objects that restricted the subject's agency and yet, within a diminished scope of experience, offered the subject a transmissible situation and sensation. One might say that Nauman's works present a communal experience of disappearance or that the possibility of community is experienced in these works as absence—as privation—thus complicating and expanding the possible elegiac connotations of works such as *John Coltrane Piece*.

For Nauman, the privacy of the studio engendered a corresponding intimacy for his work's "public" and in turn promoted an empathetic response in a small but selective audience. As he told Jan Butterfield, "I don't think that it bothers me that the pieces are not for many people, because the way I work, it seems that I am doing them in the studio for me or for the small number of people who come to the studio, so it really is one-to-one. … However, most of the people that came to the studio are sympathetic anyway (you can really feel that quickly)."[28] Nauman's sustained anxiety and interest in questions of privacy and the narrowing of public experience may be seen as a critical engagement with what Richard Sennett has called the "intimacy society," a cultural condition in which "closeness between persons is [seen] as a moral good" and "social relationships of all kinds are [seen as being] real, believable, and authentic the closer they approach the inner psychological concerns of each person."[29] For Sennett, the intimate society represents a betrayal of the modern and in particular Enlightenment-based tradition of the public sphere and civic engagement. Yet rather than merely reflecting this particular cultural condition of late modernity, Nauman's works may also suggest a stringent and intense attempt to sustain some sort of authentic, if drastically contracted, public experience at a moment when publicness itself, and the artist's relationship with his or her public in particular, seemed endangered.

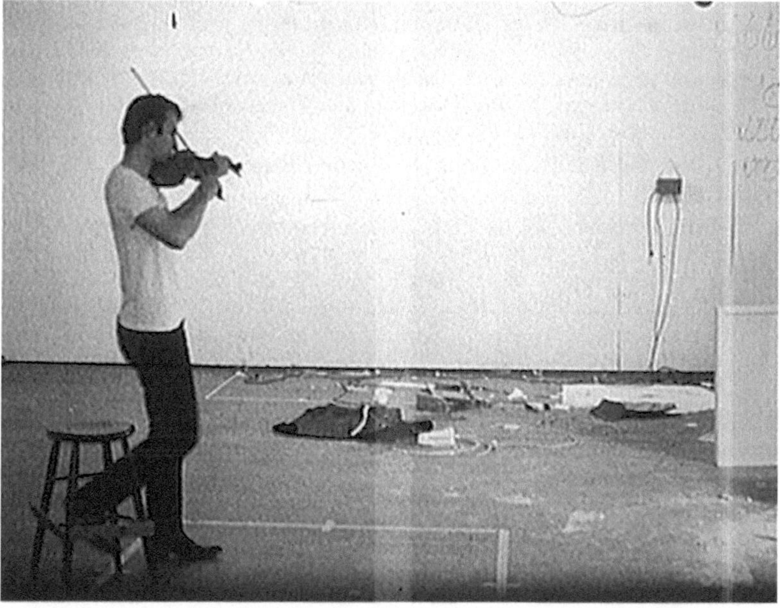

Playing a Note on the Violin While I Walk around the Studio, 1967–1968. 16-mm film (black-and-white, sound). 400 feet, approx. 10 min. Distributed by Electronic Arts Intermix. Image courtesy Sperone Westwater, New York.

Considering this possibility, Nauman's distinctive concern with barriers (walls, floors, and screens), marshaling them as sites to be transcended and yet that can also incorporate the subject, may imply an almost hysterical desire for communion in the fragile intimate society of postmodernity. In works such as *Playing a Note on the Violin While I Walk around the Studio* (1967–1968), and *Flesh to White to Black to Flesh* (1968), Nauman seems to drain the esteemed performance tradition of the solo of its most prized attributes, transforming a moment when the single artist demonstrates his or her technical mastery and personal individuality into a repetitive and emotionless task that more often than not occludes any signs of the artist's personality. Through these works, Nauman's art makes intimacy seem perverse or even grotesque, reminding the viewer of the privation at the base of our culture's cherished privacy.

Notes

1. *Bruce Nauman Going Solo* was commissioned by the Douglas F. Cooley Memorial Art Gallery, Reed College, to accompany the exhibition *Bruce Nauman, Basements*, on view from January 27 to March 9, 2012. The exhibition was curated by Stephanie Snyder, John and Anne Hauberg Curator and Director of the Cooley, who edited this essay.

2. Nauman, in Willoughby Sharp, "Nauman Interview, 1970," in Bruce Nauman, *Please Pay Attention Please: Bruce Nauman's Words*, ed. Janet Kraynak (Cambridge, MA: MIT Press, 2003), 129.

3. Nauman, in Lorraine Sciarra, "Bruce Nauman, January, 1972," in Nauman, *Please Pay Attention Please*, 169. Michael Auping has more recently noted the centrality of this theme in the artist's oeuvre: "Throughout his career, Nauman grappled with the tension between private thought and public exposure—one of the great dilemmas facing the modern artist who is challenged to be intensely personal in a very public way" ("Sound Thinking," *Artforum* 43, no. 5 [January 2005]: 160).

4. Nauman, in Jan Butterfield, "Bruce Nauman: The Center of Yourself, 1975," in Nauman, *Please Pay Attention Please*, 182. The artist goes on to say, "We really want to expose the information, but, on the other hand, we are afraid to let people in."

5. Nauman, in Ian Wallace and Russell Keziere, "Bruce Nauman Interviewed, 1979 (October 9, 1978), in Nauman, *Please Pay Attention Please*, 191.

6. Frederic Perls, Ralph F. Hefferline, and Paul Goodman, *Gestalt Therapy: Excitement and Growth in the Human Personality* (New York: Julian Press, 1951), 3. For a discussion of the influence of this book on Nauman, see Marco De Michelis, "Spaces," in *Bruce Nauman, Topological Gardens*, ed. Carlos Basualdo and Michael R. Taylor (New Haven, CT: Yale University Press, 2009), 67–71. Nauman acknowledges his interest in the book in his interview by Lorraine Sciarra, "Bruce Nauman, January, 1972," 166.

7. Perls, Hefferline, and Goodman, *Gestalt Therapy*, ix.

8. Nauman described the exercise in Perls, Hefferline, and Goodman's book as promoting situations where "you can't relax following resistances" (quoted in Coosje van Bruggen, *Bruce Nauman* [New York: Rizolli, 1988], 228).

9. "Instructions for a Mental Exercise" was originally written in 1969, titled "Untitled (Project for Leverkeusen)," and published under this title in the journal *Interfunktionen* 11 (1974): 122–124.

10. The text of *Body Pressure* is reprinted in Nauman, *Please Pay Attention Please*, 83–85.

11. *Body Pressure* also reveals the central concern for bodily projection and incorporation in various of Nauman's works. My understanding of Nauman's engagement with bodily projection is deeply informed by Gabrielle Gopinath's reading of his work in her unpublished essay "Bruce Nauman's Astral Projections."

12. Rosalind Krauss, "Video: The Aesthetics of Narcissism," *October* 1 (Spring 1976): 53–55. And while the critic suggests at the end of her essay that this move into narcissism might have larger cultural implications in general, her interest is more in terms of the question of sustaining modernist tenets of medium specificity in the face of the distinctly dispersed apparatus of the video format.

13. In an interview by Sharp, Nauman notes that "the enclosed circuit functions as a kind of electronic mirror" (Willoughby Sharp, "Interview with Bruce Nauman, 1971 [May 1970]," in Nauman, *Please Pay Attention Please*, 150).

14. Nauman, in Chris Dercon, "Keep Taking It Apart: A Conversation with Bruce Nauman, 1986 (July 12, 1986)," in Nauman, *Please Pay Attention Please*, 310. In an essay addressing the recent trend in using the artist's body as a sculptural medium, Willoughby Sharp notes: "Generally the performance is executed in the privacy of the studio. Individual works are mostly communicated to the public through the strong visual language of photographs, films, videotapes and other media, all with strong immediacy of impact" ("Body Works," *Avalanche* 1 [Fall 1970]: 14).

15. Nauman, in Dercon, "Keep Taking It Apart," 309.

16. For a discussion of this transformation in studio practice, see Caroline Jones, *Machine in the Studio: Constructing the Postwar American Artist* (Chicago: University of Chicago Press, 1996). Michael R. Taylor, in his essay "Bruce Nauman: Mapping the Studio, Changing the Field" (in *Topological Gardens*, ed. Basualdo and Taylor), states that "Nauman's work … simultaneously challenges and reinforces the twentieth-century notion of the artist's studio as a private, almost sacred space, where the creative act takes place within an atmosphere of solitude and reflection" (49).

17. Nauman, in Wallace and Keziere, "Bruce Nauman Interviewed, 1979," 194.

18. In "Video: The Aesthetics of Narcissism," Krauss notes that in the 1970s artists' capacity to present work in public via reproductions and dissemination in the media was "virtually the only means of verifying its existence as art" (59).

19. Nauman, in Sharp, "Interview with Bruce Nauman," 148.

20. Nauman, in Michele de Angelus, "Interview with Bruce Nauman, May 27 and 30, 1980," in Nauman, *Please Pay Attention Please*, 272.

21. David Joselit, *Feedback: Television against Democracy* (Cambridge, MA: MIT Press, 2000), 21.

22. Nauman, in Dercon, "Keep Taking It Apart," 309.

23. Ibid., 313.

24. The deeply parodic nature of Allan and Saul's personas suggest that the possibility of communication with a mass (or even moderately large) public was not really an issue in the program. Even if there was a sizable audience for the "show," it is hardly likely that many watched it, let alone understood it. In fact, Nauman noted that he was not particularly interested in bringing his work to "a wider audience." (Nonetheless, in his interview by Sharp, Nauman remarked that he would like to do something for network TV: "I'd like CBS to give me an hour on my terms … to present some boring material" [Sharp, "Interview with Bruce Nauman," 152]).

25. Nauman, in Sharp, "Nauman Interview," 113–114.

26. Nauman, quoted in van Bruggen, *Bruce Nauman*, 18. In an interview by Jan Butterfield, Nauman describes a similar effect in *Floating Room* of 1972, in which "people seemed to either have pretty much the same experience or they were blocking it out" (Butterfield, "Bruce Nauman: The Center of Yourself," 179).

27. Nauman, in Sharp, "Nauman Interview," 113.

28. Nauman, in Butterfield, "Bruce Nauman: The Center of Yourself," 180–181.

29. Richard Sennett, *The Fall of Public Man: On the Social Psychology of Capitalism* (New York: Vintage, 1978), 259.

Deceptive Practice

Jeffrey Weiss

"I was interested in the idea of lying, or not telling the truth," Bruce Nauman said in 1980.[1] He was speaking of *Wax Impressions of the Knees of Five Famous Artists*, a work of 1966 that contradicts itself in two ways. To begin with, it is made of fiberglass and polyester resin, not wax; moreover, the five indentations displayed across its surface were produced by Nauman's own knee.[2] For all its artlessness, *Wax Impressions* is a gloss on two forms of identity: the material identity of the object and the personal identity of its author.

The knee—as opposed to, say, the hand, a conventional metonym for the artist—is an odd choice. Perhaps it was intended to evoke, with mock solemnity, a ceremony in which the celebrity artist kneels to submit himself to a higher authority. If so, *Wax Impressions* may concern Nauman's conflicted relationship to professional art making: "I was working very little, teaching a class one night a week," he said in 1970, speaking of having left art school in 1966, "and I didn't know what to do with all that time. I think that's when I did the first casts of my body and the name parts and things like that. … I was forced to examine myself and what I was doing there."[3] In that context, the act of kneeling—performed five times in a row—is both self-inflating and self-deprecatory. The joke, however, is private: the artist conceals himself behind the lie.

The cast impression belongs to a sequence of mechanistic operations that occurred throughout the first two decades of Nauman's work. The operations are practical in their original purpose, but for Nauman they

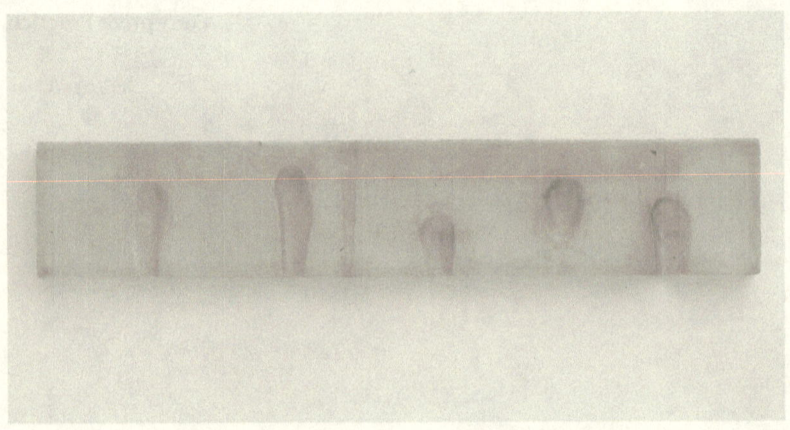

Wax Impressions of the Knees of Five Famous Artists, 1966. Fiberglass, polyester resin. 15⅝ × 85¼ × 2¾ in. (39.7 × 216.5 × 7 cm). San Francisco Museum of Modern Art, the Agnes E. Meyer and Elise S. Haas Fund and Accessions Committee Fund: gift of Collectors' Forum, Doris and Donald Fischer, Evelyn Haas, Mimi and Peter Haas, Pamela and Richard Kramlich, Elaine McKeon, Byron R. Meyer, Nancy and Steven Oliver, Helen and Charles Schwab, Norah and Norman Stone, Danielle and Brooks Walker Jr., and Pat and Bill Wilson. Photograph: Bruce Nauman.

perform no conventional role; accordingly, an inventory of the artist's works from this period reveals various utilitarian devices being put to absurd use. Some of the works are casts or templates, serving to replicate or copy. In *Neon Templates of the Left Half of My Body Taken at Ten-Inch Intervals* (1966), for example, clamplike templates purport to retain the form of the now absent body around which—according to the work's conceit—they were formed. Another device is the "storage capsule," which takes the shape of the body—or, grotesquely, the body fragment—that it is imagined to hold; *Storage Capsule for the Right Rear Quarter of My Body* (1966) is a galvanized-iron receptacle of that kind. Another is the spatial passage, which takes multiple forms: corridor, tunnel, channel, trench, and shaft. Some works in this category, such as *Live-Taped Video Corridor* (1970) and *Corridor Installation with Mirror* (1971), invite participants to walk the length of an extremely constricted space. Others ask us to imagine ourselves inside: in *Three Dead-End Adjacent Tunnels, Not Connected* (1981), the tunnels—ducts of plaster and wood—are too small to be entered, although Nauman identified these objects as "models" for large projects to be realized in the future.[4] Finally, Nauman also names a device that could be said to signify template, cast, capsule, corridor, tunnel, trench, and shaft all together: the trap. Two large time-lapse photographs are designated as such: in *Light Trap for Henry Moore, No. 1* and *No. 2* (1967), the artist used a flashlight to spin a continuous line of light, creating cocoonlike images of his own body.

The origin of the English word *deceive* traces back through Old French (*decevoir*) to the Latin verb *decipere*, which in turn is derived from two words: *de*, or "from," and *capere*, to "take," "seize," or "ensnare." To be deceived, then, is to be ensnared or trapped. The etymology suggests that "the idea of lying"—that is, the concept of deception in Nauman's work—is partly intrinsic to the work's realization as object or device. Put differently, Nauman's sculptural objects possess forms predetermined by functions; in turn, their implementation can be assigned to various types of taking—to holding and withholding, to containment and detainment. Language associates these actions with the state of having been defrauded, deluded, or misled. The act of lying is figured by the physical action of catching or having caught.

⋆ ⋆ ⋆

Varieties of deception make fleeting but significant appearances in art after 1960. Robert Morris's *Three Rulers* (1962) is a wall plaque bearing three yardsticks that hang from hooks.[5] The objects look store bought (and therefore readymade) but were actually fabricated by hand. Conspicuously, however, they differ in length, undermining the reliability on which standardization depends. (Made of gray-painted wood, they look, at first glance, like metal objects—a second lie.) In the context of advanced art practice, false "rulers"—surely a punning reference to figures of authority—insinuate a decline of trust or, more specifically, of aesthetic faith.

Jasper Johns made *Liar*, a work in gray encaustic and Sculp-metal on paper, in 1961. The title word is emblazoned in capital letters twice at the top of the work, once right side up, once inverted: LIAR. Together the two resemble a printed word accompanied by the plate or block used to make it. In fact, a note in the upper margin indicates that in another version of the work the inverted LIAR could take the form of a "wood block with raised letters." Writing in 1962, Leo Steinberg described the work's chief attributes as "the paint that denotes nothing but painting" and the simple "device for printing a useful word." *Liar*,

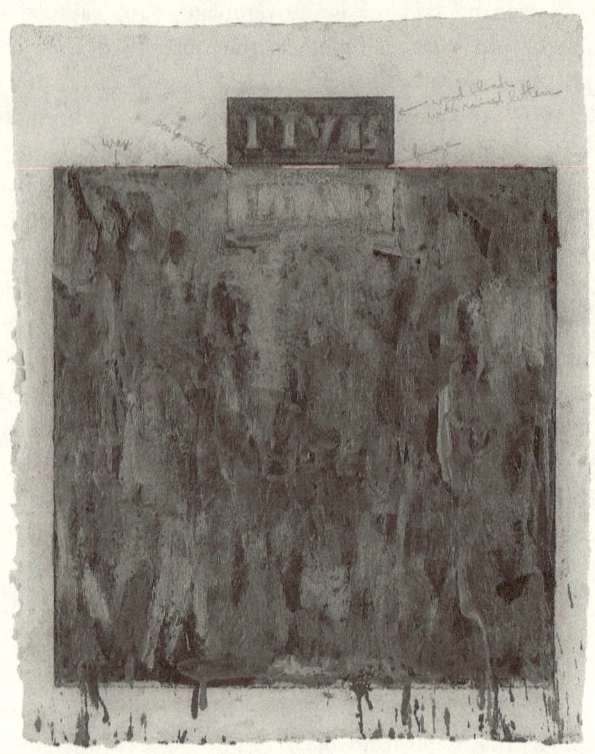

Jasper Johns, *Liar*, 1961. Encaustic, Sculp-metal, and graphite on paper. 21¼ × 17 in. (54 × 43.2 cm). Collection of Gail and Tony Ganz, Los Angeles. Art © Jasper Johns/Licensed by VAGA, New York. Photograph: Jamie Stukenberg, Professional Graphics, Inc., Rockford, IL.

he concluded, is "an implacable presence and a gaping metaphor generated by crude literal means."[6]

One historical context for *Liar* is that of painting practice itself, with reference to the legacy of the previous generation. The abstract expressionism of the 1940s and 1950s had delivered a battery of fundamental material strategies to Johns and his circle; nonetheless, with its faith in abstraction as a vehicle for heroic content, it had also proven to be an illusive model. Johns's *Liar* challenges the signifying capacity of paint as medium. Moreover, it presents the word LIAR in the form of a double: shown inverted and reversed (a method of addressing language that Nauman would soon adopt), the word as object is deprived of its discursive function; yet, as a result, its meaning—the meaning of *liar* as "counterfeit or false prophet"—is actually reduplicated. With respect to both painting and language, then, *Liar* signifies a conflict between fact and fiction, deception and faith, and does so according to the terms of an exercise in logic that dates back to ancient Greece, the liar paradox: If a liar labels himself a liar, is he then telling the truth?

Nauman's *Liar* is *Untitled (Model for Room in Perspective)* of 1966. This work achieves an illusion of three-dimensional space through a rudimentary application of one-point perspective. The title asks us to imagine that we are gazing into an empty room, yet due to an optical trick that typifies this sort of schematic image, *Model for Room* can be read in two opposing ways: as the image of a receding interior, into which we see from a slightly elevated vantage, or as the image of a protruding solid, which we view from below. This instability is related to that of a Necker cube, a simple exercise in visual perception.[7]

Nauman's work, however, is not, like the Necker cube, a bodiless diagram: made of fiberglass and polyester resin, with traces of the unrefined process of its making visibly exposed, it is a tangible object.[8] Its dimensions (28¾ by 25¾ by 8 inches) are those of an easel picture or sculptural plaque. Further, more than simply an image on a planar support, the work as object is physically shaped to correspond to the distorted representation—rather than the actuality—of the "room." Given the conventions of linear perspective, a system for projecting a spatially convincing representation of the built world onto a flat plane, *Model for Room* requires a fixed beholder. Yet in its shallow dimensionality and its conspicuous surface, the work solicits close inspection from multiple vantages, thanks to which the illusion of the depicted space is defeated.

In that it serves illusion, perspective is a form of deceit. It shows us something that isn't there or exaggerates something that is. Various groups of Nauman's works from the early to mid-1970s address the distortions of linear perspective in the context of real space. The works in one such sequence are identified by the phrase "forced [or 'enforced'] perspective." The term refers to techniques of visual distortion in photography and film that collapse or attenuate the perception of distance or scale. Forced perspective is also used in architecture: for example, the design of a staircase can exaggerate its height and length by reducing the size of the stairs as they ascend, thereby attenuating the appearance

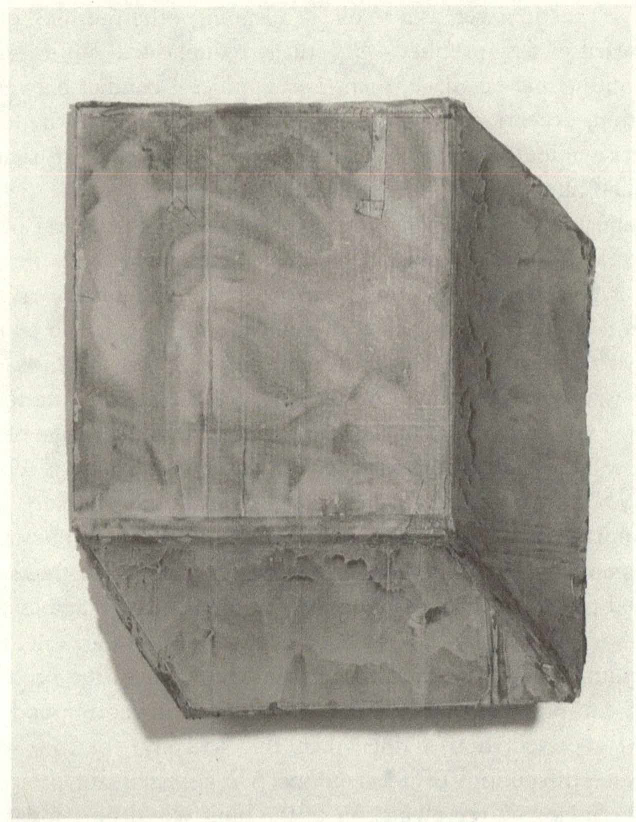

Untitled (Model for Room in Perspective), 1966. Fiberglass, polyester resin. 28¾ × 25¾ × 8 in. (73 × 65.4 × 20.3 cm). Kunstmuseum Basel. Photograph: Martin P. Bühler.

of perceptual diminution through space. Nauman's forced-perspective works consist of groups of blocklike rhombohedrons in steel, plaster, or stone, distributed in various combinations across the floor. Like cubes, these blocks have six equal faces, but each block leans as much as ten degrees off its vertical axis. The installations are intended to induce in the beholder an unstable impression of the room. By deviating slightly from a cubic form, the rhombohedral blocks warp the beholder's sensation of the regularity of the space.

Works of this kind solicit a mobile observer, as early reviews suggest.[9] A large drawing for one installation bears inscriptions that face four directions, implying that the installation itself is to be engaged from multiple vantages. Yet Nauman has described the works as "more visual than … physical": "you can stand in one spot and they do their thing to you."[10] In the installations, the distortions of perspective produce an estrangement heightened by this pull between a fixed vantage and a mobile one. With its deviation from the verticality of the cube, Nauman's block resembles the representations of cubes in illustrations for treatises on orthogonal or parallel projection, in which the cube is rendered on paper as if it were seen obliquely. Having been "forced," the distorted block seems to belong to the world of graphic representation. Yet in moving through ambient space, the beholder could arrive at a position from which a forced block would look cubic.

★ ★ ★

Linear perspective was first systematically applied to pictorial representation in Italy during the fifteenth century, when it was codified as a method for achieving unprecedented accuracy in the visual description of space. Nonetheless, as a form of veracity, perspective is acutely vexed. "In the eyes of Renaissance commentators," writes Robin Evans, "perspective was a deception because it distorted true measure; because, that is, it departed from the inalienable truths of Euclidean geometry. In the eyes of many of its twentieth-century detractors perspective is suspect because it imposes Euclid on the way we see." Eventually, philosophers and social critics—including Maurice Merleau-Ponty, Michel Foucault, and Jacques Lacan—variously characterized perspective as a form of subjugation, less an objective system of spatial representation than "an attempt to capture and colonize" our sense of sight.[11]

While techniques of perspective lay fallow during a large part of the history of twentieth-century aesthetic practice, the idea of perspective was recuperated for art after 1960, when it was critically engaged as a form of artifice—a falsehood invented to serve truth. In an unpublished text of 1967, Robert Smithson invoked the application of perspective to mapping and surveying practices, characterizing the concept of spatial infinity—a conceit on which perspective depends—as the source of an uncanny existential predicament for the perceiving subject:

> Natural space is not infinite. The surveyor imposes his artificial spaces on the landscape he is surveying, and in effect produces perspectival projects along the elevations he is mapping. In a very

> nonillusionistic sense he is constructing an illusion around himself because he is dealing directly with literal sense perceptions and turning them into mental conceptions.[12]

Smithson's conclusion reverses the relation between actuality and the projected image in Nauman's leaning blocks, but its implication is identical: tools of perception are not tools of cognition; they influence or model our relation to what we see but not necessarily to what we know. Smithson's account describes perspectival illusion as a "mental conception," an artifice within which the surveyor (who acts to determine position, border, and distance) is confined—a cage or trap.

Nauman wrote various texts for the forced-perspective works. The most elaborate, a seven-part composition included in the installation *The Consummate Mask of Rock* (1975), is an extended analysis of psychic pain. The text is explicitly based on the circular logic of Rock–Paper–Scissors, a children's game in which two participants use hand gestures representing each of the title's three elements, with each element possessing the potential to dominate another: rock breaks scissors; scissors cut paper; paper covers rock. Nauman subjects a narrow set of words and phrases to a permuting scheme of this kind that reshuffles the hierarchy among them. The basic elements are listed first; they include mask, fidelity, truth, life, cover, pain, need, desire, and human companionship, among others. The artist then employs them to compose a numbered sequence of propositions concerning self-concealment and self-exposure in a context of desire and shame:

> 1. This is my mask of fidelity to truth and life.
> 2. This is to cover the mask of pain and desire.
> 3. This is to mask the cover of need for human companionship.
> 4. This is to mask the cover.
> 5. This is to cover the mask.
> 6. This is the need of cover.
> 7. This is the need of the mask.
> 8. This is the mask of cover of need.
>   Nothing and no
> 9. No thing and no mask can cover the lack, alas.
> 10. Lack after nothing before cover revoked.
> 11. Lack before cover

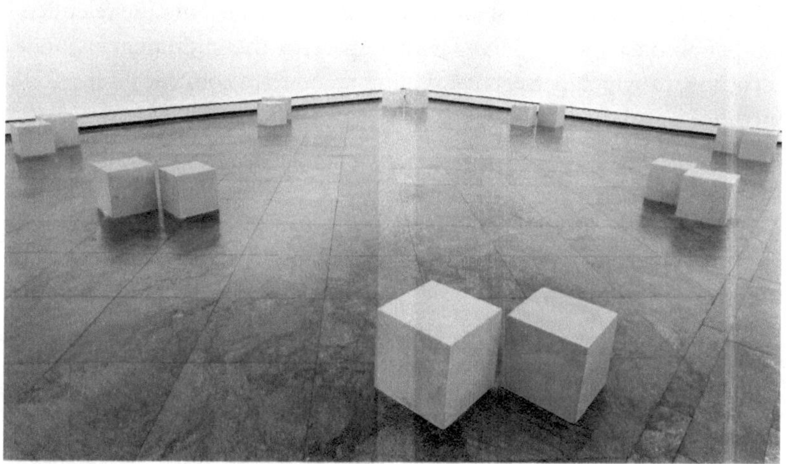

The Consummate Mask of Rock, 1975. Installation of sculpture and text. Sculpture: limestone. Eight 15-in. (38.1 cm) cubes; eight 14-in. (35.6 cm) cubes; approx. 360 × 360 in. (914.4 × 914.4 cm) overall. Text: typewriting, graphite, paper, and tape on paper. 39½ × 19½ in. (100.3 × 49.5 cm), framed. Private collection. Image courtesy Sperone Westwater, New York.

paper covers rock
rock breaks mask
alas, alack …

Nauman's text ends in despair. Proposition 18: "This is my painless mask that fails to touch my face but floats before the surface of my skin my eyes my teeth my tongue." Proposition 21, the final one: "PEOPLE DIE OF EXPOSURE."[13]

In his reading of *The Consummate Mask of Rock*, one critic cautions against ascribing existential significance to the work. Rather, he detects a "convoluted pattern or vortex of distortions which incarnates the generic nothingness in the abyss of each personal lack."[14] Yet, historically speaking, allegories of identity dating from antiquity to the modern era (the figure of Nemo, or "no man," for example, or that of the "double") have long made ample room for abyssal voids of this kind. In any case, we observe that Nauman annotated the drawing for *Forced Perspective II* (1975) with the words "FORCED PERSPECTIVES: OPEN MIND/

CLOSED MIND/PARALLEL MIND/EQUAL MIND/(analogy + symbolism)." Inexorable repetition obstructs the narrative conventions of allegory, but it does not obviate the existential so much as distill it from the relentlessness of abstract means. Here, with respect to the authoritarian model according to which perspective is illusion and trap, constructed space is a province of solitude.

* * *

Nauman's early objects represent a mechanics of withholding and ensnarement. The devices he uses—cast, capsule, corridor, tunnel, and the like—are forms of traps, objects of confinement, restraint, displacement, and other states of estrangement. With their dead ends, "false perspectives," and forced-space involutions, these objects and installations openly belie the immediate aesthetic inheritance of minimal art. From the presumptions of clarity and literalism that attend the minimalist object, Nauman extracts a set of false claims; the precise geometry of his work openly serves, instead, irrational or perverse ends.

In 1989, Nauman said the chief concern of *The Consummate Mask of Rock* was artistic self-representation: "What is masked and what is not—that tension between what is given and what is held back."[15] I take the mechanics of this description—the relation between giving and withholding—to be an extension of the operations of the early devices. Indeed, in the same interview, the artist used those very terms to account for one such device: the sculptural mold, which he used to cast fiberglass objects in 1965. From the casting process (in which the mold reverses the object it is made to cast), Nauman extrapolated implications for the work's content: "I like the way front/back confuses the information. Not knowing what you're supposed to look at keeps you at a distance from the art while the art keeps you at a distance from me; the combination produces a whole set of tensions one can learn to exploit."[16] The distancing function of concealment—of front and back—in Nauman's formulation is a sort of duplicity, which, with its implication of double or two-faced behavior, recalls the analogical origin of the word *deception*—the word's figural dependence on the operation of the trap.

A principle of twofoldedness, then, governs Nauman's recourse to the device: an object or form is derived from a procedure that can be said both to put forth and to conceal or misrepresent. The principle even supports a kind of epistemology. At times, Nauman intensifies his status as unreliable narrator by identifying a form of discontinuity that lies within his work overall, an element represented, he says, by "two kinds of information." Speaking in 1980 of a corridor work, for example, where the beholder is confronted with a live-feed surveillance image of himself or herself on a video monitor, the artist explains, "You have a piece of visual information and a piece of kinetic, or kinesthetic, information and they don't line up. … The piece is finally about that."[17] According to Nauman, these oppositions produce "tensions": between sensation and image; between private and public space; and, in the case of the tunnels, between the sculptural object and its function as maquette. Using an analogy he had devised ten years earlier to describe the live feed, Nauman compares the effect to that of "going up the stairs in the dark and either having an extra stair that you didn't expect or not having one that you thought was going to be there—that kind of misstep that surprises you every time it happens. Even when you knew how those pieces were working."[18] Ultimately, the work's deception, once exposed, is supported by the willing suspension of disbelief.

* * *

Nauman's *Thumb Start* (2013) is based on the illusion of the "floating finger," a simple effect that we can perform by holding our hands before our eyes while focusing on a point beyond them, causing the appearance of a finger suspended in space. In the work, a video in which the artist's hands are seen in superimposed images from both front and back against a white ground, Nauman engages in a simple counting exercise. Corresponding fingers on each hand (four fingers plus thumb) are extended in changing combinations; these combinations are recited by the artist—"combinations of one," "combinations of two," and so on through five—in a deadpan incantation. By superimposing images, the video simulates the rudimentary optical effect of the floating finger. The projected image is an illusion of an illusion, producing a double disembodiment: that of the hands, which are cropped at the wrist, and that of the detached finger—an eerie, even grotesque figment.

Thumb Start opposes illusion (the floating finger) to plainness (the recitation of numbers). It also opposes body to sense. Hand gestures can constitute a language of signs, yet the work's form—counting, repetition, rote labor, and a certain awkwardness of execution—frustrates symbolic meaning. For Friedrich Nietzsche, "truths are illusions about

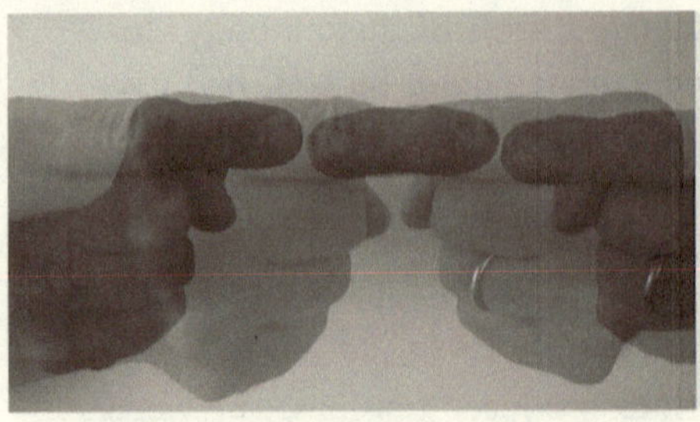
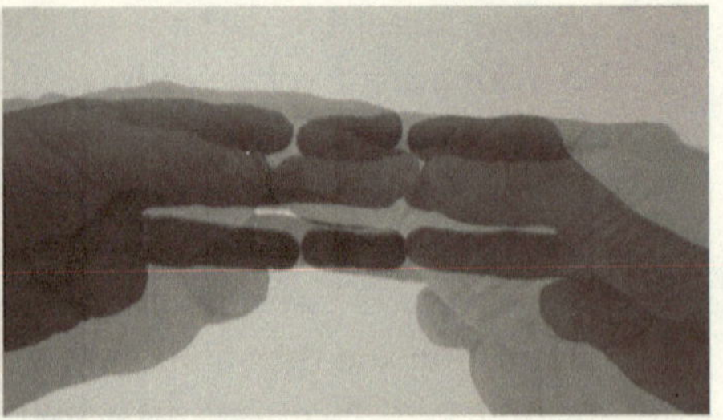

Thumb Start, 2013. High-definition (HD) video installation (color, mono sound, continuous play, synchronous loop); two HD video sources, two HD video projectors, two speakers. 4 min., 21 sec. Image courtesy the artist and Sperone Westwater, New York.

which one has forgotten that this is what they are; metaphors which are worn out and without sensuous power; coins which have lost their pictures and now matter only as metal, no longer as coins."[19] In Nauman's recent work, the artist submits his aging body to a variety of prosaic activities and tasks, as if staging an attempt to retrieve the long-lost legitimacy of expressive means. Yet the logic of the practice continues to hold: abstraction still traps the real, and deception still underwrites an entropic theory of knowledge.

Notes

1. Nauman, in Michele de Angelus, "Interview with Bruce Nauman, May 27 and 30, 1980," in Bruce Nauman, *Please Pay Attention Please: Bruce Nauman's Words*, ed. Janet Kraynak (Cambridge, MA: MIT Press, 2003), 250.

2. See ibid.

3. Nauman, in Willoughby Sharp, "Nauman Interview, 1970," in Nauman, *Please Pay Attention Please*, 117–118.

4. See de Angelus, "Interview with Bruce Nauman," 269, 276–77. See also Christopher Cordes, "Talking with Bruce Nauman: An Interview, 1989," in Nauman, *Please Pay Attention Please*, 368.

5. The obvious model for Robert Morris's *Three Rulers* is Marcel Duchamp's *Three Standard Stoppages* (1913–1914), a demonstration of what Duchamp described as "canned chance" (*The Complete Works of Marcel Duchamp*, ed. Arturo Schwarz [New York: Delano Greenidge Editions, 1997], 595).

6. Leo Steinberg, "Jasper Johns: The First Seven Years of His Art" (1962), in *Other Criteria: Confrontations with Twentieth-Century Art* (Chicago: University of Chicago Press, 2007), 19.

7. The Necker cube was named for Louis-Albert Necker, the Swiss crystallographer who published the illusion in 1832.

8. The history of perspectival and "oblique" drawing distinguishes between diagram (transparent two-dimensional rendering) and model (embodied representation) in this way. See Massimo Scolari, *Oblique Drawing: A History of Anti-perspective* (Cambridge, MA: MIT Press, 2012), chap. 6.

9. See, for example, Kenneth Baker, "Bruce Nauman at Castelli, Sonnabend, and Sperone Westwater Fischer," *Art in America* 65, no. 2 (March–April 1977): 111.

10. Nauman, in Robert C. Morgan, "Interview with Bruce Nauman" (1987), in *Bruce Nauman*, ed. Robert C. Morgan (Baltimore: Johns Hopkins University Press, 2002), 267.

11. Robin Evans, *The Projective Cast: Architecture and Its Geometries* (Cambridge, MA: MIT Press, 2000), 124–125.

12. Robert Smithson, "Pointless Vanishing Points" (1967), in *Robert Smithson: The Collected Writings*, ed. Jack Flam (Berkeley: University of California Press, 1996), 358–359.

13. Bruce Nauman, "The Consummate Mask of Rock, 1975," in Nauman, *Please Pay Attention Please*, 86–87.

14. Sławomir Masłoń, "Nauman: Deprivation and Overload," in *Stating the Obvious: Celan—Beckett—Nauman* (Katowice, Poland: Silesia University Press, 2012), 93–95.

15. Nauman, in Cordes, "Talking with Bruce Nauman," 373.

16. Ibid., 350.

17. Nauman, in de Angelus, "Interview with Bruce Nauman," 264–265. On the implications of information theory for deception or misdirection in Nauman's work, see Janet Kraynak, *Nauman Reiterated* (Minneapolis: University of Minnesota Press, 2014), 67–87.

18. Nauman, in de Angelus, "Interview with Bruce Nauman," 264.

19. Friedrich Nietzsche, "On Truth and Lie in an Extra-moral Sense" (1873), in *The Portable Nietzsche*, ed. and trans. Walter Kaufmann (New York: Penguin Books, 1976), 46–47.

Small Fires Burning: Bruce Nauman and the Activation of Conceptual Art

Taylor Walsh

In 1964, Ed Ruscha's *Various Small Fires* was published in an edition of four hundred and sold for the retail price of around $3. The slim, offset-printed volume was Ruscha's second artist's book, and it helped to solidify the structure that would define his photographic output. The cover text provides a frank synopsis of the pictures inside—fifteen slightly grainy photos of commonplace, domestic-scaled fires.[1] Each minor blaze emanates from a familiar household source: a gas stove's burner, a Zippo lighter, a candle in a china holder, a faintly lurid splay of hot dogs browning on a barbecue.

Reissued several times and sold in specialty stores around the country, Ruscha's publication was priced to move and open to multiple readings. "After a book leaves here," he said, "it's for whatever anyone wants to use it for."[2] His remark implies an invitation, or even a tacit challenge—one that fellow California artist Bruce Nauman relished in a book of his own. Four years after *Various Small Fires* appeared, Nauman used his copy for kindling, ripping out the pages to ignite them one by one, then photographing the charred remnants on his studio floor. He brought the negatives to a print shop in San Francisco to order an edition at his own expense, and arranged the shots to form an oversize, foldout grid.[3] Subjecting Ruscha's work to an aggressive form of circular logic, Nauman made a book about burning a book about burning.

As a work of art predicated on another's cancellation, Nauman's *Burning Small Fires* (1968) owes a clear debt to Robert Rauschenberg's example. *Erased de Kooning Drawing* (1953) has come to signify a passing

VARIOUS

SMALL

FIRES

Ed Ruscha, cover of *VARIOUS SMALL FIRES*, 1964. Artist's book. 7 × 5½ inches (17.8 × 14 cm). © Ed Ruscha. Courtesy Gagosian.

of the torch, as an aesthetic of withdrawal supplanted abstract expressionism's loaded gesture.[4] Yet Nauman's book comports less well with narratives of generational conflict. Ruscha was the more famous artist but only four years Nauman's senior, so *Burning Small Fires* amounts more to a fraternal rivalry than to an Oedipal one. The significance of the work is more ambivalent, its motivations less secure, and the statements furnished by the artists themselves don't help to pin it down. Asked to comment on Nauman's unauthorized take, Ruscha laughed it off, saying, "Everything gets its due, right? … I think he liked *Various Small Fires*."[5] Nauman, for his part, gave an even more clipped account: "*Burning Small Fires* was a response to Ed Ruscha's book," he would recall.[6]

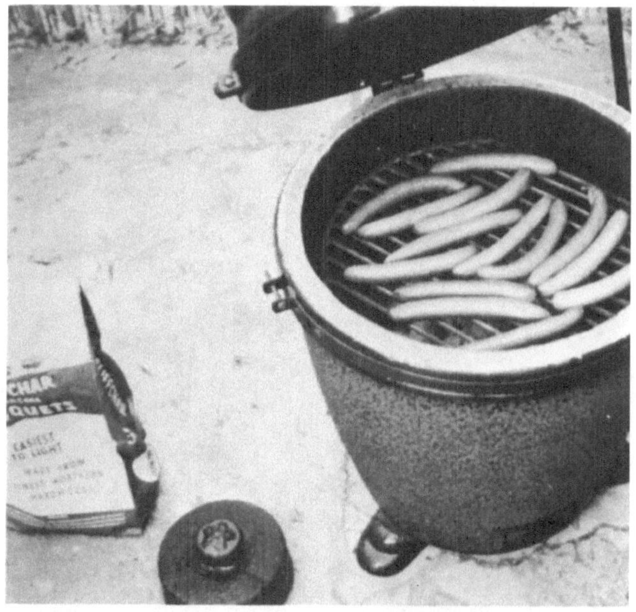

Ed Ruscha, interior page from *VARIOUS SMALL FIRES*, 1964. Artist's book. 7 × 5½ inches (17.8 × 14 cm). © Ed Ruscha. Courtesy Gagosian.

These were the only public comments the artists made about the incident, and neither is particularly illuminating: Nauman's bland characterization of his work as a "response" glosses over the damage done, and Ruscha's genial spin too hastily resolves critique into compliment.[7] Such reticence also parallels the art-historical neglect of *Burning Small Fires*, which has been treated as a minor skirmish, best appreciated at the level of anecdote. But Nauman's book has an urgency of execution that repays critical attention, and marks it as a peculiarly contentious episode in the annals of West Coast art.

The work's antagonism was rare for Nauman, though its citational aspect was not. "I think what I've tried to do," he told Marcia Tucker, "is to make art that wasn't an extension of or in opposition to other art."[8] Yet *Burning Small Fires* is clearly at odds with the sui generis feel he sought, and it joins a small group of 1960s works conceived in explicit dialogue with his peers. His first year out of art school, 1967, saw several such commemorations: *William T. Wiley or Ray Johnson Trap*, *Westermann's Ear*, *Light Trap for Henry Moore*.[9] The Nauman scholarship has taken an interest of late in these acts of aesthetic tribute—what Jo Applin

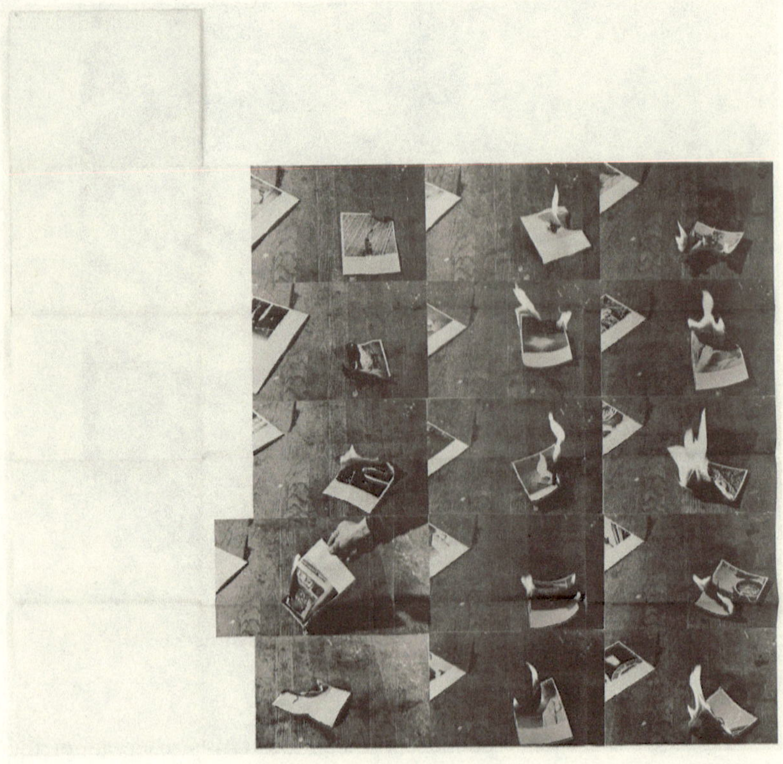

Interior from *Burning Small Fires*, 1968. Artist's book. One sheet: 37⅛ × 49 in. (94.3 × 124.5 cm), folded to 12½ × 9½ in. (31.8 × 24.1 cm). Publisher unknown, San Francisco. Edition size unknown. Image courtesy of bpk Bildagentur/Kunstsammlung Nordhein Westfalen, Düsseldorf. Photo by Achim Kukulies/Art Resource, NY.

refers to as "potlatch exchanges" and Robert Slifkin calls "non-parodic, sympathetic memorialization."[10] Nauman's attitude toward each dedicatee has a slightly different cast: the works for Westermann and Johnson are deemed "affectionate" and "playful," while the Moore is "elegiac."[11] But all three are safely classified as gestures of homage, born of fascination or a genuine respect. With *Burning Small Fires*, Nauman reaches once more for another artist's oeuvre, but the previous dynamics of quotation and inheritance no longer seem to apply. The Ruscha book is subject to much harsher appraisal, unraveled from within, making *Burning* the most rigorous—and scathing—of Nauman's appropriations.

Ruscha's text gives both fodder and the rationale for its own assault, as Nauman cannibalizes a work of conceptual art to expose its blind spots. For although it has never been read as such, *Burning Small Fires* was a timely project—loosely adhering to existing conventions lifted from both art and activism. On the surface, each photobook has all the hallmarks of conceptual practice: rule-bound procedure, systematic recording, grayscale color scheme, deadpan gaze. But where Ruscha claims to treat burning as "absolutely neutral"—an "introverted" and "*meaningless*" subject—Nauman restores some of the ritual power that fire then held in the culture of protest.[12] This essay measures the distance in tone and technique between the original work and its destructive double, as an early-'60s aesthetic of relentless banality gave way to more volatile forces. If we read Nauman's book in the terms laid out by the visual vocabulary of its time, the work becomes more closely entwined with the events of that tumultuous decade, in which both the image and the act of burning played decisive roles.

★ ★ ★

Both artists begin their books innocuously enough: their card-stock covers list three-word titles that dictate their contents in advance. As Margaret Iversen's scholarship on Ruscha has emphasized, his titles serve as a set of instructions, a kind of design brief or governing framework that the photographs realize after the fact.[13] Nauman was likely familiar with a 1965 item in *Artforum* in which Ruscha stressed this unusual order of operations: "The title came before I even thought about the pictures. … [It] became like a fantasy rule in my mind that I had to follow."[14] The elder artist would return time and again to this pose of "simply following through": "The books were easy to do once I established the format. … [E]ach [picture] could be plugged into a system I had."[15]

So Ruscha's titles are shortened directives mandating what's to come, though in his books that action is merely implied, while Nauman adds the verb. Ruscha begins with *various*—a hazy adjective that conveys open quantity and disparate quality—while Nauman foregrounds the act of *burning* with his use of the present participle. That focus on the expenditure of energy—on "process"—feels indebted to his contemporary Richard Serra, whose *Verb List* (1967–1968) tallied the physical labors from which his work would spring.[16] But Nauman's book also belongs to a less-codified lineage of artistic uses of fire. A sampling from 1968 alone captures its signifying range: from Fluxus artist Ben Vautier's *Total Art Matchbox*, with instructions to "use these matchs [*sic*] to destroy

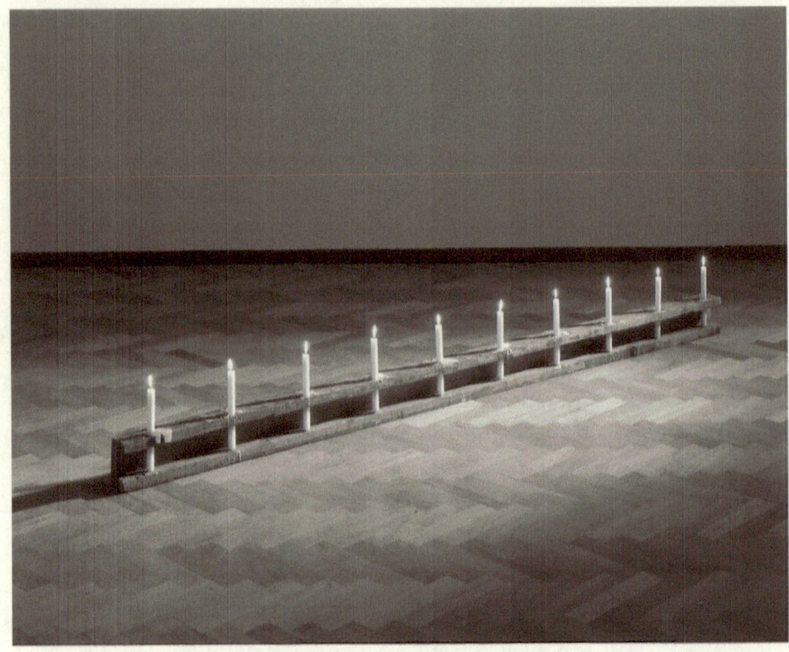

Richard Serra, *Candle Piece*, 1968. Wood with candles. Wood support: 5 × 144 × 13½ inches (12.7 × 365.8 × 8.9 cm); height with candles varies. Collection Stedelijk Museum Amsterdam.

all art [in] museums," to Lawrence Weiner's written appeal to detonate firecrackers in the corners of a gallery, to Serra's *Candle Piece*, the post-minimal precedent that Nauman is sure to have known.[17] *Candle Piece* attempts to rid sculpture of metaphor, letting hot wax behave as it will. Yet, as Benjamin Buchloh has noted, the work carries a somewhat "archaic inflection," as an air of the devotional still clings to this industrial altar.[18] Like the Serra, Nauman's work investigates the mechanics of a controlled burn, but his illicit doings undercut the solemnity of Serra's, leavening *Candle Piece*'s manner as he radicalizes its steps.

That use of real fire as an agent of change has a catalyzing function.[19] *Burning Small Fires* mirrors the Ruscha text's premise and shares in its task-based, automatic quality. The structural kinship between the two books is amplified by a chain of formal echoes, as Nauman singes Ruscha's photographs in the same spot where the original fire appeared. A great deal of stagecraft has gone into Nauman's seemingly reckless act, and each photograph's careful setup permits us to scrutinize these symmetries.[20] When process is superimposed over image, the indexical traces of actual fires threaten to consume their fixed portrayals: the flare shot from a benzene canister is reverse ignited, the S-curved flame from a book of matches is twinned by its real-time counterpart, and a lit cigar is reduced to ash along with the head of the man who smokes it. Such wickedly precise duplications seem to underline the work's derisive stance, but the paired flames also help draw distinctions between the artists' respective projects. Ruscha's benign combustions strike the viewer as routine; each *Various Small Fire* is unremarkable, sanctioned and contained. Nauman's decision to burn a book, then, is more deviant by far, an intentional destruction of property that verges on iconoclasm.

Nauman seems to own up to this hectoring tone through a quirk of cover design, wrapping the title around the book's spine to nudge several letters onto the back. "Burning Small Fires" is thus legible only when the book is splayed open; otherwise, it reads "urning all ires." Breaking words in strange places slows down comprehension and makes this simple phrase difficult to parse. Nauman's use of wayward spacing recurs in subsequent books, *CLEA RSKY* and *L A AIR*, each a bound stack of monochromes shot as long exposures of cloudless atmosphere.[21] But "urning all ires" is more sophisticated wordplay, engaging the aural register. Like Marcel Duchamp's assisted readymade *L.H.O.O.Q.*, the abridged title looks like nonsense but hangs together when spoken aloud. "Urning" mines the slippery relation between appearance, sound, and sense—an errant spelling that toys with meaning and lets us free-associate. The idea of "earning ire" is consistent with the hostility of Nauman's gesture, and perhaps this phonetic reading admits to the perversity of the act. Or it may have been directed at the object of his own "ire," as if to say that Ruscha's book deserved what it got.[22]

Book burning often signifies the quashing of dissent, conjuring thoughts of fascist purges or *Fahrenheit 451*.[23] But with *Various Small Fires*, Ruscha had published nothing to warrant the censor's match—nothing coarse or divisive or galling; no significant statements of any kind. Briony Fer has linked Ruscha's archival impulse to the format of the list: a series of loose elements rattled off in no particular order.[24] Grouped without hierarchy or transition, Ruscha's photographs made "a non-statement with a no-style," he insisted, comprising "absolutely neutral material ... simply a collection of 'facts.'"[25] His pages form a

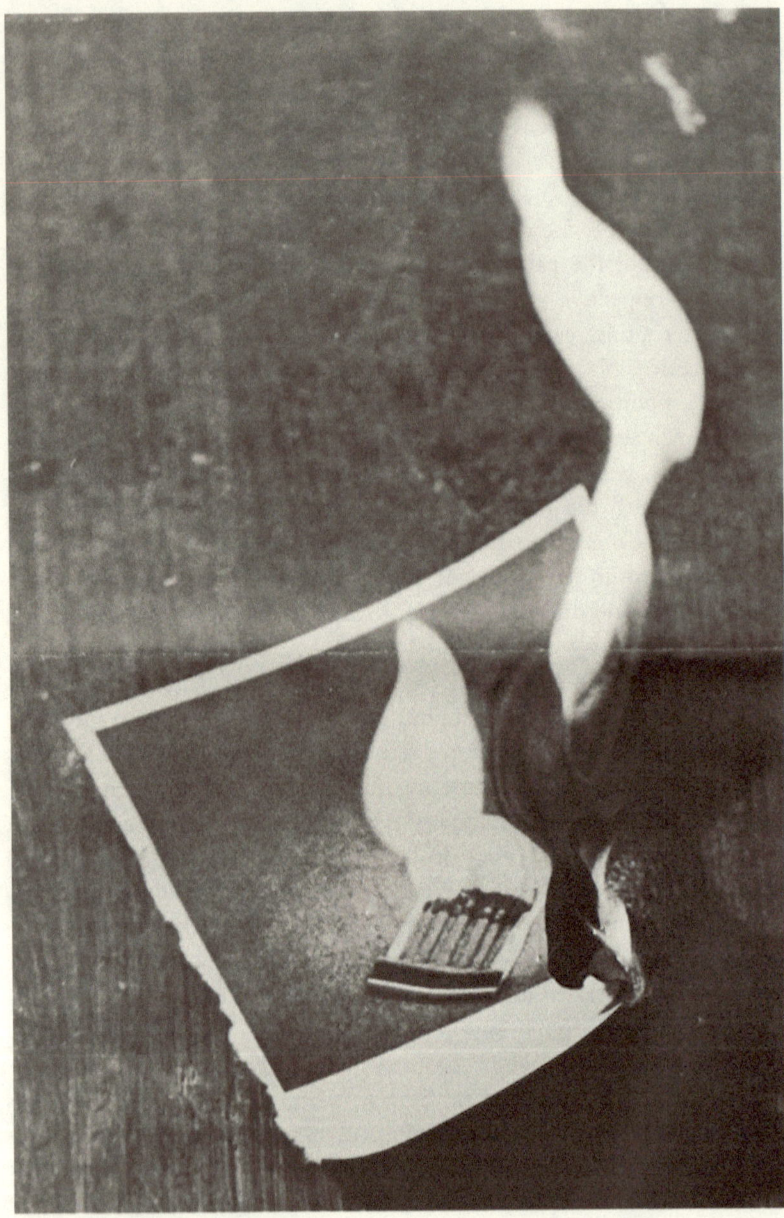

Interior detail from *Burning Small Fires*, 1968. Artist's book. One sheet: 37⅛ × 49 in. (94.3 × 124.5 cm), folded to 12½ × 9½ in. (31.8 × 24.1 cm). Publisher unknown, San Francisco. Edition size unknown.

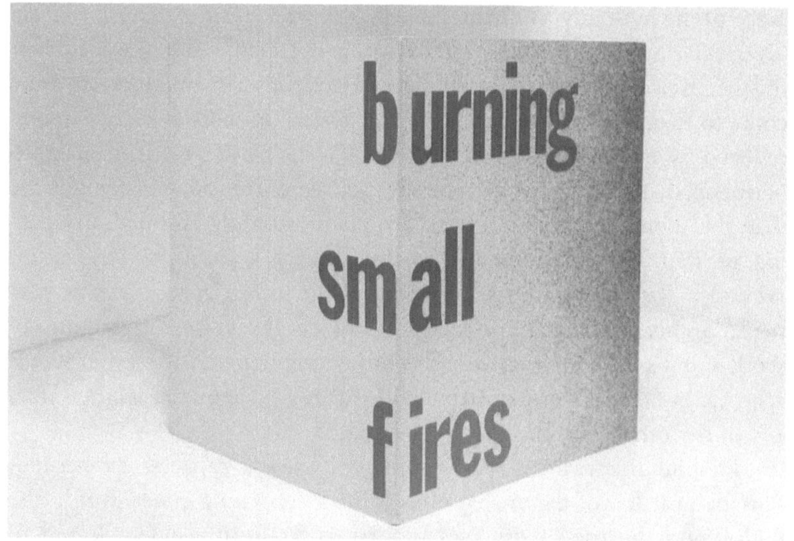

Cover of *Burning Small Fires*, 1968. Artist's book. One sheet: 37⅛ × 49 in. (94.3 × 124.5 cm), folded to 12½ × 9½ in. (31.8 × 24.1 cm). Publisher unknown, San Francisco. Edition size unknown.

matrix of waiting compartments into which anything can be slotted, so the books become strings of interchangeable parts that refuse to add up to a narrative. Describing his arbitrary selection criteria in 1973, Eleanor Antin said the artist was "committed to … a casual, slight structure, with apparent idiosyncrasy and superficial dopiness."[26] The deliberate whimsy that Antin describes is heightened by *Various Small Fires*'s final shot of a glass of milk—an odd, perplexing exception that proves the inscrutability of the rule.[27] The milk is a fly in the ointment, inserted just to throw things off, and it's the only page of the text that Nauman doesn't burn. Skipping over this non sequitur lets Nauman uphold the logic of his own project and could betray a certain distaste for the randomness of Ruscha's.

Of course, within the field of limitless options, patterns do emerge, and Ruscha's best-known books plot a topographic survey of his adopted city. The artist treats the architecture of Los Angeles as a kind of "ready-made,"[28] and photography merely as a vehicle for capturing its low-slung façades and urban sprawl.[29] Each book follows a formula in which some unit of measure—either vague or unduly specific—precedes a piece of the built environment: *Some Los Angeles Apartments*, *A Few Palm Trees*, *Nine Swimming Pools*, *Thirty-Four Parking Lots*.[30] Any one specimen of stucco-clad housing feels trifling and generic. Yet in aggregate they come to manifest LA's defining trait: an overall monotony only partially relieved by tawdry surface details. But *Various Small Fires* is even more hermetic than these cursory guidebooks, venturing no farther outside than the suburban patio. Each drab vignette is tightly cropped, presenting its item free of context—isolated against a more or less vacant ground.[31] Ruscha himself acknowledged the airless quality of this particular archive, saying: "The image of fire has always been strong in my work and it's just culminated in this little book here. … It kind of stands apart … because it's more introverted, I guess, … more *meaningless* than any of the other [books]."[32]

Despite the real hazards burning poses—its capacity to harm—Ruscha's catalog of flammable objects has a deadening effect. But in the mid-1960s, the use of fire as a motif was far from accidental, and to classify it like pools or palm trees required the suppression of key examples to keep the archive neutral. Certainly from Nauman's vantage in 1968, Ruscha's roster of apolitical flames would seem to rely on constitutive exclusions. The setting of fires was endemic to the period's upheaval, and its image figured prominently in the visual culture of the era. The struggle for civil rights across the United States incited tragic retaliations, including the fire-bombing of a Freedom Riders' bus in Alabama in 1961, and Malcolm Browne's iconic photo of a Vietnamese monk's self-immolation won a slew of awards in 1963 and '64.[33] Closer to home, the Watts riots of 1965 brought widespread arson to Los Angeles, leaving parts of the city ablaze for several days. As Joan Didion recounted in 1968, "At the time of the Watts riots what struck the imagination most indelibly were the fires. For days one could drive the Harbor Freeway and see the city on fire. … The city burning is Los Angeles's deepest image of itself."[34]

Such fires were deadly and devastating, tied to the decade's most pressing conflicts—yet even small fires could be politically consequential. The practice of burning draft cards began in 1964, the year Ruscha's book was made, and intensified in the period leading up to Nauman's version.[35] This performative act of resistance became a federal offense in 1965—a law that quickly backfired, as the tactic only increased in vehemence and visibility.[36] Soon such images would grace the covers of national magazines, from the left-leaning San Francisco–based journal *Ramparts* to that most mainstream weekly, the *Saturday Evening Post.*[37] The disembodied hands of the *Ramparts* cover—draft cards cocked "in a kind of New Left salute"[38]—bear a striking resemblance to Nauman's own, as it breaches the largest cell of an otherwise uniform grid, holding a smoldering Ruscha photo of a stovetop.

Indeed, the figure of pinched fingers clutching a flaming slip of paper became emblematic of antiwar sentiment, repeated across a range of printed matter and distilled into a logo for the peace movement. A 1968 leaflet promoting "National Turn in Your Draft Card Day" features a militant Statue of Liberty, who flashes a peace sign and trades her customary torch for a burning card. And the *Fuck the Draft* poster—then in wide circulation—voiced disgust with conscription in no uncertain terms, pairing that caustic slogan with a photograph of a young man completing the act.[39] Nauman's dealings with Ruscha risk coming off as an insular prank, a one-liner whose cleverness is quickly exhausted. But the work has an intuitive linkage with more activist maneuvers, tapping into the antiauthoritarian vein so central to the '60s. *Burning Small Fires* rhymes its recursive gesture with the iconography of civil disobedience.

If there is a political valence to Nauman's reading of Ruscha, it is redoubled in his choice of medium. Though *Burning Small Fires* presents as a book, its pages cannot be thumbed through. The reader who opens it does not find the typical discrete leaves bound along an axial spine, but rather a jarringly oversize poster that unfurls to 16 times the cover's measurements.[40] The awkwardness of this ballooning interior recalls Claes Oldenburg's ode to "art that unfolds like a map … which expands like an accordion, which you spill dinner on, like an old table cloth."[41] Adopting the book's exterior guise while its contents extend beyond it, Nauman denies the singularity and tactile communion afforded by Ruscha's volumes. And while *Burning Small Fires*'s vestigial cover interferes with proper hanging, the sheer size of the poster alludes to its destination on a wall. In 1968, the year that Nauman's book was published, Sol LeWitt began drawing directly on the wall and remarked: "The wall is understood as an absolute space, like the page of a book; [but] one is public, the other private."[42] If Ruscha's scale is intimate, Nauman's is architectural, accommodating a social, collective reception in place of an individual reader.

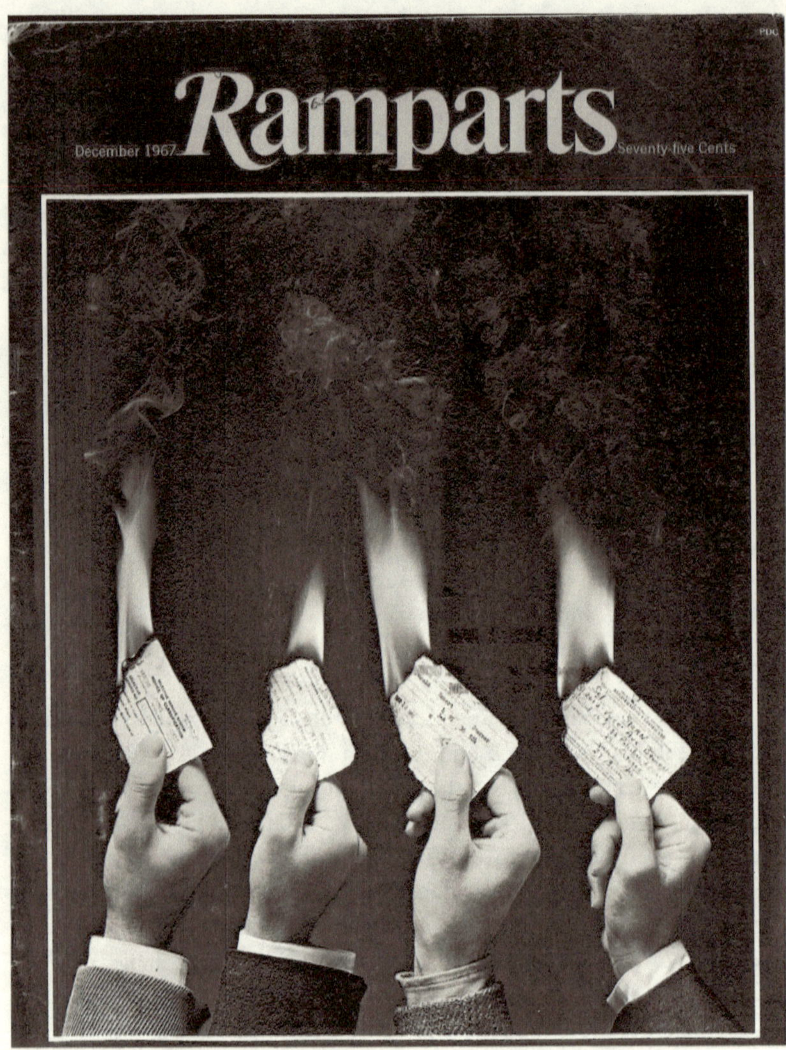

Cover of *Ramparts* magazine, December 1967.

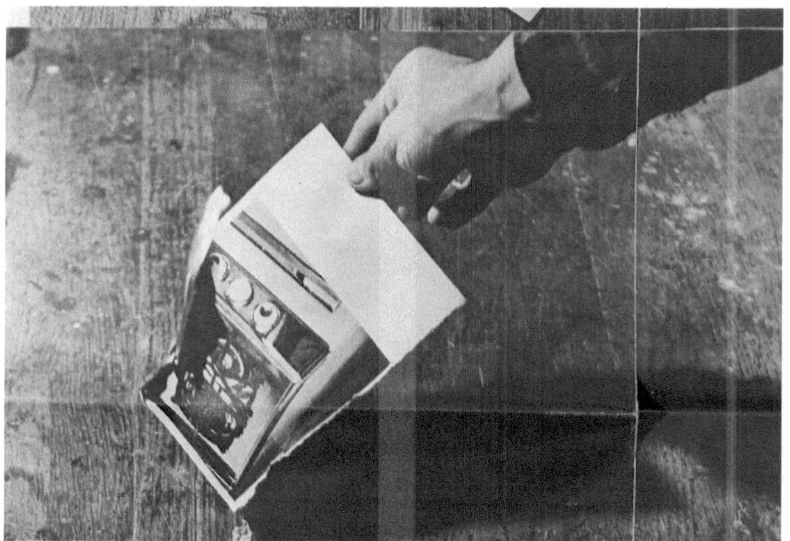

Interior detail from *Burning Small Fires*, 1968. Artist's book. One sheet: 37⅛ × 49 in. (94.3 × 124.5 cm), folded to 12½ × 9½ in. (31.8 × 24.1 cm). Publisher unknown, San Francisco. Edition size unknown.

That Nauman would be drawn to the poster format in the late 1960s is not surprising: commentators referred to 1968 as the year of "postermania" and "the poster craze."[43] From Haight-Ashbury to the Museum of Modern Art, the medium was experiencing a swift resurgence, as US sales figures topped $1 million per month and artists took increasing notice.[44] A low-cost, nimble conveyor of messages, the poster had a particular currency among the youth and antiwar movements. *Burning Small Fires* is free of text and somewhat cryptic in intention, so it skirts the poster's usual directness and any hint of propaganda. But its dimensions alone subtly channel the format's long-standing ties to agitation,[45] as what first appears to be a standard artist's book conceals a more public form of address.

Ruscha's books have been read as touchstones of early conceptual art, not least because of their commercial printing techniques and ease of dissemination.[46] The book contributed to conceptualism's vision of the art world as decentered and democratized, joining the magazines, postcards, and other ephemera that bypassed the gallery system. Distinct

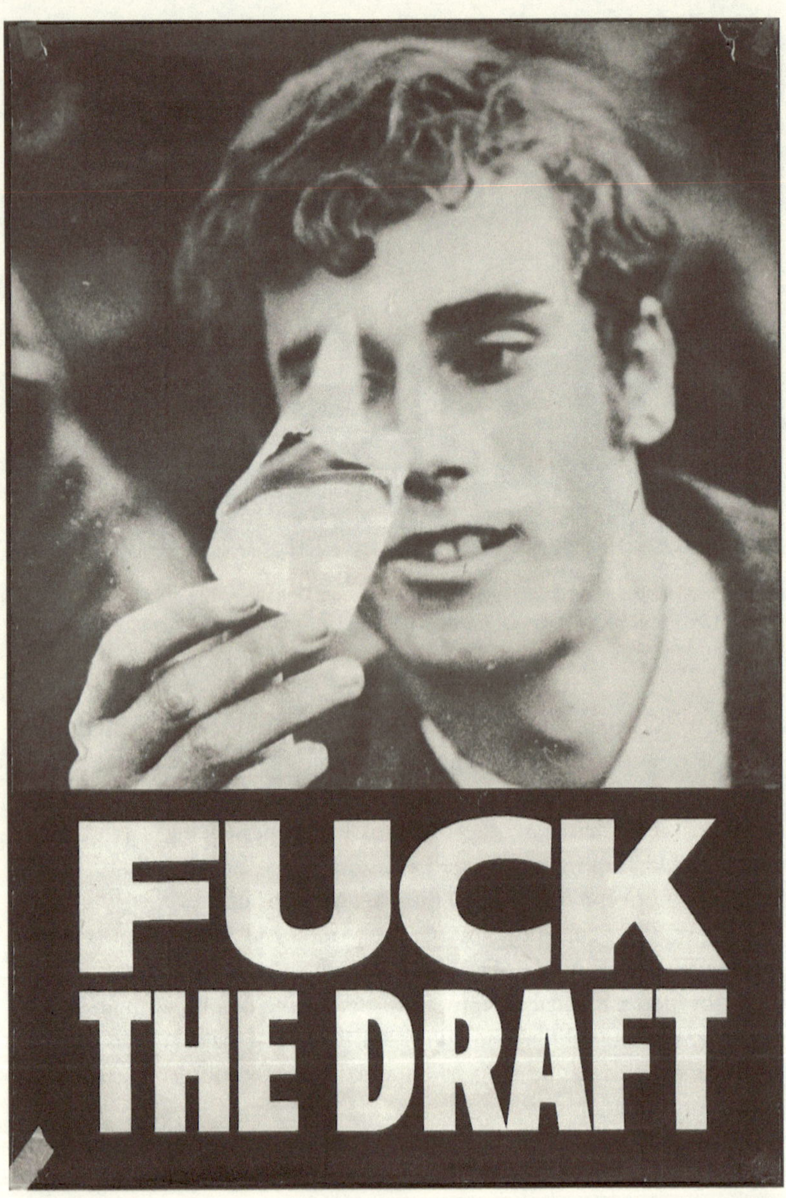

Kiyoshi Kuromiya, *Fuck the Draft*, 1968. Offset lithographic poster. 30 × 20 in. (75.6 × 51.2 cm). Published by the Dirty Linen Corp. Image courtesy University of Michigan Library (Special Collections Library, Joseph A. Labadie Collection).

from earlier models of the *livre d'artiste* that maintained an aura of the exceptional, the humble paperbacks of the 1960s challenged the art market's overvaluation of the unique and precious object. But for all the utopian potential of the book as populist multiple, such works were often beset by a nagging hermeticism—the aversion to significant reference seen in Ruscha's low-stakes fires. And from an early date, critics struggled to square conceptualism's egalitarian forms with its tautological, indifferent content.

By the 1970s, some of the genre's chief proponents had noted this discrepancy. No less a champion of conceptual art than Lucy Lippard ended her anthology *Six Years* with a caution—against the "ghetto mentality" that would sequester it in "a narrow and incestuous art world."[47] In the following decades, these objections were sharpened and refined as artists and historians worked to gauge the movement's legacy. Echoes of Lippard can be heard in Jeff Wall's chagrin at what he terms conceptual art's "terrible contradiction": its inability "to reinvent social content through its socialization of technique."[48] Victor Burgin offered an even more damning verdict, balking at photoconceptualism's "disavowal of modern history" and its "total failure to be about anything of consequence."[49] Wall may well have had Ruscha's books in mind when he railed: "The grey volumes of conceptualism are filled with somber ciphers, which express primarily the *in*expressibility of socially critical thought in the form of art."[50]

The sense of letdown fueling these critiques is intensified with hindsight, but I would argue that such skepticism is already latent in *Burning Small Fires.* By subjecting Ruscha's book to the kind of violence it refuses to show, Nauman alludes to the limits of that model and to the real consequences of burning. Yet any contemporary reference remains oblique, haunting his piece at the margins. As Julia Bryan-Wilson's important work on the art of the Vietnam era has confirmed, adversarial politics could take "forms not legibly antiwar in any conventional way,"[51] and the historian's challenge is to restore these period meanings to an object without overreading. To be clear: I would not go so far as to assign intention to the comparison with draft cards I've drawn, nor is it my aim to rebrand Nauman's book as a pacifist manifesto. Although his Bay Area, art-school milieu was a hotbed of antiwar activism, his on-the-record statements do little to clarify his own involvement with the counterculture.[52] Such citations would have to be inferred by a Vietnam-era viewer primed to see them, emanating—almost subliminally—from the object's form and structure.

To ascribe a politics to an artist as guarded as Nauman is a tricky business, and critics have shied away from doing so until his work of the 1980s, with quasi-commemorative sculptures such as *South America Triangle* (1981) that he says were inspired by accounts of torture.[53] The Nauman literature tends to lean on biography to shore up its interpretive claims, alleging only what can be secured through the books he's read, the assertions he's made.[54] Political readings thus come easily to these ominous hanging chairs; less so to his art of the '60s, where such direct evidence is lacking. My efforts to link the early work to the world need a more speculative tack. Yet this conjecture may be the only line of access to what's undecidable in the art—the stinted allusions to social reality that Nauman is at pains to dissemble.

In *Burning Small Fires* and other work of this period, the language game provides that cover. Puns, palindromes, and other lexical inversions appear wholly self-contained: orderly (if useless) "pragmatic-like exercises" with foreseeable results.[55] But even when couched within a rational matrix, Nauman's content still provokes—the system manages to deliver something in excess of its own stiff parameters. To make art, he has said, "you just make these rules which are arbitrary and follow them and get the effect of an emotional impact."[56] Take his 1968 drawing *RAW/WAR*, a study for a six-foot neon sign.[57] The word *war* is spelled out three times in tiers of sans-serif capitals. Each alphabetic character is formed by an open penciled outline, some left blank inside and others saturated with red pigment, presenting the word as both a transparent carrier of meaning and a dense material presence. The red letters spell *war* across the bottom and in an upward diagonal, which also reads from the top down as the reversed word: *raw*. Exposing the adjective contained in (and masked by) the noun, *RAW/WAR* exploits the dispassionate logic of linguistic permutation. Yet his anagrammatic choice of words is far from innocent or uninflected, and Nauman hints at something radical in their reversibility. He has said he envisioned this wartime message "not only as a sign but as an irritant,"[58] and in that context it calls to mind the stripping effects of napalm. *Raw* may be a weak descriptor for the subject of war, but something in the pairing stirs, exacting a tenuous accord between hazy thoughts of armed combat and the viscera of an open wound.

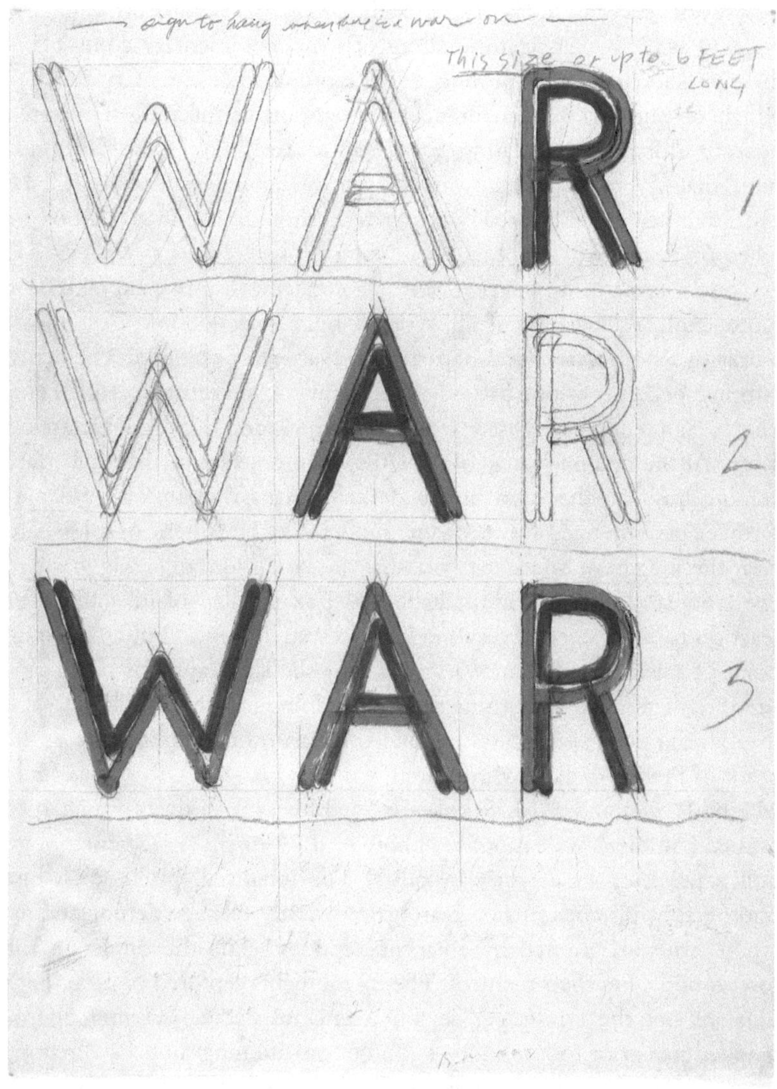

RAW/WAR, 1968. Pencil, colored pencil, and watercolor on paper. 30 × 22 in. (75.5 × 55.8 cm). Froehlich Collection, Stuttgart. Image courtesy Froehlich Collection, Stuttgart.

Works such as *RAW/WAR* and *Burning Small Fires* arrive at the political as if by chance. Intimations of social commentary come off as merely incidental—a by-product of the wordplay's "elementary device," which obscures a "hidden drama."[59] A surplus of meaning is secreted beneath a dry and calculating guise, and darker tidings issue from gestures that try to seem throwaway arch. Structural order can still be evocative, as these layered works attest, though Nauman cannot be relied on to tell us what precisely is being evoked.[60]

Soon enough, however, California conceptualism would take on a more explicitly partisan slant, typified by a selection of West Coast works that both derive and depart from Nauman's example. The act of burning becomes more patently topical in the performances of Terry Fox, a San Francisco–based artist who knew and admired Nauman's work. At the opening party of a 1970 exhibition, Fox incinerated a rare jasmine bush on the lawn of the Berkeley Art Museum.[61] The flamethrower he employed was the same model used by American soldiers to clear the jungles of Southeast Asia, and the symbolism of laying waste to live tropical flora was unmistakable. As Fox recalled of his audience's reaction to the piece, "Everyone likes to watch fires … but at a certain point people realized what was going on—the landscape was being violated. … It was the same thing they were doing in Vietnam."[62]

Social unrest also infiltrates conceptual art more emphatically in the work of Fred Lonidier, who—along with his UC San Diego colleagues Martha Rosler and Allan Sekula—trained his camera on more charged events. Lonidier's wall-mounted photo grid *29 Arrests* (1972) documents police presence at an antiwar rally.[63] The serialized, black-and-white photographs pit cops in riot gear against mostly teenage demonstrators, whose arms are pinned by adjacent deputies while the officer in the foreground takes their pictures. The 29 moments captured on Lonidier's film are not the arrests per se, but scenes of detainees being photographed just prior to booking—a kind of on-site mug shot. By directing his gaze over the cops' shoulders—creating a picture within a picture—Lonidier uses police protocols to frame his own images, redoubling that disciplinary vantage.[64] The title's arbitrary numerical limit is clearly patterned on Ruscha, but Lonidier angles Ruscha's flippant subsets toward more socially conscious ends. Yet while *Burning Small Fires* exposes similar deficiencies in the Ruscha book that came before it, it does not rely on simple substitution. Where Lonidier swaps Ruscha's trivial content for images of state power and its abuses, Nauman enacts a ruinous rehearsal of Ruscha's own method. The fires Nauman sets leave behind an affective remainder—they trigger the afterimage of other blazes, beyond the confines of the domestic hearth.

Burning Small Fires has no agenda to push, no desire to intervene; Nauman's work hardly resembles political art by any of the usual criteria. But his dissident take on Ruscha's book registers a broader climatic shift, a mounting urgency that distinguished the first half of the decade from the second. Allan Kaprow's comments on this turn are helpful here; as he told *Art in America* in 1967, "Artists don't have to illustrate current events to respond to their pressures. If the sensibility of the sixties is warming, I suspect it will get even warmer."[65] *Burning Small Fires*

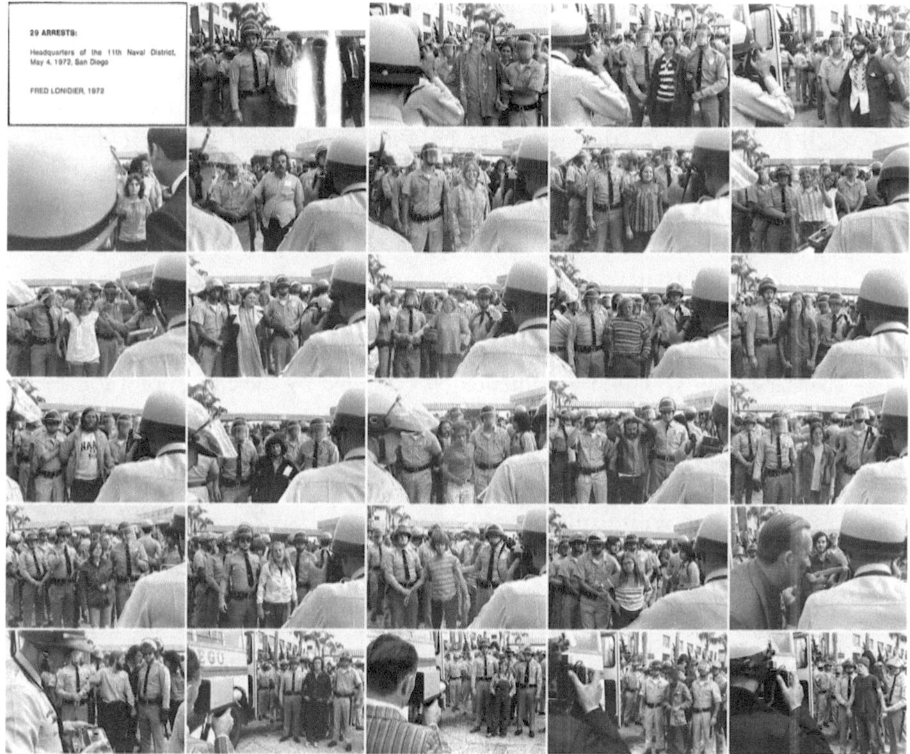

Fred Lonidier, *29 Arrests*, 1972. Text panel and 29 black-and-white gelatin silver prints. Each 5½ × 8½ (12 × 21.6 cm). Image courtesy of the artist and Michael Benevento, Los Angeles, and Essex Street, New York.

attests—almost literally—to the escalation Kaprow predicts, restoring to Ruscha's anodyne flames a bit of productive volatility.

* * *

Arguing that Bruce Nauman's book consumes *Various Small Fires*, wrecking it through repetition, this essay has drawn (perhaps too sharp) a line between the original and its assailant. The Ruscha text, as I've described it, is all ironic detachment, the Nauman more dynamic and engaged—and their conflicting approaches to a shared subject do stem from a difference of artistic temperament. But more significant still is the length of time that separates the two, a brief but crucial interval in which flames took on more dire connotations. At issue here is the image's susceptibility to change, as developments outside the sphere of art color its reception after the fact. Consider Ruscha's picture of a cigarette lighter, the sixth "small fire" in his book. An uncapped Zippo sprouts a tepid flame, clasped by a man's hand at an attractive diagonal like a product in a print ad. This 1964 book's leveling procedures made each fire as tame as the next. But by 1968, a photo of a pocket-size lighter would have carried significantly more weight, as the device had acquired new cultural meaning in just a few short years.[66]

The turning point can be dated precisely to August 3, 1965, when reporter Morley Safer's footage of a burning village was broadcast on the evening news.[67] During a raid on the hamlet of Cam Ne, believed to harbor Viet Cong, marines "lit up" all 150 dwellings and killed a 10-year-old boy. The TV audience was stunned by the image of a soldier raising his Zippo to a thatched roof, and the use of such a banal instrument made the scene all the more disturbing.[68] In military parlance, that brand name soon became a catchall for fiery havoc: Navy vessels outfitted with flamethrowers were known as "Zippo boats," and the teams sent on search-and-destroy missions armed with lighters were called "Zippo squads."[69]

Zippo lighters were standard issue for American GIs, and the gadgets themselves also came to serve a talismanic function. Their metal casings could be engraved with aphorisms or private mantras—sayings that were often jingoistic and brutal, with a dose of gallows humor. Some servicemen even inscribed their lighters with an admission of their most grisly purpose, variants of "Let me win your heart and mind or I'll burn your goddamn hut down."[70]

Thus the image of the Zippo became broadly identified with the atrocities of this particular war. A final example comes in the form of a broadsheet from 1967, which poses the grim rhetorical question "Would you burn a child"? Its vertical column of stacked photographs contrasts two instances of burning, pitting a staged, Ruscha-like tableau of a Zippo against a press photo of napalm-scarred flesh. Designed by Jeff Schlanger for the Week of Angry Arts, the poster was "plastered all over New York" and attracted considerable attention—conflating the cigarette lighter's "small fire" with bodily peril on a devastating scale.[71]

The Zippo's conversion to a makeshift weapon takes place in the interim between the two books, the same four-year span in which draft-card burning became a preferred strategy for rejecting that violence. Ruscha's 1964 inventory of blazes keeps fire at a chilly remove. But by 1968, the year of Khe Sanh and the Tet Offensive, that nonchalance was no longer tenable, and Nauman's burnt offerings recast mundane imagery as something more potent and fraught.[72] *Burning Small Fires* trashes the Ruscha in its own manner of operation, but renders that template

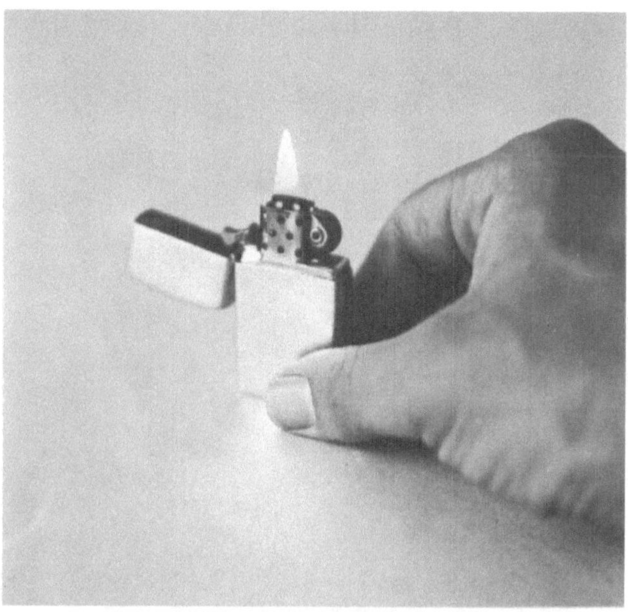

Ed Ruscha, interior page from *VARIOUS SMALL FIRES*, 1964. Artist's book. 7 × 5½ inches (17.8 × 14 cm) © Ed Ruscha. Courtesy Gagosian.

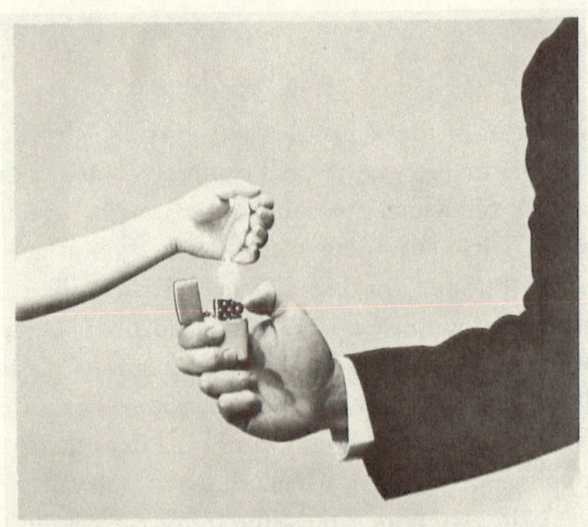

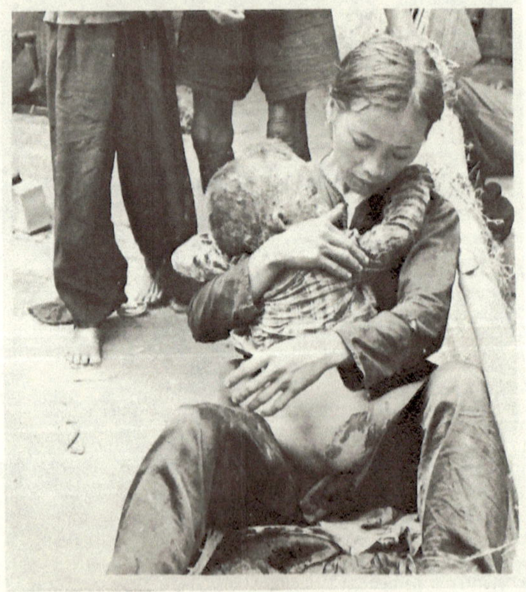

Jeff Schlanger, *Would You Burn a Child?* 1967. Offset lithographic poster. 21¼ × 8½ in. (54 × 21.6 cm). Image courtesy Jeff Schlanger.

newly porous to the politics of the day. Burning paper was of grave importance at the time, and I don't think Nauman did it lightly—letting conceptualism go down in flames also forced the genre to confront what it would rather repress. The searing intensity of his attack on the Ruscha is what brings it up to date, allowing the visuals of protest to occupy its rigid forms. With *Burning Small Fires*, Nauman intuits what would take years to speak aloud—that conceptual art must be activated if it was to become "the art of the Vietnam War."[73]

Notes

1. The book's final shot—of a glass of milk—is accounted for on its title page (which reads "Various Small Fires and Milk"), though the cover makes no mention of it.

2. Ruscha, in A. D. Coleman, "My Books End Up in the Trash" (1972), in Ed Ruscha, *Leave Any Information at the Signal: Writings, Interviews, Bits, Pages*, ed. Alexandra Schwartz (Cambridge, MA: MIT Press, 2002), 46.

3. Juliet Myers, Nauman studio, phone interview by the author, August 2, 2017.

4. This 1953 drawing was not widely shown or discussed until the mid-1960s. Rauschenberg first recounted the work's backstory in a 1964 profile (Calvin Tomkins, "Moving Out," *New Yorker*, February 29, 1964, quoted in Lawrence Alloway, *American Drawings* [New York: Solomon R. Guggenheim Museum, 1964], n.p.), and John Cage described this act of "additive subtraction" in a text Nauman would have likely read (John Cage, "Jasper Johns: Stories and Ideas," in *A Year from Monday: New Lectures and Writings* [Middletown, CT: Wesleyan University Press, 1967], 75). Nauman would have had occasion to see *Erased de Kooning* in person at San Francisco State College in 1967 as part of the touring exhibition *Art in the Mirror*, organized by Gene Swenson for the Museum of Modern Art, New York.

5. Ruscha, in Coleman, "My Books End Up in the Trash," 52.

6. Nauman, in Christopher Cordes, "Talking with Bruce Nauman: An Interview, 1989," in Bruce Nauman, *Please Pay Attention Please: Bruce Nauman's Words*, ed. Janet Kraynak (Cambridge, MA: MIT Press, 2003), 363.

7. In a recent unpublished conversation, Christophe Cherix also questioned Ruscha about *Burning Small Fires*, and the artist's answer remained unchanged: he "was flattered" (Ed Ruscha, interviewed by Christophe Cherix, January 24, 2012, Oral History Program, transcript 24, Museum of Modern Art, New York).

8. Nauman, quoted in Marcia Tucker, "Bruce Nauman," in Jane Livingston and Marcia Tucker, *Bruce Nauman: Work from 1965 to 1972*, exhibition catalog (Los Angeles: Los Angeles County Museum of Art, 1972), 31–32.

9. Nauman graduated with his MA from the University of California at Davis in the spring of 1966, and spent the next two years teaching part-time at the San Francisco Art Institute and making work in a series of rented studios.

10. Jo Applin, "Hauntings: Bruce Nauman," in *Eccentric Objects: Rethinking Sculpture in 1960s America* (New Haven, CT: Yale University Press, 2012), 115, and Robert Slifkin, "Now Man's Bound to Fail, More," *October* 135 (Winter 2011): 64.

11. Joan Simon calls *Westermann's Ear* "an affectionate, open-ended portrait" ("Nauman Variations: Back to the Future," in *Bruce Nauman*, exhibition catalog [London: Whitechapel Art Gallery, 1986], 16); and Jane Livingston noted *William T. Wiley or Ray Johnson Trap*'s "mood of playful occultism" ("Bruce Nauman," in Livingston and Tucker, *Bruce Nauman*, 15). Slifkin refers to Nauman's "elegiac pathos" in "Now Man's Bound to Fail, More," 69.

12. Ruscha, in John Coplans, "Concerning *Various Small Fires*: Edward Ruscha Discusses His Perplexing Publication" (1965), in Ruscha, *Leave Any Information*, 26, and Ruscha, in Coleman, "I'm Not Really a Photographer" (1972), in Ruscha, *Leave Any Information*, 52, emphasis in original.

13. Margaret Iversen, "Auto-Maticity: Ruscha and Performative Photography," in *Photography after Conceptual Art*, ed. Diarmuid Costello and Margaret Iversen (Chichester, UK: Wiley-Blackwell, 2010), 16.

14. Ruscha, in Coplans, "Concerning *Various Small Fires*," 23.

15. Ruscha, in Henri Man Barendse, "Ed Ruscha: An Interview" (1981), in Ruscha, *Leave Any Information*, 212. Similar claims appear in published exchanges from 1972, 1977, and 1985. See Ruscha, in David Bourdon, "Ruscha as Publisher (or All Booked Up)," in Ruscha, *Leave Any Information*, 41; Ruscha, in Diane Spodarek, "Feature Interview: Edward Ruscha," in Ruscha, *Leave Any Information*, 75; and Ruscha, in Bernard Brunon, "Interview with Edward Ruscha," in Ruscha, *Leave Any Information*, 251.

16. Nauman and Serra's acquaintance dates at least to Serra's visit to Nauman's studio in the summer or early fall of 1966.

17. The Weiner instruction is taken from his 1968 artist book *Statements*. Serra discusses *Candle Piece* in a 1968 article that also profiled Nauman, explaining that "its entire aesthetic—time and so on—is contained within it" (quoted in Howard Junker, "The New Art: It's Way, Way Out," *Newsweek*, July 29, 1968, 64).

18. Benjamin H. D. Buchloh, "Process Sculpture and Film in the Work of Richard Serra" (1978), in *Richard Serra*, ed. Hal Foster with Gordon Hughes (Cambridge. MA: MIT Press, 2000), 6.

19. In his brief catalog entry on *Burning Small Fires*, Phil Taylor characterizes Nauman's book as "the catalytic conversion of representation into action" (in *Various Small Books: Referencing Various Small Books by Ed Ruscha*, ed. Jeff Brouws, Wendy Burton, and Hermann Zschiegner [Cambridge, MA: MIT Press, 2013], 34).

20. "Playing with fire" in this manner would (ironically) require a great deal of advance planning as the precariousness of the exercise demands close observation and perfect timing. An unruly force that consumes its host, fire is fugitive by nature, leaving Nauman one shot to get each picture before ruining his source material. The individual photographs that make up *Burning Small Fires* are then subject to further mediation, tiled edge to edge in a grid formation and rephotographed from above. This collage technique—borrowed from aerial-reconnaissance missions—was a favorite of Nauman's, as seen in large-scale works such as *Composite Photo of Two Messes on the Studio Floor* from the previous year. Nauman's friend and collaborator Jack Fulton recalls spreading those individual prints (taped together) across the very floor they picture, then photographing the ensemble while perched on top of a ladder (Jack Fulton, interviewed by the author, Kathy Halbreich, and Magnus Schaefer, San Rafael, CA, January 28, 2016, and technical notes by Fulton, February 15, 2016). This was likely the procedure for creating *Burning*'s tidier grid, though Fulton was not involved in the book project.

21. Nauman's younger brother Craig recalls that the photographs for *CLEA RSKY* (1967–1968) were taken on a camping trip to the desert by leaving the shutter of a Hasselblad camera open, trained on a patch of sky. See written statement by Craig Nauman, July 24, 2008, Nauman artist's file, Museum of Modern Art Library, New York.

22. Or, as James Nisbet puts it, the text succeeds at both "setting up agonistic relationships ('ires'), and ultimately taking ownership of them (through the homophone 'earning')" ("Environmental Abstraction and the Polluted Image," *American Art* 31, no. 1 [Spring 2017]" 20).

23. Ray Bradbury's 1953 novel was adapted into a popular François Truffaut film in 1966, reviving that dystopian parable for the Vietnam generation.

24. See Briony Fer, "List," in *The Infinite Line: Re-making Art after Modernism* (New Haven, CT: Yale University Press, 2004).

25. Ruscha, in Barendse, "Ed Ruscha: An Interview," 217, and Ruscha, in Coplans, "Concerning *Various Small Fires*," 26.

26. Eleanor Antin, "Reading Ruscha," *Art in America* 61, no. 6 (November–December 1973): 69.

27. Ruscha adds another eccentric visual coda to *Nine Swimming Pools and Broken Glass* (1968)—a dissonance he likens to "a yapping puppy running through a church full of people listening to a sermon" (interview by Barbara Radice, *Flash Art*, 1975, quoted in Clive Phillpot, "Sixteen Books and Then Some," in *Edward Ruscha, Editions, 1959–1999: Catalogue Raisonné*, ed. Siri Engberg [New York: Distributed Art Publishers, 1999], 64).

28. This conflation with the Duchampian readymade dates to the earliest review of a Ruscha book; see Philip Leider, "Review of *Twenty-Six Gasoline Stations*, by Ed Ruscha," *Artforum* 2, no. 3 (September 1963): 57.

29. For Ruscha, photography was purely functional, a tool to do a job. When asked if it mattered that he photographed the fires personally, Ruscha replied, "No, anyone could. … I went to a stock photograph place and looked for pictures of fires, there were none. It is not important who took the photos, it is a matter of convenience, purely" (in Coplans, "Concerning *Various Small Fires*," 25). The Getty Research Institute houses a first edition of *Various Small Fires* that Ruscha inscribed to the LA collector Betty Asher, with a handwritten addendum that reads "credit: page 15 photo by Betty Asher" (Special Collections, N7433.4.R951 V37 1964, Getty Research Institute, Los Angeles)—so that indifference to authorship is borne out in his slotting of a friend's snapshot in among his own.

30. Ruscha recognized something stingy—what he called "a certain *blackness*"—in the caps he placed on his numbered series: "Like '26 Gasoline Stations'—26 is so specific that it's almost cruel. … Limits on things and specifics such as 26 are hard and tough and I like to use them wherever I can" (unpublished interview by Ultra Violet, July 6, 1971, Margery Mann Papers, roll 1869, frame 00461, Archives of American Art, Washington, DC).

31. Kevin Hatch notes this aspect of Ruscha's framing in "'Something Else': Ed Ruscha's Photographic Books," *October* 111 (Winter 2005): 114.

32. Ruscha, in Coleman, "I'm Not Really a Photographer," 52, emphasis in original. Ruscha also later confirmed that "*Small Fires* came at a time when I needed to come inside. It's my only interior book. The rest are all exteriors" (in Howardena Pindell, "Words with Ruscha" [1973], in Ruscha, *Leave Any Information*, 61).

33. Browne's photograph of Thich Quang Duc, shot in Saigon on June 11, 1963, was named World Press Photo of the Year in 1963 and won the Pulitzer Prize for International Reporting the following year. In a gruesome act of emulation, two American antiwar activists followed suit, self-immolating in front of the Pentagon and the United Nations headquarters within several days of one another in 1965.

34. Joan Didion, "Los Angeles Notebook," in *Slouching toward Bethlehem* (1968; reprint, New York: Farrar, Straus & Giroux, 2008), 220.

35. The first recorded instance occurred on May 12, 1964, when twelve students in New York burned their draft cards and coined the phrase "We won't go." See Sherry Gershon Gottlieb, *Hell No, We Won't Go! Resisting the Draft during the Vietnam War* (New York: Viking, 1991), xix.

36. Mere nonpossession of one's draft card was already a violation of the Selective Services Act punishable by law, but an additional amendment singled out this specific anti-induction measure, granting it a level of agency beyond the symbolic. The targeted ban on draft-card burning had the anxious marks of an emergency measure, passing the House 393 to 1 and clearing the Senate by a voice vote with no opposition; predictably, this flare-up over the First Amendment became an invitation to challenge the law. See Dean Alfange Jr., "Free Speech and Symbolic Conduct: The Draft-Card Burning Case," *Supreme Court Review* 1968 (1968): 6.

37. The *Saturday Evening Post*'s flaming draft card was an artist's rendering, but the *Ramparts* documents were real—belonging to four of the journal's editors, their names clearly visible. The display attracted government attention, and the four were called before a federal grand jury (though ultimately never indicted). See Sidney E. Zion, "Four *Ramparts* Editors Facing Draft Card Burning Prosecution," *New York Times*, July 18, 1968.

38. "The Press: Magazines," *Time*, December 1, 1967, 58.

39. A primly worded item in *Life* magazine described *Fuck the Draft* but dared not speak its name, calling it "the poster to end all posters-against-the-draft ... it advises, simply and obscenely, what should be done to [it]" (Roger Vaughan, "The Defiant Voices of S.D.S.," *Life*, October 18, 1968, 90). The poster was printed by the Dirty Linen Corp. (a pseudonym used by designer "Steve" Kiyoshi Kuromiya) in Philadelphia but distributed widely via mail order ("one for $2, two for $3, or five for $5") in alternative newspapers such as the *Los Angeles Free Press* and the *Berkeley Barb*.

40. Closed, Nauman's book measures 12½ by 9½ inches; unfolded, it is 38 × 50 inches. Ruscha's original text, a mere 7 by 5½ inches, is dwarfed by comparison.

41. Claes Oldenburg, "I Am for Art," in *Store Days: Documents from the Store, 1961, and Ray Gun Theater, 1962*, ed. Emmett Williams (New York: Something Else Press, 1967), 40. The concertina format of Ruscha's famous *Every Building on the Sunset Strip* (1966) may also be a relevant precursor, though its linear pleats splay out (and fold back up) in a much tidier, less-confounding manner.

42. LeWitt, quoted in Anne Rorimer, "Siting the Page: Exhibiting Works in Publications—Some Examples of Conceptual Art in the USA," in *Rewriting Conceptual Art*, ed. Michael Newman and Jon Bird (London: Reaktion Books, 1999), 11. That first wall drawing was also executed in a politicized context: the Paula Cooper Gallery's inaugural show organized by Lucy Lippard in 1968, *Exhibition to Benefit the Student Mobilization Committee to End the War in Vietnam.*

43. See Manuel Gasser, "The Poster Craze," *Graphis* 24, no. 135 (1968): 52. The *New York Times* went so far as to declare the poster the signature graphic expression of the era: "No development in the popular visual culture of the nineteen-sixties has been more striking than the revival of the poster" (Hilton Kramer, "Postermania," *New York Times Magazine*, February 11, 1968).

44. The exhibition *Word and Image: Posters and Typography from the Graphic Design Collection at the Museum of Modern Art*, January 25–March 10, 1968, featured hundreds of posters from art nouveau to the present day and offered a fine-art correlate to the more grassroots versions cropping up on college campuses and at protest rallies.

45. For an early survey that inserts the 1960s "poster of protest" into a radical tradition dating to the broadsheets of Martin Luther, see David Kunzle, *American Posters of Protest 1966–70 (Art as a Political Weapon)* (New York: New School Art Center, 1971), 5.

46. Although the term *conceptual art* had not been coined at the outset of Ruscha's bookwork, his modest publications are credited with launching the movement in early anthologies such as Ursula Meyer's *Conceptual Art* (New York: Dutton, 1972) and Lucy Lippard's *Six Years: The Dematerialization of the Art Object …* (New York: Praeger, 1973) as well as in Benjamin Buchloh's canonical essay "Conceptual Art 1962–1969: From the Aesthetic of Administration to the Critique of Institutions," *October* 55 (Winter 1990): 119–122. And while the "conceptual" label applied to Ruscha is anachronistic, the artist didn't fight it. In an unpublished interview by Barbara Rose around 1970, he granted: "I think my work is probably related a lot to what the attitudes of the so-called Conceptual artists are"—namely, "documentation, and the use of a camera, the printing media, making a work of art that … has a straight immediacy to it, [and] it's not in the gallery" (interview transcript, c. 1970, p. 7, Barbara Rose Papers, Box 1, Folder 34, Getty Research Institute, Los Angeles).

47. Lucy Lippard, "Postface," in *Six Years*, quoted in Blake Stimson, "The Promise of Conceptual Art," in *Conceptual Art: A Critical Anthology*, ed. Alexander Alberro and Blake Stimson (Cambridge, MA: MIT Press, 1999), xlii. In a later essay, Lippard would train this critique on the artist's book in particular, characterizing the format's ascendance in the 1960s as "part of a broad, if naïve, quasi-political resistance to the extreme commodification of artworks and artists. Accessibility and some sort of function were an assumed part of their *raison d'être*. Still, despite sincere avowals of populist intent, there was little understanding of the fact that the accessibility of the cheap, portable form did not carry over to that of the contents. … [W]e failed to realize that, however neat the package, when the book was opened by a potential buyer from 'the broader audience' and she or he was baffled, it went back on the rack" ("Conspicuous Consumption: New Artists' Books," in *Artists' Books: A Critical Anthology and Sourcebook*, ed. Joan Lyons [Layton, UT: Visual Studies Workshop Press, 1985], 50).

48. Jeff Wall, *Dan Graham's Kammerspiel* (Toronto: Art Metropole, 1991), 21–22.

49. Victor Burgin, "The Absence of Presence: Conceptualism and Postmodernism" (1984), in *The End of Art Theory: Criticism and Post-modernity* (Atlantic Highlands, NJ: Humanities Press International, 1986), 50. Benjamin Buchloh shares Burgin's jaundiced view, stating as fact that "conceptualism acknowledged from the start the relative opacity, if not outright inaccessibility, of socio-political realities to photographic documentation" ("Cosmic Reification: Gabriel Orozco's Photographs," in *Gabriel Orozco* [London: Serpentine Gallery, 2004], 75).

50. Wall, *Dan Graham's Kammerspiel*, 19.

51. Julia Bryan-Wilson, *Art Workers: Radical Practice in the Vietnam War Era* (Berkeley: University of California Press, 2009), 8.

52. Nauman was not untouched by the spirit of protest that swirled around him. He kept company with the inflammatory painter Peter Saul, appeared in Robert Nelson's satirical 1968 film *War Is Hell*, and contributed to group exhibitions to raise funds for antiwar causes (such as *Number* 7, curated by Lucy Lippard at Paula Cooper, and *Art for the Moratorium* at Castelli, both in 1969). But Nauman was not a joiner, not one to publicly take sides—where his peers signed on to the Peace Tower in Los Angeles or the Collage of Indignation in New York, no such clear affiliations can settle the question of his personal politics.

53. Coosje van Bruggen's influential monograph dates the entrance of political allusion to the early '80s (*Bruce Nauman* [New York: Rizzoli, 1988], 21), and that periodization is a commonplace in the Nauman literature. Even as close an observer of his career as Marcia Tucker would claim that "Nauman's move away from art concerns to more political and social concerns began as early as 1970" ("Some Notes on Bruce Nauman's Videos," unpublished manuscript, c. 1986, Marcia Tucker Papers, Box 68, Folder 1, 2004.M.13, Getty Research Institute, Los Angeles). So my contextualist reading of *Burning Small Fires* is also a bid to revise this aspect of Nauman's historiography, arguing that his work begins to have social resonance from an earlier date than has been widely acknowledged.

54. Nauman provides clear sources for this series of suspended, empty chairs: the description of life under Latin American dictatorship in *The Return of Eva Perón*, a novel by V. S. Naipaul, and *Prisoner without a Name, Cell without a Number*, a memoir by Jacobo Timerman (Nauman, in Joan Simon, "Breaking the Silence: An Interview with Bruce Nauman" [1988], in Nauman, *Please Pay Attention Please*, 331 [reprinted in this volume]; van Bruggen, *Bruce Nauman*, 21). One or the other of these books is invariably cited in scholarly treatments of the sculptures.

55. The phrase "pragmatic-like exercises" is Christopher Cordes's from an unpublished essay on language games in Nauman's prints, c. 1980, p. 3, Castelli Gallery Records, Box 78, Folder 19, Archives of American Art, Washington, DC.

56. Nauman, in Lorraine Sciarra, "Bruce Nauman" (1972), in Nauman, *Please Pay Attention Please*, 162.

57. The watercolor drawing, in the Froehlich Collection, is one of several variations on this theme. Between 1968 and 1970, Nauman returned to this motif in a second drawing, his first mature lithograph, a neon sign, and a cryptic metal box (now lost) rigged with flashing lights that blinked out the phrase *raw war* in Morse code.

58. Nauman, in an unpublished interview by Brenda Richardson, June 21, 1982, typescript, Richardson's personal papers.

59. See Bruno Corà's fine explication of the tensions at play in *RAW/WAR* ("Bruce Nauman," *Domus* [August 1977]: 52). The artist Glenn Ligon has recently advanced a similar reading of Nauman's video *Violin Tuned D.E.A.D.* (1969), in which he inexpertly plays only those open strings, to shrill effect. Ligon suggests that this plaintive, "discordant note can be heard as a soundtrack to the war in Vietnam or the brutal violence faced by civil rights workers" ("Glenn Ligon: *What We Said Last Time* and *Entanglements*," press release, Luhring Augustine Gallery, February 27–April 2, 2016).

60. For a nuanced discussion of the affective dimension that erupts within the structuralist aesthetic of the 1960s, see Eve Meltzer, *What Systems We Have Loved: Conceptual Art, Affect, and the Antihumanist Turn* (Chicago: University of Chicago Press, 2013).

61. The action/performance *Defoliation* occurred on March 16, 1970, on the opening night of curator Brenda Richardson's forward-looking exhibition *The Eighties*.

62. Fox, interviewed by Willoughby Sharp (1970) and Robin White (1979), quoted in Constance Lewallen, "Terry Fox," in *Terry Fox: Articulations (Labyrinth/Text Works)*, exhibition catalog, ed. Constance Lewallen (Philadelphia: Moore College of Art and Design, 1992), 15.

63. The work's full title is *29 Arrests: Headquarters of the 11th Naval District, May 4, 1972, San Diego*.

64. The historic entanglement of photography and criminality—with the camera as an apparatus of state control—would be brilliantly theorized by Allan Sekula in "The Body and the Archive," *October* 39 (Winter 1986): 3–64). Benjamin J. Young discusses *29 Arrests*' visual alignment with law enforcement in "Documents and Documentary: San Diego, c. 1973," in *The Uses of Photography: Art, Politics, and the Reinvention of a Medium*, exhibition catalog, ed. Jill Dawsey (San Diego: Museum of Contemporary Art San Diego, 2016), 130.

65. Kaprow, response to a questionnaire issued by Barbara Rose and Irving Sandler, "Sensibility of the Sixties," *Art in America* 55, no. 1 (January–February 1967): 45.

66. I thank Mignon Nixon for this suggestion.

67. Millions of viewers saw this dispatch from Vietnam on the *CBS Evening News with Walter Cronkite*, and media outlets summarized it at length. See "TV's First War," *Newsweek*, August 30, 1965; "Burning of Village Described," *New York Times*, August 4, 1965; and "Justify Viet Hut Burning: Marines Report Those Hit Are Red Centers," *Chicago Tribune*, August 6, 1965.

68. The broadcast so enraged President Johnson that he made violent threats to the network and summoned Safer to the White House for more intimidation. See Todd Gitlin, *The Whole World Is Watching: Mass Media in the Making and Unmaking of the New Left* (Berkeley: University of California Press, 1980), 276.

69. See Edward S. Herman, *Atrocities in Vietnam: Myths and Realities* (Philadelphia: Pilgrim Press, 1970), 19, 83–84, and first-person accounts in Vietnam Veterans Against the War, *The Winter Soldier Investigation: An Inquiry into American War Crimes* (Boston: Beacon Press, 1972). The command "Zippo the joint"—in which a sergeant directs an infantryman to burn a hut—also appears in one of the first fictionalizations of the American presence in Vietnam. See William Wilson, *The LBJ Brigade* (Los Angeles: Apocalypse Press, 1966), 28.

70. In the decades after the war, these personalized Zippos became increasingly valuable memorabilia and, more recently, objects of study for historians of material culture. For detailed treatments, see Sherry Buchanan, *Vietnam Zippos: American Soldiers' Engravings and Stories, 1965–1973* (Chicago: University of Chicago Press, 2007), and Michael P. Corey, "The Vietnam War Zippo Lighter: An Entry Point for Examining Personal, Interpersonal, Collected, and Collective Memory Making," PhD diss., New School for Social Research, 2009.

71. The poster's contents were also narrated in detail in the pages of *The Nation*, where Max Kozloff approvingly deemed it a step toward "the crystallization of [visual] metaphor

and language which would kindle an audience toward an anti-war purpose" ("… A Collage of Indignation," *The Nation*, February 20, 1967, 251). Grace Paley incorporated her own observations of protestors toting the same placard through Washington Square into the story "Faith in a Tree," published in the *New American Review* 1 (1967) and collected in Grace Paley, *Enormous Changes at the Last Minute: Stories* (New York: Farrar, Straus & Giroux, 1974), 75–100.

72. Of course, if images of fire can become more politicized over time, they can also become less; Nauman's book may strike most present-day observers as just as cool and detached as Ruscha's. The subtlety of reference in *Burning Small Fires*—conjuring draft cards, but indirectly—becomes harder to detect with age, as the protest images that it echoes fade from collective memory.

73. Joseph Kosuth periodizes conceptual art thusly in his essay "1975" (1975), cited in Bryan-Wilson, *Art Workers*, 198.

Index of Names

Note: Pages in italics indicate illustrations.

www.ingramcontent.com/pod-product-compliance
Lightning Source LLC
LaVergne TN
LVHW091133080826
845145LV00008B/2133

9780262535670